Three American Plays

by
Maxwell Anderson
and
Laurence Stallings

New York
Harcourt, Brace and Company

PRINTED IN THE U. S. A.

CONTENTS

WHAT PRICE GLORY *5*
FIRST FLIGHT *93*
THE BUCCANEER *183*

WHAT PRICE GLORY

A Play in Three Acts

What Price Glory was presented in 1924, at the Plymouth Theatre, under the direction of Arthur Hopkins, who appended the following note. The stage settings were designed by Woodman Thompson. The cast was as follows:

CORPORAL GOWDY	*Brian Donlevy*
CORPORAL KIPER	*Fuller Mellish, Jr.*
CORPORAL LIPINSKY	*George Tobias*
FIRST SERGEANT QUIRT	*William Boyd*
CAPTAIN FLAGG	*Louis Wolheim*
CHARMAINE DE LA COGNAC	*Leyla Georgie*
PRIVATE LEWISOHN	*Sidney Elliott*
LIEUTENANT ALDRICH	*Fay Roope*
LIEUTENANT MOORE	*Clyde North*
LIEUTENANT SCHMIDT	*Charles Costigan*
GUNNERY SERGEANT SOCKKEL	*Henry G. Shelvey*
PRIVATE MULCAHY	*Jack MacGraw*
SERGEANT FERGUSON	*James A. Devine*
A BRIGADE RUNNER	*John J. Cavanaugh*
MONSIEUR PETE DE LA COGNAC	*Luis Alberni*
ANOTHER BRIGADE RUNNER	*Arthur Campbell*
BRIGADIER GENERAL COKELEY	*Roy La Rue*
A COLONEL	*Keane Waters*
A CAPTAIN	*William B. Smith*
A LIEUTENANT	*Fred Brophy*
ANOTHER LIEUTENANT	*Thomas Buckley*
A CHAPLAIN	*John C. Davis*
TOWN MAYOR	*Alfred Renaud*
SPIKE	*Keane Waters*
PHARMACIST'S MATE	*Thomas Sullivan*
LIEUTENANT CUNNINGHAM	*J. Merrill Holmes*
LIEUTENANT LUNDSTROM	*Robert Warner*

A COLONEL, A CAPTAIN, A LIEUTENANT, ANOTHER LIEUTENANT } Headquarters Staff

NOTE

What Price Glory is a play of war as it is, not as it has been presented theatrically for thousands of years. The soldiers talk and act much as soldiers the world over. The speech of men under arms is universally and consistently interlarded with profanity. Oaths mean nothing to a soldier save a means to obtain emphasis. He uses them in place of more polite adjectives.

The authors of *What Price Glory* have attempted to reproduce this mannerism along with other general atmosphere they believe to be true. In a theatre where war has been lied about, romantically, effectively—and in a city where the war play has usually meant sugary dissimulation —*What Price Glory* may seem bold. The audience is asked to bear with certain expletives which, under other circumstances, might be used for melodramatic effect, but herein are employed because the mood and truth of the play demand their employment.

WHAT PRICE GLORY

ACT I

SCENE ONE

*A room in a French farmhouse—now a U. S. Marine com-
pany headquarters. A couple of desks covered with
maps and papers. Several scattered chairs. Three
runners sit talking and smoking, very much at ease.
LIPINSKY is seated at one end of bench, KIPER at the
other; GOWDY is sitting on a stool near KIPER.*

GOWDY. Well, where the hell did you come from?

KIPER. Who, me? I come from every place I've been to.

GOWDY. Yeah, well, where you been to?

KIPER. Me? I've been to China, Cuba, the Philippines,
San Francisco, Buenos Ayres, Cape Town, Madagascar . . .
wait a minute—Indiana, San Domingo, Tripoli, and Black-
well's Island.

LIPINSKY. Ever going home?

KIPER. Who, me? I can't go anywhere without going
home.

GOWDY. By the time this war's over you ought to be
pretty near ready to marry and settle down.

KIPER. There ain't going to be any after-this-war. Anyway, I got married after the last two wars and when I get

5

through paying my debt to Lafayette, I'm through settling down. I never have settled down in so many hick towns in my life.

LIPINSKY. What became of them two broads?

KIPER. My wives?

LIPINSKY. Yeah.

KIPER. The first one never knew my last name, and when I left town she was out of luck.

GOWDY. And the next one?

KIPER. Ain't I signing the payroll for her every month? A twenty-dollar allotment, and she gives it to a fireman in Buffalo. Here I am saving democracy, and he's turning in a twenty-bell alarm the first of every month.

GOWDY. That's a waste of cash, the way I look at it. It stands to reason when a girl gets rid of one bozo she's looking for another. Now why does the late unlamented finance that little game? There's no justice in that.

KIPER. Who said it was justice? It ain't justice; it's alimony.

GOWDY. Well, alimony's all right if you're well fixed; hell, a girl ought to have some fun! I don't want a girl to quit living just because she ain't living with me, but the guy that's getting his ought to pay for it. What do you want to pay alimony for?

KIPER. What did you want to come to France for? It's the same reason why I pay alimony. So's to see the rest of the girls. Join the Marines and see the girls—from a port-hole.

GOWDY. God! I came to France because I had a brain-storm one day and signed on the dotted line.

LIPINSKY. There ain't but one man in the world that came to France to see the mam'selles, and that's the skipper.

When there's women around the skipper's got trick eyes like a horsefly.

KIPER. The old man? Say, he can't look at a mam'selle without blushing. Compared to me he's an amateur. He don't know the difference between a Hong-Kong honky-tonk and a Santo Domingo smoongy.

LIPINSKY. No, oh, no! I suppose women is an open book to you. You're damn well right—a code book.

KIPER. Yeah, you're damn well right. When I was in Turkey with that landing party the Sultan had to hunt through his harem with a flashlight to find a decent-looking girl, and when I left China the Yangtse was full of the bodies of virgins that drowned their beautiful selves because I was shipping over. And when I was in Spain the king of Spain put an ad in the paper offering a reward for the return of the queen.

GOWDY. What did you do?

KIPER. Took her back for the reward.

LIPINSKY. Huh! I notice you've got Cognac Pete's daughter, too.

KIPER. If I had the skipper's uniform and his Sam Browne belt, I could take that little wench away from him before you could say squads right! You ain't never seen it done. The skip's full of wind.

GOWDY. Anyway, Flagg's got Pete's kid sewed up—and she's as pretty a little frog as ever made a dish of frog's legs.

KIPER. Pete's kid! The poor little tart! What could she do? Ain't the skipper billeted there? God! I guess even Lippy could make a kid if she slept on the other side of a paper wall.

LIPINSKY. God! I don't know. Ain't it the truth some

guys just naturally walk away with women? Damned if I could ever do it!

KIPER. Take one good long look at yourself and you'll see why. There ain't many as unfortunate as you are. I guess there ain't anybody handicapped with features like them there.

LIPINSKY. Sometimes I think it's features, and sometimes I think it's luck. Once I spent three hundred dollars on a dame at Asbury Park in two days, and she keeping her damn chum with her all the time. Finally I got the extra one so drunk she couldn't tell her own name, and I ditched her. Then this broad I was trying to make insisted on riding on the merry-go-round. . . . God! the merry-go-round. Nothing else would satisfy her. She'd rung ducks till it rained ducks. She'd shot up more powder in shooting galleries than's been shot in this war, and she wanted to ride on the merry-go-round! So we got on the merry-go-round, and I threw her into a chariot and I piled on a horse. She hollers, "Whoopee, whoopee, let's do it again!" Jeez, I had spent three hundred bucks and I said, "Now, honey, let's not ride any more. Come on, let's do what you promised." She said she would after one more turn on the merry-go-round. So I, like a bloody fool, tries to save twenty cents by catching a brass ring. Son-of-a-bitch! I fall off and break my leg!

KIPER. My God!

LIPINSKY. Yes, sir. I broke my leg.

GOWDY. You certainly have had your share of tough luck.

LIPINSKY. So when the captain walks off with the top soldier's girl I say to myself, maybe there's luck in it. Maybe the breaks favored him. They never did favor me.

GOWDY. Any skipper can walk off with any top soldier's girl in my opinion. Say, maybe that's the lowdown on why the sergeant left.

KIPER. Naw—he was too damn good. Regimental took him. We'll probably get a lousy replacement. Probably get a corporal with ten years' experience chasing prisoners at Portsmouth. Soon's the new sergeant gets here the skip's going on ten days' leave.

LIPINSKY. Yeah? Where?

KIPER. Paris.

LIPINSKY. You going with him?

KIPER. Yep.

LIPINSKY. Some guys have all the luck.

[*The door opens.* SERGEANT QUIRT, *the very picture of an old-timer, enters and looks quickly around. All rise.*]

QUIRT. L Company?

KIPER. Company Headquarters.

QUIRT. Where's the company commander?

KIPER. Just stepped down the street. Will be back soon.

QUIRT. He's going on leave?

KIPER. Right.

QUIRT. What's his name?

KIPER. Captain Flagg.

QUIRT. Whew!

KIPER. You know him?

QUIRT. Do you?

KIPER. Yes, sir!

QUIRT. Company Headquarters. Looks like a God damn reception room to me.

KIPER. We aim to please.

QUIRT. Yeah, to please yourself. Well, listen, I'm the new top soldier here. Who's the company clerk?

LIPINSKY. I am, sir.

QUIRT. Clear this jam out of here and let's have a look at what you're doing.

LIPINSKY. Will you get the hell out?—and don't come back till you're sent for. [KIPER *and* GOWDY *go out.*]

QUIRT. I've been ten kilometers west of you. Took the wrong turn.

LIPINSKY. Here's the map. That's the only road there is, and we can't use it. The damn thing is one long shell-hole from last May.

QUIRT. Jeez!

LIPINSKY. That's what they all say.

QUIRT. Don't you ever clean these galleys?

LIPINSKY. We don't do anything else.

QUIRT. You haven't got a police sergeant, I suppose?

LIPINSKY. We've got an acting corporal. Old Hennessey was bumped off last time up.

QUIRT. Spud Hennessey?

LIPINSKY. That's the soldier.

QUIRT. Tough for Spud to go. A grand soldier. Too damn finicky, though.

LIPINSKY. We've gone to hell for chow since he left.

QUIRT. That's queer. I never knew Flagg to let his men go to hell.

LIPINSKY. Not his fault. These cooks are no good. Hennessey was acting mess sergeant, too.

QUIRT. That's like old times.

LIPINSKY. Yeah?

QUIRT. Say, if the skipper's going ashore they'd better get him out of here before he gets too drunk to navigate.

I've seen him shove off with a liberty party and spend a forty-eight-hour leave sleeping it off on the beach.

LIPINSKY. It's the same skip, all right. You know him.

QUIRT. I'll say I do. . . . I think I'll look him up. Where's he likely to be?

LIPINSKY. Damned if I know. He might be at Pete's place. Anybody can tell you where that is—just this side of the river.

QUIRT. All right. I'll find it. [*Goes out briskly. After he has gone,* LIPINSKY *goes to the door and whistles.* KIPER *and* GOWDY *come in.*]

LIPINSKY. Did you take a slant at the amphibian?

GOWDY. Yeah.

KIPER. What of it?

LIPINSKY. He's our new papa.

KIPER. So he says.

LIPINSKY. He's soldiered with the skipper before. Says he never saw the chief sober.

KIPER. Is he hard-boiled?

LIPINSKY. There's only one place in the world they boil them as hard as that, and that's the Tropic of Cancer.

KIPER. What does he know?

LIPINSKY. This God damn army's going to run right from now on or get off on its ear.

GOWDY. He must have used some language on you?

LIPINSKY. Not a word, and I'm not going to give him a chance, either.

KIPER. Scared, huh?

LIPINSKY. You meet a top with two glass eyes, a slit across his face for a mouth and a piece out of his ear, and you might just as well heave out and lash up. That bird could curse the hide off a whole Senegalese regiment.

[CAPTAIN FLAGG *enters and comes to chair above table.*
He is a fine, magnificently endowed man.]

FLAGG. 'Tenshun! [*Reading report which he picks up
from table.*] Where's that first sergeant?

KIPER. Went out looking for you, sir.

FLAGG. Scatter and find him, a couple of you. [LIPINSKY,
GOWDY, *and* KIPER *start out.*] Stay here, Kiper. [KIPER
comes back.] Damn him, why couldn't he sit still? [LIPIN-
SKY *and* GOWDY *go out.*] What's he like?

KIPER. Tough.

FLAGG. Yeah? I hope he damn well hangs the whole
damn company up by the thumbs. About time we had a
little discipline around here.

KIPER. Yes, sir.

FLAGG. "Yes, sir!" "Yes, sir!" Shut your trap, will
you?

KIPER. Oh, yes, sir.

FLAGG. Go to hell! Everything packed?

KIPER. Absolutely.

FLAGG. Bike working? Side-car trimmed?

KIPER. Tuned it up this morning.

FLAGG. Well, we're going ashore as soon as I see the new
top soldier, you understand? And we don't stop for anything smaller than shell-holes!

KIPER. Ay, ay, sir!

FLAGG. Go sit down! Go read a book! You make me
nervous. [KIPER *sits.* CHARMAINE *slips in. She is a drab.*
FLAGG, *who is busy at the desk, does not see her at first.*
He looks up impatiently.] Well, hello! hello! What are
you doing here? You better run along back to your papa.
Listen, *mon amie,* you better beat it back to *le père,* understand?

CHARMAINE. Why? [*She comes nearer.*]

FLAGG. Well, I'm busy.

CHARMAINE. You are going away.

FLAGG. So that's it. Kiper, did you tell the kid I was going away?

KIPER. No, sir, she saw me with your musette bag.

CHARMAINE. The sergeant went away. He is not coming back. Now you go away. You are not coming back.

FLAGG. As far as the sergeant's concerned, you're quite right, dearie; but as far as I'm concerned, you're dead wrong. The sergeant isn't coming back. We have a new sergeant, see? But I am coming back.

CHARMAINE. *Oui?*

FLAGG. *Oui, oui, oui!*

CHARMAINE. No. You are such a lovely liar. You don't want to make me cry. So you lie a little—*n'est-ce pas?*

FLAGG [*takes her by shoulders*]. I'm not lying, Charmaine. I don't know how I can prove it to you, but I'm telling the solemn truth. [*A knock on the door.*] See who that is, and keep him out, whoever it is.

KIPER [*opens the door, goes out, and returns*]. It's Lewisohn, third platoon replacement. He wants permission to speak with you, sir.

FLAGG. What about?

KIPER. Lost something, sir.

FLAGG. Let him in. [LEWISOHN *enters. He is a pale little boy.*] Let's have it quick, soldier.

LEWISOHN [*saluting*]. Beg pardon, sir. [*Very much scared.*]

FLAGG. What do you want?

LEWISOHN. The truth is, sir, I've lost my identification tag.

FLAGG. What? What? Lost what?

LEWISOHN. My identification tag.

FLAGG. Well, I thought I'd been around a good deal, and I've had 'em ask me to show 'em where they live and button up their pants for them and put on their little night-drawers, but I'm a son-of-a-gun if this isn't the first time anybody has ever asked me to help him find his identification tag!

LEWISOHN. Sorry, sir. I—I thought it was— I . . .

FLAGG. What did you think?

LEWISOHN. I thought it was important, sir.

FLAGG. And what, may I ask, made you think it was important?

LEWISOHN. In case I was—ah—hit, sir. They wouldn't know who I was. I thought maybe it would matter.

FLAGG. Matter?—to whom?

LEWISOHN. Well—to keep the records—or to my folks.

FLAGG. Listen, boy, why did you ever leave your home and come over here?

LEWISOHN. Why, to fight, sir.

FLAGG. Yeah. Well, you'll get a chance, don't you worry, and for God's sake learn to act like a man. Never mind your identification tag. If you want to know what your name is look in your hat.

LEWISOHN. Yes, sir.

FLAGG. By the way, what is your name?

LEWISOHN. Louis Lewisohn.

FLAGG [to KIPER]. Make a note of that, Kiper. [KIPER *makes a note in the book he carries in his pocket.*] Now, anything else? Hope you got a good room with a view and running water and everything.

LEWISOHN. No, sir. [*Swallowing a lump in his throat.*]

FLAGG. No? I'm surprised. Well, go on outside and swear at me a while. It'll do you good, and that's what I'm here for. I'm here to keep you in hot water till you're hard-boiled. See? You can go.

LEWISOHN. Yes, sir. [*He salutes and goes.*]

FLAGG. Make a note of that, Kiper, and get him a new tag if they have to build a new factory in Hoboken to turn it out. The God-forsaken fool's dying of grief away from mother. Got it?

KIPER. Yes, Captain Flagg.

FLAGG. Then step outside and guard that door a minute. [KIPER *salutes and goes out, closing the door carefully.* FLAGG *then turns to* CHARMAINE.] Now, you little she-woman, what do you want?

CHARMAINE. You are going away.

FLAGG. Damn it, I'm not going away. I'm going to Paris—coming back in eight days. Eight days in Paris, see, then I come back.

CHARMAINE. The sergeant did not come back.

FLAGG. My God, child, get this! The sergeant is not coming back. I am coming back. We have a new sergeant, see?

CHARMAINE. Oui?

FLAGG. Oui, oui.

CHARMAINE. No. I think the captain does not love me, not any more?

FLAGG. Girlie, I love you fit to kill. I love you no end, same as always. Come here. [*She puts her arms around his neck.* FLAGG *takes her in his arms.*] You're as sweet as Burgundy, and you've got a kick like triple sec. Sure I love you. Everybody loves you. I love you, dearie girl, but I don't trust you.

CHARMAINE. You take me to Paris? Yes? Take me to Paris?

FLAGG. No. I guess not.

CHARMAINE. But I'm so unhappy when you go away.

FLAGG. Yes, you are! I wish you were. Why, you little Geisha [*chucking her under the chin*], if I didn't wear captain's stripes you wouldn't know me from the K.P.'s.

CHARMAINE. No, dear Captain Flagg. [*Her arms on his shoulders. She runs a hand through his hair.*] It is true, I shall be so lonesome. I shall be all alone at the inn, crying every day to break your heart.

FLAGG. You'll be dancing all night and flirting all day with the Y.M.C.A. boys, you mean. Ain't it so?

CHARMAINE. Oui. But you could take me. I can't be good—unless you take me. I want to be good for you. We could have so good time—in Paris.

FLAGG. No, I can't take you. But listen. [*Takes hold of her shoulders.*] While I'm gone you wait for me. Remember, you're my girl, see? Just my girl, and you wait for me, see?

CHARMAINE. *Oui*, I will.

FLAGG. And listen to this [*putting her away*]. If I find out you've been running with some one else, I'll break you in two, see? [*He makes the motion of breaking something.*] Now, will you be good while I'm gone?

CHARMAINE [*coming into his arms*]. *Oui, monsieur.*

FLAGG. That's better. You know what I mean?

CHARMAINE. *Oui.*

FLAGG. That's right, little kitten, purr. . . . And remember, I don't trust you any further than I can see you. Now run along. [FLAGG *turns to table, but* CHARMAINE *follows him.*]

CHARMAINE. But you will take me to Paris?

FLAGG [*seating himself on edge of table, he beckons her with his finger and takes her on his knee, between his legs*]. You ever been to Paris?

CHARMAINE. *Non. . . .*

FLAGG. Well, there's a river in Paris.

CHARMAINE. *La Seine.*

FLAGG. Yeah, the Seine. That's where they drown little girls like you. Every time the police catch a little girl in Paris, they drown her in the Seine. You can't go there. They'd drown you.

CHARMAINE. It is not true.

FLAGG. It is true. I'll tell you another thing. There's nothing to eat in Paris, no food but horses; no wine, only water. No young girls, only old women. Some of the girls they drown in the Seine; some they make into sausages for the generals. Paris is full of generals that won't eat anything but young girls. You can't go to Paris.

CHARMAINE. You are full of lovely lies. Oh, it is not true.

FLAGG. Uh, you don't know Paris.

CHARMAINE. Oh, but I know these captains and sergeants! They do not ever put anything, what you say, past me. But, oh, I love you for a lovely liar! [*Embraces him.*] And I will be good; I will, *vraiment!*

FLAGG. That's a good girl. Now you go back to Papa Pete's. Stay home nights. Wait for Captain Flagg. Kiss me good-bye. [*She kisses him.*] Now run along. [*She goes.*] Kiper!

KIPER [*coming in*]. Yes, sir.

FLAGG. Have you found that sergeant yet?

KIPER. He's coming with Lipinsky, sir.

FLAGG. Tell him to damn well get a wiggle on.

KIPER [*to* QUIRT, *outside*]. He's waiting for you, sir.

[LIPINSKY *enters with* QUIRT.]

QUIRT [*saluting*]. Captain Flagg?

FLAGG [*returns salute and remains seated, not even glancing at* QUIRT]. Hello, Sergeant. Where've you been all day?

QUIRT. Ten kilometers west by mistake.

FLAGG. Do you know our lay-out?

QUIRT. I've got a general idea.

FLAGG. What kind of a hole were you in over there?

QUIRT. Much the same as yours, only we had a road.

FLAGG. Do you think you can handle this company? It's a rough crowd of old men and little baa-lamb recruits. [*He still does not look up.*]

QUIRT. It's an army, ain't it? Sure.

FLAGG. I damn well hope you can. We're in a devilish sector here, and it's going to be worse when we move up again. We just hold half a town; the Heinies hold the other half. It rains grenades most of the time. About half our men are green replacements. They damned near ruined us in that last tour of duty. You'll have to whip some of 'em into shape before we go up. Close order drill is best.

QUIRT. Half of 'em raw?

FLAGG. Over half.

QUIRT. Well, I've seen worse.

FLAGG. Now, I'm going on leave, you see. Eight days. While I'm gone you feed 'em up and give 'em hell. Teach 'em where they are. Make 'em so bad they'll eat steel rather than get another dressing from you. Make 'em hard, but don't break 'em. Give 'em eats and about eight hours of drill and guns a day. They're mostly Bible Class boys, and God knows most of 'em haven't got long to live.

QUIRT [*takes step toward table*]. Cut the comedy, Captain. You must know me.

FLAGG [*rising, looks at* QUIRT *for the first time*]. Yeah? I'm a cuckoo if it ain't the old Hoppergrass!

QUIRT. Thought you didn't know me. Well, I'm glad to meet you again, Captain Flagg.

FLAGG. Kiper——

KIPER. Yes, sir.

FLAGG. Step out and tell all platoon commanders to report here at once.

KIPER. Ay, ay, sir. [*Exits.*]

FLAGG. Well, Quirt, I'm glad to see you, because if there was ever a good soldier needed I need one here, and you're as good as there is ; but I'm damned if I take any particular joy in meeting you again. You've been poison to me everywhere I've served with you.

QUIRT [*at right of table*]. Same to you, I'm sure, and many of 'em. Personally I'd as soon meet a skunk in a dugout, and officially I don't think much of your crew. I broke you the first time in China, and you broke me in Cuba. You're in a position to break me now, and if you didn't need me worse than the wildcat needed what he didn't have, you'd break me again.

FLAGG. I'd see you in hell before I'd break you, and you know it. I'll give you exactly what you deserve, and as long as you're straight we'll get along, always providing we don't have to shake hands. If that's understood, why, take hold. The company's yours.

QUIRT. Well, before I take hold, let me get one more remark in the record. I wish to God I could jump your damn gang. I've heard of it all along the line. You've got a rabble, and I know it. I saw it coming into Is-sur-Tille once when you didn't see me. A shambling bunch of hams that wouldn't salute anything under a general.

FLAGG. All right, and what's my outfit's rating at regimental?

QUIRT. Oh, I got to hand it to you. You can hypnotize 'em. They'd start out to cut their way to Berlin if you gave the word. But, my God, they ain't much to look at, Captain Flagg.

FLAGG. Well, teach 'em to salute if it'll make you feel any happier, Hoppergrass. And before the platoon commanders get here, there's one thing I'd like to ask you. What did you do with the little girl?

QUIRT. What little girl?

FLAGG. You damn well know what little girl.

QUIRT. It's a small world, Captain Flagg, but the number of soldiers' sluts is numerous.

FLAGG. I was a corporal under you in China. You broke me to get her.

QUIRT. You were a damn fool. You'd have married her if it hadn't been for me, and be running a laundry now with the seat of your pants hanging down between your knees.

FLAGG. What happened to her?

QUIRT. What happened to the battleship *Maine?*

FLAGG. My God . . .

QUIRT. I broke you in China. I admit I broke you for that little Chink. And when I served under you in Cuba you got even. That's why I'm still a sergeant. [*A knock at the door from* KIPER.] Let it go at that.

FLAGG. Kiper?

KIPER [*outside*]. Ay, ay, sir!

FLAGG. Bring 'em in. [KIPER *opens the door and follows into the room* LIEUTENANTS ALDRICH, MOORE, *and* SCHMIDT, *and* GUNNERY SERGEANT SOCKEL. *They salute. They line up.*] Gentlemen, this is First Sergeant Quirt, who is in charge. This is Lieutenant Aldrich; this is Lieutenant Moore, and this is Lieutenant Schmidt, and you'll remember Sockel from Cuba. He's commanding the fourth platoon.

QUIRT [*turns to* SOCKEL]. Hello, Joe. How's tricks?

SOCKEL. Pretty good. How's yourself? [*They smile broadly, two old-timers among green lieutenants.*]

QUIRT. Ticking like a clock.

FLAGG. Aldrich, you're senior here, aren't you?

ALDRICH. Yes, sir. Two days ahead of the others.

FLAGG. You'll be in command here. Ask Quirt for any advice you need. I'll be back Wednesday week. . . . Now, men, Sergeant Quirt here is one of the best God damn soldiers that ever destroyed a memorandum receipt. I've soldiered with him around the world, and there isn't a finer, cleaner, smarter Marine afloat than Quirt—when he's sober. As long as he's sober, he'll run this outfit—whether I'm here or absent; but Quirt loves the bottle; and when he's drunk he's the lousiest, filthiest bum that ever wore a uniform. When drunk, he's worse than I am, and you know damn well I don't allow anybody to get as bad as that. If he tanks up I'll break him. I've broken him once, and he knows I'll do it again. The first raw crack he makes will find him drilling in the rear rank of Sockel's platoon, drilling like a tramp with a broom for a rifle. Get that, Aldrich; the first time you find him down in the square with his face in the dirt in front of all these young nipple-nursers, you lock him up and keep him locked up till I return.

ALDRICH. Yes, sir.

FLAGG. Give him his head, and let him have anything he wants, and don't forget he's forgotten more about being a soldier than any of you college boys will ever know. But if you're wise you won't play cards with him, and before you lend him any money you'd better kiss it a last long farewell. That's all. Kiper, have you got the waterproofs in that side-car?

KIPER. Ay, ay, sir.

FLAGG. Give her a spin, and we'll shove off. [*Picks up cap and stick from table and goes out, followed by all save* QUIRT.]

[*Off stage, the motorcycle clatters. The* LIEUTENANTS *shout farewell.* QUIRT *goes up to right window, looks out, and then sits at table, takes out dice, and practices a few turns. He holds the dice up to his eyes and then spins.* QUIRT *whistles "Pretty Baby."*]

QUIRT. Seven, baby. [*He smiles with satisfaction.*] Look at those acrobats act. You got to treat the old man right, now. [*There is a light tap on the door to left.* QUIRT *puts dice in pocket and looks at map.*] Come in. [CHARMAINE *enters.*]

CHARMAINE. *Le capitaine—il est parti?*

QUIRT. Just left. Don't cry, little one.

CHARMAINE. *Le nouveau sergeant. N'est-ce pas?*

QUIRT. *N'est-ce pas* is right.

CHARMAINE. I wanted to see the captain.

QUIRT. Just too late, sorry to say. [*Looks at her for first time.*] You one piecie captain's fella boy? You captain's fella?

CHARMAINE. *Le capitaine? Mais non!*

QUIRT. I'll bet it's *mais non*. Say, ain't you Cognac Pete's daughter?

CHARMAINE. *Oui*. You stay at Pete's?

QUIRT. Sure. [*Pause*.] *Et vous?*

CHARMAINE. *C'est mon père*.

QUIRT. Uh-huh. I thought so. [*Rises; crosses to her*.] Well, baby, you better stick to me, and you'll have another papa.

[*A terrific commotion begins outside. A vociferous Irish voice is heard shouting over and over again, "I'll get that lousy German son-of-a-bitch, I'll get the German bastard," while* LIPINSKY *and* GOWDY *yell, "Cut it out, you loafer. Dry up, dry up or you'll get yours."* LIPINSKY *opens the door.* CHARMAINE *steps back. The shouting is audible only when door is open*.]

LIPINSKY. Sergeant, there's a drunken Mick named Mulcahy raising hell outside. Can't do a thing with him. Got blood in his eyes for a guy from Cincinnati.

QUIRT [*sternly, out of the corner of his mouth, not looking at him*]. Tell him to pipe down. [LIPINSKY *goes out. Door closes; shouting stops.* CHARMAINE *goes toward door*.] Better not go out there now, honey. Some rough language is taking place out there. [LIPINSKY *reënters. Shouting is started again*.]

LIPINSKY. Sergeant, the Mick's sitting on Gowdy, and I can't pull him off.

QUIRT [*quietly, as before*]. Tell him to pipe down. [LIPINSKY *goes out. Shouting stops.* QUIRT *crosses to* CHARMAINE.] You going to promenade *avec moi* tonight? Down by the canal? Under the lime trees?

CHARMAINE. No. [*She is trembling*.]

QUIRT. No? Captain's own private darling, huh? Say,

you're a damned pretty frog. For a frog, I don't know as
I ever saw a prettier.

[*The hullabaloo redoubles outside.* Lipinsky *comes in
again.*]

Lipinsky. Shall we lock him up, Sergeant?

Quirt. Drag him in.

[Lipinsky *and* Gowdy *drag in a huge, red-raced Irishman
and stand him groggily on his feet below* Quirt.]

Mulcahy. That damn Nussbaum from Cincinnati is a
German spy, and I'll have his guts out of him before I'm
through.

Quirt [*quietly*]. Mulcahy, pipe down.

Mulcahy. I tell you that Nussbaum is a German spy!
I'll get the lousy German and every German out of Cincinnati. . . .

[*The* Sergeant *plants one squarely on* Mulcahy's *jaw.
He goes down like a log.*]

Quirt [*still out of the corner of his mouth*]. Drag him
out.

[Lipinsky *and* Gowdy *take him by arms, turn him around,
and drag him out.* Quirt, *rubbing his knuckles, crosses
back of table to* Charmaine, *who is smiling at her won-
derful hero with the powerful punch.*]

Quirt. Why, hello, Pittsburg, you love me? [*They embrace and hold a long kiss.*]

CURTAIN

Scene Two

Late afternoon, eight days later. The scene is unchanged.
Lipinsky *is lying along bench, smoking a cigarette and*

trying to sleep at the same time. KIPER enters, singing at the top of his voice. LIPINSKY's cap is down over his eyes. POLICE SERGEANT FERGUSON is at table toward back, working over papers; he is smoking a pipe.

KIPER.   Mademoiselle from Armentière, *parlez-vous?*
Mademoiselle from Armentière, *parlez-vous?*
Mademoiselle from Armentière——
Hullo, hullo—Jee-zus. [*Puts musette bags in corner.*]

LIPINSKY.   Knock off that chat. [*On bench; doesn't move.*]

KIPER.   Say, are you running this God damn army?

LIPINSKY.   You're damn well right, I'm running this army.

KIPER.   Well, you had better God damn well snap out of it. You're relieved.

LIPINSKY [*sitting up*].   Skipper come back?

KIPER.   Almost. He's at the Last Chance.

LIPINSKY.   Still soaked?

KIPER.   He ain't soaked. He's just the drunkest bum you ever saw in your life.

LIPINSKY.   Trying to whip the world?

KIPER.   Naw, just quiet drunk. Looks out of those eyes of his like two red holes in the snow.

LIPINSKY.   How's Paris?

KIPER.   Never got that far. Washed ashore at Bar-le-Duc.

LIPINSKY.   Yeah? Good time?

KIPER.   Pretty good the first day.

LIPINSKY.   What'd you do the rest?

KIPER.   You see, it was this way. The skip and me was promenading, and he was swinging that damn little Pekin swagger-stick of his when up comes an M.P. "Sorry, sir," says the M.P.; "Corps commander's regulations, sir, no swagger-sticks." The skip says, "Well, and who, may I ask, is the corps commander? Tell him he can take his lousy army and sell it for cheese." "Sorry, sir," says the M.P. "Corps commander's regulations, sir, and I'll have to take that stick away from you." "All right," says the skip, whirling the stick around his head, "pitch in, soldier, pitch in!"

LIPINSKY. Did he take it away?

KIPER. Aw, take it away! Listen to the poor nut. I spent the next six days of my leave detained as a material witness for attempted manslaughter.

LIPINSKY. I guess the skip didn't draw much?

KIPER. Draw hell! Didn't I swear this yellow-bellied M.P. came up and knocked him into the road?

LIPINSKY. Yeah?

KIPER. And the court looks at this M.P. and says, "Right face! Take him away and give him ten days, bread and water."

LIPINSKY. Serve him right, the Boy Scout! They ought to take away those guys' whistles before they blow themselves to death. And speaking of whistles, this new top of ours don't do nothing else at all besides blow a whistle. It's been one bloody formation after another ever since you left.

KIPER. Is that the kind of hombre he is?

LIPINSKY. He's a sea-going son-of-a-bitch. He ain't sit down since he was here. He's got the first platoon down in the village now taking up the dirt from the courtyard with teaspoons. You can't get in the chow line until you catch twenty horse-flies. He seen Cooper pulling a fag at reveille this morning. What's Cooper doing now? Boy, following the ponies, following the ponies. *He's* out collecting apples.

KIPER. Well, the skip will make him cut that stuff. Me and the skip ain't going to see the little boys bullied.

LIPINSKY. You and the skip, yeah. But say, the skip and this top soldier are going to tangle pant-legs over another little matter before they have been together one day.

KIPER. What t'hell!

LIPINSKY. This horny pelican is going aboard the skip's old hooker every night.

KIPER. Down at Cognac Pete's house?

LIPINSKY. Parking his dogs in Pete's kitchen every night with that little black-eyed frog sitting in his lap lighting his pipe.

KIPER. If the skip finds that out there'll be a noise like you'd throw a tom-cat in a dog pound.

[*Enter* SERGEANT QUIRT.]

QUIRT [*to* KIPER]. Where's Captain Flagg?

KIPER. Last Chance.

QUIRT. What the hell do you mean, coming in here without him? What do you think you're paid for?

KIPER. I tried to argue with him, Sergeant, and he picked me up and threw me out the window. Lucky for me it was open.

QUIRT. Go get him. Don't argue. Get him. Take Lippy along. [LIPINSKY *and* KIPER *start, hesitate, and talk.* QUIRT *starts toward chair above table.*]

[LIEUTENANT ALDRICH *enters.*]

ALDRICH. Heard the skipper was aboard.

QUIRT [*turning to* ALDRICH]. Grounded on the last bar.

ALDRICH. Yeah?

QUIRT [*to* KIPER *and* LIPINSKY, *who hurry off*]. Cast off,

will you? Travel! Hit the deck! [*To* ALDRICH.] Sending
out a salvage party. He's full to the scuppers.

ALDRICH. All I hope is he comes in mild and goes to sleep.
He's got too damn much talent for raising hell to suit me.

QUIRT. You ought to seen him in China. Straight as a
mast, muscled like a gorilla, Christian as hell. Good deal of
liquor has flowed under his belt since then.

ALDRICH. Expect any trouble?

QUIRT. What do you mean?

ALDRICH. This here now little wild woman.

QUIRT. I don't know what's your game.

ALDRICH. Oh, all right! Just the same, you'd be a damn
sight wiser to lay off, in my opinion.

QUIRT. Lay off what?

ALDRICH. Charmaine.

QUIRT [*turning to* ALDRICH]. Are you thinking of making this a three-handed game?

ALDRICH. I am not.

QUIRT. Because if you are, all I got to say is, help yourself to whatever you can get. It's love in a manner of
speaking, and it's certainly war. Everything dirty goes.

ALDRICH. Suit yourself. You've known him longer than
I have.

QUIRT. He's got a grudge against me, I don't mind telling you. And I ain't wasting any ardent affection on him.
If it hadn't been for him, I'd had a company of my own. I
didn't know she was his meat when I first saw her. But when
I found out, d'you think I'd apologize and back out the door
out of deference to him? I says, Kippy-dope, you're mine!

ALDRICH. Yeah—but do you know what I heard at mess
today?

QUIRT. Nope.

ALDRICH. Well, now listen. I didn't intend to mix into this unless it was necessary, but Schmidt got it straight yesterday that old Cognac Pete was going to prosecute some soldier or other for corrupting Charmaine's morals.

QUIRT. Charmaine's what? Jeez, that's good!

ALDRICH. Maybe so. Just the same, he's got a case.

QUIRT. He has not.

ALDRICH. No? Suppose he gets you before a court martial? It's a hanging matter if he wants to push it. You know the regulations.

QUIRT. You mean he's after me?

ALDRICH. I don't know who he's after. You—or Flagg. Has Cognac anything on you?

QUIRT. Well, they might hang me once as a sort of lesson to me.

[*Motorcycle clatters outside.*]

ALDRICH. Well, there you are. Suppose he takes it to headquarters? Where's Quirt then? Sitting pretty?

QUIRT. Well, I just resign all rights and interests in the ma'am'selle and avoid possible complications.

ALDRICH. Fine. There's Kiper already. If Flagg's with him, for God's sake use a little diplomacy.

[*Outside,* FLAGG *in drunken voice says,* "*Get out of my way, Kiper.*" *Noise of* KIPER *being pushed.*]

QUIRT. Diplomacy, with that? [FLAGG *enters, coat in hand and hair mussed. He still carries stick.* LIPINSKY *and* KIPER *follow. All stand at attention until the* CAPTAIN *is seated.*]

ALDRICH [*saluting*]. How are you, Captain Flagg?

FLAGG. I'm a wreck, that's what I am! I'm an epoch-making disaster! You see before you, Mr. Aldrich, one of the seven great calamities of the world!

QUIRT. Hope you had a pleasant leave, sir.

FLAGG. Well, I didn't. Held for carrying a stick. Picked up the second day by one of Pershing's Sunday School teachers. By God, he must think he's running a day nursery! . . . What's happened?

QUIRT. Not a thing.

FLAGG. Boys in shape?

QUIRT. They'll do. Three more days, and I'd risk them on the line.

FLAGG. Try and get three days. If we aren't digging in somewhere before then, I'll pay the Russian national debt out of my salary. How much do you think I spent in Bar-le-Duc?

QUIRT. How much did you have?

FLAGG. Eight hundred francs, and I got a chance to get rid of thirty. Here's the whole roll. Does anybody want it? Just my luck to have to move in again with seven hundred and seventy francs on me and get bumped off. [*A knock at the door by* BRIGADE RUNNER.] Come in. [*A* BRIGADE RUNNER *enters.*]

THE RUNNER. Captain Flagg?

FLAGG. Right here.

THE RUNNER. From Captain Simpson, sir. He wanted you to know the "G One" crowd is on the way over.

FLAGG. Tell him I'm much obliged. Anything else?

THE RUNNER. That's all. How do I get to the Twelfth?

FLAGG. Show him, Kiper. [KIPER *and* THE RUNNER *salute and go out.* FLAGG *starts to button his coat.*] Damn headquarters! It's some more of that world-safe-for-democracy slush! Every time they come around here I've got to ask myself is this an army or is it a stinking theosophical society for ethical culture and the Bible-backing uplift! I

don't want that band of Gideons from headquarters. Now
you watch that door. Watch it! In ten minutes we're going
to have another of these round-headed gentlemen of the old
school here giving us a prepared lecture on what we're fighting the war for and how we're to do it—one of these bill-
poster chocolate soldiers with decorations running clear
around to his backbone and a thrilling speech on army
morale and the last drop of fighting blood that puts your
drive over to glorious victory! . . . The side-whiskered
butter-eaters! I'd like to rub their noses in a few of the
latrines I've slept in, keeping up army morale and losing men
because some screaming fool back in the New Jersey sector
thinks he's playing with paper dolls. [*A knock.*] Well,
come in, come in. [LIEUTENANT MOORE *enters.*] Hello.

MOORE. How are you, Captain Flagg? Hope you liked
Bar-le-Duc?

FLAGG. Ever been there?

MOORE. Once.

FLAGG. Ever put in much time in the redecorated chicken
stable where they detain the A.W.O.L.'s?

MOORE. Afraid I never saw it, sir.

FLAGG. Well, you haven't missed a great deal. They
whitewashed the damn shanty right over the hen manure.
Phew! I can smell it yet. If I'd stayed there another day
I'd have laid an egg.

MOORE. Tough luck! But what I really wanted to say,
sir, was, there's an old fellow outside here who wants to see
you about his daughter. He seems to think somebody's
taken advantage of her.

FLAGG. Somebody in this outfit?

MOORE. Yes, sir.

FLAGG. Took advantage of the girl, huh?

MOORE. That's what he says.

FLAGG. He means she took advantage of her opportunities and now he's taking advantage of his. What's the old boy's name?

MOORE. Can't quite make it out, but it seems to be Pete something or other. Are there any Pete's in France? Sounded like Cognac Pete.

FLAGG. Yeah?

MOORE. Sounded like it.

FLAGG [*rising, perturbed*]. Well, wait a minute. Cognac Pete's, huh? Is the girl with him?

MOORE. No.

FLAGG. Hell!

QUIRT. Think fast, Captain. Think fast.

FLAGG. Quirt, do you know anything about this?

QUIRT [*starting to leave*]. Not a thing.

FLAGG. You leaving us?

QUIRT [*unembarrassed*]. A few orders to make out, sir. [*He grins.*] Can't very well work here, you see.

FLAGG. I'm damned if I see. Sit down and spill your ink. And if you've put up a game on me, you crawling crab . . .

QUIRT. Me? What have I got to do with it? Think fast, Captain, think fast.

FLAGG. Damn it, send him in, and we'll see. [MOORE *goes out.*] Hell!

QUIRT [*laughing*]. Think fast, Captain. Don't forget to think fast.

FLAGG. You sit where you are, you hyena; and laugh, damn you, laugh. [*Enter* COGNAC PETE, *an ancient nut-brown Frenchman, very polite and humble, followed by*

Moore *and* Kiper. Moore *and* Pete *stand by table.* Kiper *sits on bench.*] Pete, what's this I hear about a complaint? What's the matter, huh? One of my men, huh?

Pete. *Oui, mon capitaine.*

Flagg. I'm damned if I can leave this damn army half a day without hell breaking loose somewhere. Come on, let's have it; spit it out.

Moore. Allay, Pete.

Pete [*speaking in an unintelligible rush of French*]. *Ah, monsieur le capitaine, je suis un vieillard; mais j'ai vécu heuresement, et mes enfants ont été toujours honnêtes, mais hélas, mon capitaine, quelque chose de terrible vient de passer, une calamité monstrueuse . . .*

Flagg [*to* Moore]. What's on the menu? Do you get anything out of that?

Moore. He says something has happened.

Flagg [*distressed*]. Does it take all that vocabulary to say something has happened in French? Well, keep going, keep going.

Moore. Allay, Pete.

Pete. *Mais, mon capitaine, voilá que les américains arrivent. Ils sont grands et forts, et ils demandent tour-jours ce qu'ils veulent. Ils ne s'accoutument pas à nos mœurs ni à nos habitudes, mais—nom de Dieu!—pourquoi choisissent-ils la seule fleur de ma vie, quand ils peuvent trouver n'importe où qu'ils vont des poules qui les desirent. Ma seule fleur, ma fleur Charmaine, ma fleur delicate!*

Flagg. What language is he talking now?

Moore. He says the soldiers take what they want, and they have trampled the one flower of his life.

Flagg. Is that all he said?

MOORE. The rest is poetry.

FLAGG [*impatiently*]. Well, tell him to omit flowers, see, omit flowers.

MOORE [*to* PETE]. *Brèvement.*

PETE. *Ma fille. Ma fille bien-aimée. Elle est défleurée. Elle est dans la boue, elle est déshonorée.*

FLAGG [*to* MOORE]. More flowers?

MOORE. No, sir. He says his daughter's been—ah—ruined [*pause*] . . . so to speak.

FLAGG. Ruined, huh? Rape or seduction?

MOORE. [*to* PETE]. *S'est-elle soumise, ou l'-a-t-on forcée?*

PETE. *Les Américains sont si forts. Ils se forcent sur elle, ils ferment sa bouche de lacon qu'elle ne peut donner l'alarme. Que peut faire la petite fille? L'Américaine est forte, elle peut se défendre, mais la française, elle est gentille et modeste et craintive et ne sait se défendre.*

FLAGG [*to* MOORE]. Now what's all that?

MOORE. Rape, sir.

FLAGG. Does he allude to any specific girl, or is he speaking of French wenches in general?

MOORE [*to* PETE]. *Comment s'appelle ta fille?*

PETE. Charmaine.

MOORE. Charmaine, sir.

FLAGG [*very seriously*]. Look here, Moore. You know as well as I do, this same little baggage has been pretty free with me. What's the old boy's game? And for God's sake, what do you think you're up to, bringing him in here?

MOORE. You mean you're . . . God, I didn't know that!

FLAGG. You didn't! You must go around here wearing blinders. You see the fix you've got me in?

QUIRT. Think fast, Captain, think fast.

MOORE. To tell the truth, I got the impression it was

somebody else.   Honest to God, I thought he said it was a
soldier . . . [FLAGG *hesitates and then gives* MOORE *a quick
look.* MOORE *is embarrassed.*]   I wasn't sure, but I got that
impression.

FLAGG. Did he name anybody?

MOORE. No.

FLAGG [*turning away*]. Well, damn her little soul.   No,
I know damn well it wasn't anybody else.   [*Turns to*
MOORE.]   Ask him how much he wants.

MOORE. How much what?

FLAGG. Money, you highbrow, money!   What do you
think he wants?

MOORE. I don't know, but if I thought he wanted money
I certainly would not have listened to him.

FLAGG. You're just a bleating babe in the woods, you
are.   That's what they all want.

MOORE. He told me he wanted the man to marry the girl.

FLAGG. Marry her!

PETE. *Elle était une petite enfant innocente, une fleur à
demiouverte.*

FLAGG. What's that?   Flowers again?

MOORE. He says she was an innocent child.

FLAGG. Listen.   You tell him I'm sure she's still an innocent girl.   Tell him Charmaine is one of the most virtuous
and respectable ladies I've ever had the pleasure of meeting.

MOORE [*to* PETE]. *Monsieur le capitaine dit que c'est
impossible et que vous vous trompez, monsieur, parceque
Charmaine est tout à fait honnête et vertueuse.*

PETE [*shaking his head*]. *Non! non! non!—je ne me
trompe pas—malheureusement c'est bien la vérité.*

MOORE. He's sure of it.

FLAGG. Ask him if he wants to bring charges.

Moore. *Désirez-vous le faire passer au conseil de guerre?*

Pete. *Conseil de guerre? Ca se peut.*

Moore. He says perhaps.

Flagg. What does he mean, "perhaps"? Ask him how much he wants.

Moore. *Il demande ce que vous voulez.*

Pete. *Mais la petite qui est défleurée—il faut qu'on la fasse honnête, et moi—est-ce donc que l'honneur de ma famille ne vaut rien? Il faut qu'ils se marient, et quant à moi—il faut me payer si je ne le fais pas passer devant le conseil de guerre. Il me faut cinq cent francs.*

Flagg. Flowers?

Moore. No, he wants the fellow to marry the girl—and he wants five hundred francs.

Flagg. I see. That's better. Tell him he can have three hundred. Tell him he can pick any son-in-law he wants out of the whole damn army.

Moore [*to* Pete]. *Elle peut choisir n'importe qui qu'il soit de toute la compagnie—et vous—vous aurez trois cent francs.*

Pete [*suddenly wildly angry*]. *Ca ne va pas! Vous vous moquez de moi, vous officiers américains. Je connais le truc—moi—de vous voir m'insulter quand il s'agit de la rapace. Alors, messieurs, j'irai au G.H.Q. et vous verrez. C'est la mort, et gare à votre peau! Me voilà qui vient vous voir ici, malheureux mais amical, et je ne reçois que des insultes. Cinq cent francs! Rien de moins, et il la marie.* [*He starts for door.*]

Flagg. Wait a minute. [Aldrich *bars the door.*] What's wrong?

Moore. He's insulted. Going to Headquarters. Five hundred, he wants; and it's a certain man, he says.

FLAGG. What man?

MOORE. *Quel homme?*

PETE [*turning, crosses in front of table; to* QUIRT, *dramatically*]. *Le voilà! Alors je m'en vais. Vous vous moquez de moi! Laissez-moi partir.*

[QUIRT *rises, knocking over chair.*]

FLAGG [*taking a step toward* QUIRT]. Quirt, what's the meaning of this?

QUIRT. Sorry, sir, I don't quite catch the drift myself.

FLAGG. Have you been around with Charmaine?

QUIRT. Charmaine? I don't think so, Captain. But I've got a poor memory for names.

FLAGG. You're a liar. You knew Charmaine was mine, and you couldn't keep your hands off her.

QUIRT. Yeah? It's getting to be a habit of mine, huh? Whaddye going to do about it, Captain Flagg?

FLAGG. Oh? What [*walks to table*] am I going to do about it?—I'm going to marry you to Charmaine and let you make an honest woman out of her! Quirt, you've taken the detail right off my shoulders, and it's your turn to think fast! [*Turns to* MOORE.] Mr. Moore, now tell the old man that the sergeant was making honest proposals and desperate love! Ask what church he belongs to, or whether he wants 'em married by the cashier of the bank. [*Turns to* QUIRT. MOORE *turns to* PETE; *they start toward the door.*] Sergeant, you arrived in the nick of time with replacements! You saved the day! The Marines have landed and have the situation well in hand! We're going to decorate you! We're going to let you hold the bag!

QUIRT. All very interesting, Captain. But how are you going to do it? I may have landed, but I don't remember seeing any article in what I signed saying you could pick my woman for me. Seems to me you'd learned that I pick my women for myself.

FLAGG. Quirt, you've signed on for a cruise with this woman, and you can't jump ship. I can tell Aldrich to stand out of the way and let that old man go to headquarters with his story about you . . . and what chance has a lousy Marine sergeant got before an army court-martial when ten majors start the iron ball rolling? Ten army majors back in Paris, who ain't going to let anybody do any seducing but themselves. Don't be a hayshaker, Quirt. You can't play guardhouse lawyer in this country. You're in the army now, with a lot of western shysters sitting in the judge advocate general's room.

QUIRT. And who's going to be witness against me? You couldn't get that little frog to swear anything. I'm too damned handsome a soldier. I'm strong with this little French broad. Told me last night, just before you come back, she never loved a soldier who loved like me. Said she wished the whole damned outfit would move away and leave us in peace. Why, she's jealous every time I have to go to formation.

FLAGG. Sergeant, in about five minutes you're going to be married; in about eight you're going to please this old man by leaving an allotment here for about two thirds of your pay in regular army style. The more you talk, the more you hang yourself up by the thumbs.

QUIRT. This ain't talk. What do you say I go get this little baby and you ask her if she'll say anything about me that ain't praise and admiration? What do you say I go get her? What do I care a whoop in hell what this old bozo says about me? I ain't seduced *him!* He's after money.

Well, I ain't got money. I don't have to carry money around in my love affairs. What do you say I go get her?

FLAGG. Of course you'll go get her. And propose marriage to her on the way, because you'll meet the wedding detail when you get here. Gowdy, go to the Y. tent and get the chaplain. [GOWDY *goes out.*] Aldrich, accompany Sergeant Quirt to the tavern and tell Charmaine that I'm giving away in marriage the handsomest sergeant in the corps. Tell her she's a woman in a thousand, because Quirt has already run away from a thousand; and if it weren't for my seeing justice done him, he'd run away from that many more. All right, Quirt, we'll be waiting for you. [QUIRT *and* ALDRICH *go out.* FERGUSON *fixes chair, returns to seat, and turns to* MOORE.] Mr. Moore, tell papa the wedding bells are going to ring, and there's money in it for him, money in it! [MOORE *seats* PETE *on stool at window; then whispers.*]

[*A knock at the door.* LIPINSKY *opens it.*]

LIPINSKY. Brigade runner, Captain Flagg.

FLAGG. Send him in. [THE RUNNER *enters.*]

RUNNER. Company commander?

FLAGG. What is it—shoving off?

RUNNER. Moving in an hour, sir.

FLAGG. In an hour?

RUNNER. Please initial. [*Offers pencil and paper.*]

FLAGG [*signing*]. You hear that, Moore?

MOORE. Yes, sir.

FLAGG [*up, and business-like*]. Going in an hour. You know what that means.

MOORE. Yes, sir.

FLAGG. Pass the word to our platoon commanders to stand in heavy packs in thirty minutes. The camions are waiting at the crossroads with ammunition. [MOORE *goes out*.] Kiper, tell Quirt to salvage all rations in the square. [KIPER *starts for door but stops as* FLAGG *says, "Wait a minute."*] Don't let on to Quirt we're going in. We'll marry him to Charmaine and march the blushing bridegroom off to war. [*Walks up and down*.]

FERGUSON. Afraid you can't marry them this evening, Captain Flagg. Chaplain very sticky on that point. Have to be married in the morning.

FLAGG. Well, then, the mayor could marry them, couldn't he? Lipinsky, go get the mayor. Who's seen the mayor today?

KIPER. Just saw him down by the bridge on a load of manure.

FLAGG. There you are, Lipinsky—load of manure, near the bridge. Get the mayor, dust him off, and bring him here toot pronto. If the chaplain can't do it, the mayor can.

[LIPINSKY *starts to go out but halts and calls " 'Ten-shun." PETE still sits on stool. In walk a* BRIGADIER-GENERAL, *one* COLONEL, *one* CAPTAIN, *and two* LIEU-TENANTS.]

THE GENERAL. Hello, Flagg. Haven't you received that order yet? Not a soul stirring on your damned street. [*All salute*.] Flagg, you run the most disreputable outfit of the brigade. I come into town to hold a staff conference and find the whole shebang asleep. What kind of platoon commanders have you got, anyway, sitting round here like a nest of hoboes when you're moving in forty-five minutes? [*The staff remains standing at attention*.]

FLAGG. Just got the order, General. We'll get off in time. Never missed a train in my life.

THE GENERAL. Well, I don't see how you do it. Camions

back two miles at the crossroads. Your men will have ammunition there, and I want every man to carry two extra bandoliers.

FLAGG. If you don't mind my saying so, General, we're the refuse of the brigade back of the line and we carry extra bandoliers into it.

THE GENERAL. Well, I'll tell you why. Division wants a line straightened that we're going to take over. Isn't straight enough for him. Where's that map? Map, Davis!

THE COLONEL [turns]. Map, Tolbert!

THE LIEUTENANT. Map, Price!

THE CAPTAIN. Where's that map? [Looks wildly around. The last LIEUTENANT to enter hands map to PRICE.] Here's the map, sir. [Hands map to GENERAL.]

THE GENERAL. Good boy, good boy. A map, after all, among you soldiers. Now, see here, Flagg [pointing to map, which he spreads out on table]. There she is, and here's the line. The corps wants it straightened out. It will take the steel, the cold steel. But they've got to have it straightened out. Give them the steel and you can do it. You'll hold the town—our half of it—and you'll get these fellows out if it takes a week. Your men are a bunch of tramps, but they can do this sort of thing.

FLAGG. Individualists, General, individualists.

THE GENERAL. Well, it's the penalty you pay for laxity. I admit it has its compensations. But you've got to give 'em the steel. You've got to run 'em down like rats. You give them the old cowering point. We've got to get them out. We want to go in there and run 'em out. We want to give 'em steel.

FLAGG. We? Staff going in there too, General?

THE GENERAL [*disconsolately*]. No—they won't risk us fellows, curse the luck.

FLAGG. That's too bad, General.

THE GENERAL. But we'll be behind you, Flagg.

FLAGG. How far, General?

THE GENERAL. We'll probably be at cemetery farm. We haven't studied the indirect fire properly yet, but we'll be behind you.

THE COLONEL [*handing bundle of posters to* GENERAL]. Beg pardon, sir; these posters.

THE GENERAL. And, Flagg, some Yankee Doodle back in Hoboken sends you some posters with his compliments.

FLAGG. Posters? What for?

THE GENERAL. To post behind the German lines—sent to all companies of this brigade.

FLAGG. My God! What are we advertising? Camels?

THE GENERAL. Oh, no! It's intelligence work. Explaining our mission over here to the German soldier. There are three hundred posters. Send a small detail through the German lines some night and tack 'em up all over the place.

FLAGG. How many men am I supposed to lose on that job?

THE GENERAL. Not one. We don't want to lose a man. But tack 'em up.

FLAGG. Yeah, that's easy to say. I'd like to tack up a few in Hoboken containing my sentiments on two-starred idiots who waste men on that kind of monkey-business.

THE GENERAL. Well, here is another thing, Flagg, the big G. one wants a prisoner out of that town of yours. Wants an officer from one of those Alsatian regiments where the deserters are filtering through. And I've got to get him.

FLAGG. Oh, don't say that, General, don't break our

hearts. I've got to get him. I knew damn well you had a bolt of black crêpe up your sleeve when you came in the door.

THE GENERAL. Hold down the losses, Flagg . . . and listen. If you send me one of those Alsatian officers in good condition I'll send your whole company back for a month's rest.

FLAGG. You mean it?

THE GENERAL. Mean it! You know me, Flagg. I'll do more if you get me an officer without a scratch. I'll give you eight days in any hotel in France. If you weren't such a bum, Flagg, I'd put you on staff.

FLAGG. I've been a bum, General, but I'm damned if I'd go on staff.

THE GENERAL [at the door]. Hold down the losses, Flagg, and give 'em the steel—and don't forget those posters, for they're damned important—and if you fetch me that prisoner you get a month's rest and eight days' leave. [The door opens. In walk the CHAPLAIN, CHARMAINE and QUIRT, MAYOR, KIPER, and LIPINSKY.] Hullo! My God, what's this? A wedding party?

FLAGG. Why, yes, General. I don't suppose we ought to wait for it, but it's a sort of special case and won't take long.

THE GENERAL. You aren't getting married, are you, Flagg?

FLAGG. Not this trip; no, sir. It's Sergeant Quirt.

THE GENERAL [turning to QUIRT]. Oh, yes, I remember Sergeant Quirt very well.

FLAGG. I didn't like to intrude company matters when you were in haste, General, but the truth is, Sergeant Quirt has expressed a wish to marry the inn-keeper's daughter here, and her father was waiting to press charges; so, you see——

THE GENERAL. Oh! Charges . . . ?

FLAGG. Personally, I'm opposed to Quirt's marrying at all, but he insists his intentions were honorable, and he's such a fine soldier I should hate to carry this old man to H.Q. with a complaint.

THE GENERAL. What's this, Sergeant?

QUIRT. A courtship, General; a love match from the start. Honorable intentions on both sides.

THE GENERAL. Sounds a little fishy to me, I must say, but go right ahead. Don't waste time.

[FERGUSON *comes forward.*]

PETE. *Monsieur le général, les Américains sont si forts—ils m'ont déshonoré—ma petite fille—ma fleur charmante—ma fleur délicate . . .*

FERGUSON. In case of a marriage, Captain Flagg, a little allotment is regulation.

FLAGG. Thanks, Fergy; I almost forgot the allotment.

QUIRT. Hell, we don't need no allotment. This is a love match.

FLAGG. Of course, it holds us up a bit, but if the General doesn't mind?

FERGUSON. A little allotment is regulation, sir.

THE GENERAL. Go ahead, go ahead.

FLAGG. Ferguson, where are those allotment blanks?

FERGUSON. Right here, sir.

THE GENERAL [*to* FERGUSON]. Make it out for two thirds of the sergeant's pay, Ferguson.

FERGUSON [*sits and fills paper*]. Yes, sir.

QUIRT [*standing, with* CHARMAINE]. I don't know about this, General.

THE GENERAL. It's for your own good, Quirt. How do you plan to get out of it, otherwise?

QUIRT. Get out of it? Didn't I tell you it was a love match?

THE GENERAL. No more talk, Sergeant; sign up or stand trial.

FLAGG. For your own good, Quirt.

QUIRT. For whose good, Captain Flagg?

THE GENERAL. Sign up, Quirt.

[FERGUSON *gives paper to* FLAGG. QUIRT *reluctantly signs.*]

FLAGG. All in order. [*Looks over paper.*] Shipshape, Sergeant Quirt. Beautiful hand you write, sir. And now, Chaplain, Sergeant Quirt is next.

THE GENERAL. Let's get it over with. And here's her father ready to give her away.

PETE. *Merci, mon général.*

THE GENERAL. A regular church wedding, and Captain Flagg can be best man.

FLAGG. Get that, Sergeant Quirt? Charmaine [*he crosses and hands her allotment papers with a bow*], keep this in a good safe place. It means money to you the first of every month.

CHARMAINE. *Merci.*

THE GENERAL. Turn on the ceremony.

CHAPLAIN. This is a little irregular.

THE GENERAL. Run it through. Sorry we can't wait to kiss the bride, Quirt. You have about twenty minutes, Flagg.

FLAGG. Right, sir.

THE GENERAL. One word, Quirt. You're going in to-night. You're going in in twenty minutes. If you take your men into the line in first-rate condition, looking like soldiers, you'll square yourself with me. Keep that in mind.

QUIRT. We're going in in twenty minutes?

THE GENERAL. Yes. We're off, men. So long, Flagg. Twenty minutes.

FLAGG. Goodbye, General.

[*All salute. The* GENERAL *and his retinue file out at door.*]

CHAPLAIN. Do you, Charmaine, take this man for your husband, to love, honor——

QUIRT. She does not, I do not, we do not. So we're going in in twenty minutes, eh—and you were going to tie me up before I knew anything about it? And I suppose if I don't marry her you'll lock me up. If you think you can take your men in tonight without a first sergeant, you lock me up. I would like to see you take this gang of tiny tots across that last two miles without a sergeant. Well, if this sergeant goes in, he goes in single; so you God damn well better make up your mind what you're going to do.

FLAGG. Well, skunk, you've got me. You win. Hit the deck.

QUIRT. Sorry, Charmaine, but I've got work to do. I can't marry you tonight, I can't marry you any God damn time at all, and if I never see you again—why, then I never see you again, understand? What's more, don't you try cashing that allotment, or by God I'll pull something that'll stop my pay for good. Get out of my way. [*He goes out. Instantly a whistle blows.*]

FLAGG. Sorry, Charmaine, but I need that sergeant. Shake a leg, you hayshakers. Pass the word for inspection in five minutes, and they'd better be shipshape. Camions at the crossroad. Extra bandoliers and V.B. grenades for the outside ranks. Don't let Quirt do all the work.

THE RUNNERS. Ay, ay, sir. [*They go out hastily.*]

PETE [*angry*]. *Sont-ils maries? Ou votre sergeant, se moque-t-il de moi?*

FLAGG. Sure, they're married.

PETE [*beats on table*]. *Prennez garde! Je viendrai!*

FLAGG [*turns—speaks ominously*]. Don't bother me. Don't get in my way, see? We're fighting a war with Germany. I don't give a damn whether he's married or not. Run along outside. [*Turns* PETE *around; spanks him.*] I'm busy. [PETE *goes out, stops near* CHARMAINE *and says*, "*Sale vache*"; *then goes out.* FLAGG *goes to table, gets his hat, turns toward the door.*] So long, Fergy. Take care of the stuff.

FERGUSON. Yes, sir. [*Turns to desk.*]

[FLAGG *starts out.* CHARMAINE *crosses to him.*]

CHARMAINE [*her hand on his arm*]. I'm so sorry. You should have taken me to Paris. I told you to take me to Paris. I could not be good all alone.

FLAGG [*takes her by shoulders*]. That's all right, Charmaine. You're a damn fine little animal. Go right on having a good time. It's a great life, and you've got a genius for it.

CHARMAINE. But you do not love me, not any more?

FLAGG. Sure I love you! Everybody loves you.

CHARMAINE. You think I am *pas bonne?*

FLAGG. Listen, Charmaine. Don't you worry any more about Quirt and me. It's a thousand to one you'll never see either of us again. I'm damned sorry I have to take your sergeant away, but this war's lousy with sergeants. There'll be thirty along in thirty days. Anyway you'll probably never see us again. Kiss me goodbye. [*They kiss.*] Now you forget me!

CHARMAINE. I never forget you.

[*A whistle blows outside.*]

FLAGG. You won't forget me? Well, if I get leave, Charmaine . . . you never can tell. [*The whistle blows twice.*] It's a hell of a war, but it's the only one we've got. [*He goes out. She stands staring after him.*]

FERGUSON [*from his table; turning*]. Well, little missy. You're a single woman *with* an allotment. There ain't many as fortunate as that.

CHARMAINE. He will come back?

FERGUSON. Which one?

CHARMAINE. The captain.

FERGUSON. Not likely. Not likely either of them will. A soldier hardly ever doubles on his trail in this war.

CHARMAINE. No?

FERGUSON. Hardly ever. And you're just as fortunate you didn't marry a soldier, darling. They're a bad lot to keep house for. I know. I've been keeping house for one regiment or another since I was as young as you are.

CHARMAINE. Oh, but they are beautiful.

FERGUSON. The girls always like them. I don't know why.

CHARMAINE. They go into hell to die—and they are not old enough to die.

FERGUSON. I shouldn't think it would matter much to you, dear. Some get killed, but plenty more come in to relieve them. Never any shortage of soldiers.

CHARMAINE. It's terrible!

FERGUSON. It's their business. Some of 'em get killed at it, same as in any trade.

CHARMAINE [*crosses to back of* FERGUSON's *chair; leans over him*]. Can I help you?

FERGUSON. No.

CHARMAINE. Tomorrow?

FERGUSON. No.

CHARMAINE. You are unkind.

FERGUSON. Just because I'm the only man around here do you think I'm going to let you bother me? You run along home and pray God to keep you out of mischief a few days. It won't do you any harm. [*He bends over his work.*]

CHARMAINE. Bon soir. [*He does not hear her.*] Bon soir!

FERGUSON. What?

CHARMAINE. Bon soir.

FERGUSON. Oh, yes, good night. [*She slowly crosses to door, looking back at him all the way. She quietly closes door, and just as she does so,* FERGUSON *very loudly says,* "Good night." *He bends over his desk, alone, writing, and sings.*]

The French they are a funny race, *parlez-vous.*

The French they are a funny race, *parlez-vous.*

CURTAIN

ACT II

*A cellar in a disputed town, a typical deep wine cellar of a
prosperous farmhouse on the edge of a village in
France. It resembles half of a culvert thirty feet in
diameter, with a corresponding curved roof and walls.
One end is open, and the other is walled up, admitting
a narrow and rather low door in the center, through
which a flight of stairs extends to the ground floor
above. This cellar is lit dimly by two candles placed
at either side of the front stage and held in bottles on
small bully-beef boxes. The rear wall can only barely
be discerned. Along the sides of this culvert are dirty
white ticks stuffed with straw for sleeping quarters, the sort of ticks headquarters detachment men
carry about with them. There are four on each side,
arranged with all the litter of miscellany a soldier carries about tucked at their heads, and with the foot of
these pallets extending into the center of the culvert.
The effect is not unlike in design that of a hospital
ward, with feet toward the center aisle. Back of
FLAGG's bunk all manner of stuff—first-aid kits, bandages, chocolates, sticks, pistols and rifles, notes, books
of memoranda, etc.*

*Two men are asleep, snoring gently—gas masks at alert
on chests, tin hats on back of heads, and heads on
floor. They are indescribably dirty, and with six or
eight days' beard.*

50

The two men are SPIKE *and* KIPER. KIPER *is on second
bunk at left,* SPIKE *on third bunk at right.* GOWDY
enters. Stirs SPIKE *with his foot.*

GOWDY. All right. Heave out and lash up. Lively now.
Rations are in. Go draw for ten. At the gray stable tonight. Take that sack there. [*Points to a muddy sack on
the floor near by.*]

SPIKE. What time is it? Rations in?

GOWDY. You heard me, Spike. Shake a leg and go draw
rations for ten men, at the gray stable near the square.
It's after two o'clock.

SPIKE. Where's Captain Flagg?

GOWDY. Down tying up Mr. Aldrich.

SPIKE. So they got him. Bad?

GOWDY. I'll say they did. A ticket home. Right arm
torn all to hell.

SPIKE. A damned dirty shame. He's lucky, though, to
get out with an arm. I'd sell 'em mine, and at the same
price. What was it—that one-pounder again?

GOWDY. No. Fuse cap from a grenade. Made a hell of
a mess on Mr. Aldrich. He was crawling on the embankment near the railway station, and somebody inside threw
him a present.

SPIKE [*now up and re-winding a spiral legging*]. A
damned swell officer, if you ask me. Taking him out tonight?

GOWDY. No. The skipper is bringing him here. Send
him out tomorrow night. He's lost too much blood to walk
it before dawn. God, it's getting on my nerves.

KIPER [*who has been awakened*]. Who? Mr. Aldrich
hit bad?

GOWDY. Pretty bad. Arm. Make a bunk for him, willya? Shake it down and pile another in the back. He'll want to sit up with it. Make up Harry's bunk.

SPIKE [*at door, about to go upstairs, turns at this*]. Harry's bunk? Why, Harry?

GOWDY. Harry's through with bunks.

SPIKE. Bumped off?

GOWDY. Worse. In the belly crossing the square. [SPIKE *goes out.*]

KIPER. Where is he?

GOWDY. The skipper rushed him back an hour ago. No use, though; Harry was unconscious—halfway—holding half his guts in his bare hands and hollering for somebody to turn him loose so he could shoot himself.

KIPER. Captain Flagg want me?

GOWDY. He said not to wake you. Might need you later on.

KIPER. A good job for me, I suppose. Jeez, with this daylight saving I ain't going to live forever, that's sure. I think I'll go crazy and get the doc to gimme a ticket.

GOWDY. Flagg's crazy now. Raving crazy. Hasn't slept for five nights. We'll be sitting on him in another night like he's had tonight.

KIPER. The whole damned universe is crazy now.

[KIPER *has come forward to* FLAGG's *bunk, smoking. Enter* PHARMACIST's MATE, *with a large clothing roll trussed up in leather straps with a portmanteau handle. He is young, pink-faced, but horribly callous, probably some kid from a medical school of 1917.*]

MATE [*looking about in the dark as he approaches* KIPER]. Flagg's company P.C.?

KIPER [*hostile;* GOWDY *sits up*]. Yeah.

MATE. Where'd I better set up shop, soldier? [*He looks about the cellar.*]

KIPER [*worried*]. What do you want to set up shop for, sailor?

MATE [*sitting down on bunk; starts unpacking, takes off helmet*]. How'd I know? This ain't my party. Flagg wants it here.

KIPER. What's he want it for tonight?

MATE. He's going to put on a little party before morning. [*He uncovers a litter of blue-rolled bandages on bunk; absorbent cotton, a jar of iodine which he unscrews, and some wooden sticks around which he begins to twist wisps of cotton for daubs.*] A little party.

KIPER. The whole damn company, I suppose, and all the engineers he can find to boot.

MATE [*professionally*]. Oh, no. He ain't got arrangements here for that many. I'd say a small party, according to the stuff they gave me at the dressing station.

KIPER [*incredulous*]. How small?

MATE [*with immense indifference, busy about his detail*]. Oh, I'd say about two operating tables. . . . [*A pause as he enjoys the effect on* KIPER.] A small party. About four couples for bridge.

KIPER. Yeah. [*Rather miserable.*] Low bridge around that lousy railroad station.

MATE. I guess so. They were passing out V.B. grenades down by the street to the station when I came through.

KIPER [*immensely friendly all of a sudden*]. Look here, sailor. You are smarter than me. . . .

MATE [*interrupting*]. Oh, no!

KIPER [*insistently*]. Oh, hell, yes! Any man smart enough not to join in them four couples is smarter than I am. Even you're smarter. Now that being the case, tell me why the hell we want the Heinies out of that God damn railway station. Leave 'em there, I say. Let 'em sit where they damned well are. They ain't going anywheres.

MATE. I can't tell you.

KIPER. Nobody can. Like as not General Pershing himself couldn't tell you about it . . . and . . . oh, sweet baby, but last night down there I swore to God so long as I lived I'd never let another German in that railroad station throw a potato masher at me.

MATE. You can throw a grenade at him.

KIPER. Sure I can. But I don't want to no more. I pitched yesterday, and my arm is sore. I know I can do it, and it ain't fun any more. I know all about Flagg's invitations to parties. I know why they all got R.S.V.P. on 'em. Right smart of V.B. grenades provided. . . .

[*Enter* LIPINSKY, *who comes down; looks first at* KIPER.]

LIPINSKY [*immediately perceiving the litter*]. Jeez, Kiper, I wish you'd keep the undertakers out of here. What's all this, Jack? [*He waves to the mate's stuff.*]

MATE [*selecting a small bandage*]. Well, this one is yours, and the rest is for your friends.

LIPINSKY [*cheerily*]. Don't try to put the bug on me. I ain't no queen bee. They ain't made one that could burst alongside of me. If they'd made it, I'd be down with the daisies long ago. I'm proof now. It's down in the cards that I'll live to see the navy at Mare Island again. [*He lights a cigarette which he has taken from* FLAGG's *bunk.*] Yes, sir, I'll live to beat the pants off that bird that sold me the wrist watch down by the main gate.

KIPER. How do you know you're going to live? Said your prayers, I suppose, and got an answer.

LIPINSKY. And who'd send me an answer?

KIPER. The great cosmic top sergeant who runs this world.

LIPINSKY. Well, I don't want any answer from that bird. He'd send the answer collect, and it would say, "Fall in and get the manure outa the French angels' backyards. Clean up heaven, you low-down Marine, so's the National Guard won't get typhoid when they all die and come here."

KIPER. There ain't any heaven. Paris is heaven enough. If I ever get outa hell, I'm certainly going to stay in heaven until I die.

LIPINSKY. Of course, there's a heaven.

MATE. On the level, now. You birds know your souls go somewheres. You've seen too many men die. A fellow is walking along, blood in his face and breath in his lungs, and whizz-eeee-zzzzz, boommmmmmmmmmmmm . . . he's down on the ground, and something's gone. Something's gone, I tell you. Something that was in that bird a minute before has left, and all you've got is a pack of bloody rags and a lot of dirt. Well, for the want of a better name, you call that something a soul . . . and you can't kid me . . . the soul's gone somewheres.

KIPER. What of it? That soul ain't any of my business. It ain't got to eat; it ain't got to run; it ain't got to stand in line ten days a week to sign the payroll. I should get on my ear about where this doodlebug in my chest is going after I die. It ain't never helped me none. It can go to hell for all I care.

LIPINSKY. Jeez, Kiper, don't talk that way around me. [Raises eyes.] It wasn't me, God; it wasn't your little Vladysek Lipinsky. Not him. He knows too damn well if he was to talk that way you would certainly make him cover up and yell for mercy before morning.

KIPER. And you were the one wasn't going to be hit a while ago.

LIPINSKY. That's why I ain't going to be hit. My little soul's all ready to turn out for every formation, boots blacked and buttons shined. A little sea-going soul that knows its top sergeant can give it a kick in the pants any time he gets ready.

KIPER. Well, if there is a God, he ain't got medicine big enough to worry me. Why the hell doesn't he win the war for one side or the other and get this mess over? I know plenty of men could win it. Flagg probably could, if you gave him the army and a barrel of whisky.

LIPINSKY. But you like the chaplain, Kiper. You said he was a swell bird the other day.

KIPER. Sure I like the chaplain. Gimme two packs of Camels two nights ago. If God was to show himself, now —come down with a bunch of angels driving a wagon-load of cigarettes, that would be something like it. The chaplain said my folks was all praying for me to come through, and for God to spare me after hearing their prayers. God, I ain't that dirty a coward! That's a case of saying, "Oh, God, don't kill our child. Kill every kid in the neighborhood, but bring the one marked Kiper safe back home. . . ." No, I don't want none of that for mine. . . . And you can take all your New Testaments with the khaki backs and throw 'em in the incinerator so far as I want anything out of 'em. I'd rather have a book of cigarette papers any time. . . . I ain't asking anybody for a damned thing in this war. And you can take all your Bible backers and psalm singers and hitch 'em to the ration wagons, if you ask me.

MATE. Well, this is all very pleasant, but I got business over in the next company now. Bad curve in the position there, and 'long toward daybreak they start hollering "First Aid" as regular as a clock. If I was you fellows I'd go out and sleep in different shell-holes tonight . . . see which one of you is right. . . . Tell your skipper I'll be back around three-thirty. [*He steps on his cigarette and prepares to go out after* QUIRT *enters, which he does.* QUIRT *enters.* SERGEANT QUIRT *is tired.*]

QUIRT. Captain Flagg here?

GOWDY. Still in the orchard . . . digging those new rifle pits. We've got nine captured Maxims there. Those birds can't change the belts, but they can tap a thousand rounds apiece by pressing the buttons in the dark. Fifteen men could hold this half of the town, the way he's got the positions staked out.

QUIRT. There'll be about fifteen holding it if this business of reconnoitering patrols keeps up. I'd like to have that divisional staff in this town one night. Still bad in the square?

GOWDY. Pretty bad. Rifles in box rest in the railway station . . . light automatics.

QUIRT. I thought Flagg got 'em out last night.

GOWDY. They filtered back in at dusk tonight. Our cross-fire couldn't stop 'em. The skipper says they are working them from pulleys from the first floor, and the railroad embankment covers them from us.

QUIRT [*stretching out and sighing as he takes off his tin hat and mops his forehead*]. Running rations down that ravine every night is the toughest job I've ever soldiered.

GOWDY. Lucky tonight?

QUIRT. Pretty lucky. Six out of ten come back. Them two Jameson boys got it from the same shell going down. Dutchy and the little Jew were hit right at the dump. Easy ones though. They'll be back in ten days.

[*A commotion at head of stairs. Enter* CAPTAIN FLAGG *supporting* ALDRICH *by gripping* ALDRICH'S *uninjured wrist over his shoulder and easing him gently down steps.* ALDRICH *is not groaning. After all, it won't hurt for fifteen minutes or so. But he is weak from loss of blood and soaked through, and is in an indescribable mess of dried blood and dirt, which appears black.* FLAGG *, who is unkempt, has no leggings or laces in his breeches, these flapping in the most disillusioning fashion about his bare legs. His blouse, an old army blouse many sizes too big and without a sign of any insignia, is tied with a piece of twine. He is bareheaded—no tin hat and no accoutrements of any sort. He is a very weary-looking man. He wears belt and holster with automatic bound to leg. As* FLAGG *enters, followed by* MATE, GOWDY *jumps up and spreads blanket on bunk.*]

FLAGG. Right here, Aldrich. [*Lowers him down on bunk. The* PHARMACIST'S MATE *follows him.* FLAGG *kneels above* ALDRICH. *The* MATE *stands.*] Gimme a stick of that dope, Holsen.

MATE. They are quarter grains, Captain.

FLAGG [*to* ALDRICH, *lying down*]. Take these two now. [*He puts two tablets from a tiny vial in the wounded officer's mouth.*] I'm putting these in your blouse. Get somebody to give you one every three hours until you are carried out.

ALDRICH.   What are they?

FLAGG.   Morphine—quarter grains——

ALDRICH [*not dramatic, just casual*].   What if I take them all when your back is turned?

FLAGG [*turning his back and crossing to his own bunk down left; sits on bunk*].   Go ahead.   It's your affair.

[*After* FLAGG *is seated on his bunk a strange sob is heard at the head of the stairs.* LIEUTENANT MOORE, *last seen in company headquarters, rushes in and goes straight over to* ALDRICH, *where he stands and looks down at his arm, and not his face.*]

MOORE.   Oh, God, Dave, but they got you.   God, but they got you a beauty, the dirty swine.   God DAMN them for keeping us up in this hellish town.   Why can't they send in some of the million men they've got back there and give us a chance?   Men in my platoon are so hysterical every time I get a message from Flagg, they want to know if they're being relieved.   What can I tell them?   They look at me like whipped dogs—as if I had just beaten them—and I've had enough of them this time.   I've got to get them out, I tell you.   They've had enough.   Every night the same way.   [*He turns to* FLAGG.]   And since six o'clock there's been a wounded sniper in the tree by that orchard angle crying "Kamerad! Kamerad!"   Just like a big crippled whippoorwill.   What price glory now?   Why in God's name can't we all go home?   Who gives a damn for this lousy, stinking little town but the poor French bastards who live here?   God damn it!   You talk about courage, and all night long you hear a man who's bleeding to death on a tree calling you "Kamerad" and asking you to save him.   God damn every son of a bitch in the world who isn't here!   I won't stand for it.   I won't stand for it!   I

won't have the platoon asking me every minute of the live-
long night when they are going to be relieved. . . . Flagg,
I tell you you can shoot me, but I won't stand for it. . . .
I'll take 'em out tonight and kill you if you get in my way.
. . . [*Starts sobbing again.*]

[GOWDY *and* KIPER *sit up.*]

FLAGG [*rising quickly as though he might kill the man,
and then putting his arm around the chap, who has clearly
gone smash for a few minutes. He speaks in a quiet, chas-
tening tone, with a gentility never before revealed*]. Here,
boy, you can't do this before all these men. [*Walks him.*]
They are rubbed up, too. You are all tuckered out with
your side of the line. Don't worry about your platoon.
We'll get them out. You turn in here. [*Walks him to bunk
on the left side of the room.* KIPER *crosses and throws
blanket on him; stops at bunk nearest entrance.*] And
dope off for a little while . . . that's it, give him a blanket,
Kiper . . . and now take it easy a while, and you can go
back to your platoon in time to stand to. Sleep it off, boy,
sleep it off. . . . You're in a deep wide hole, and shells can't
get you. Sleep it off. [FLAGG *crosses to his own bunk,
lights cigarette at candle, seats himself on bunk.* GOWDY
rests head on arm. QUIRT *kneels on floor, gets a piece of
chocolate out of his pocket; rises, as though his legs were
asleep. He carries his helmet. He crosses and tosses candy
to* MOORE.]

QUIRT. Just a little chocolate I bought off a Y.M.C.A.
wagon down at the base. [QUIRT *is sympathetic and begins
to talk nervously.*] I got hit myself once. In Nicaragua.
We were washed up before we made a landing. I was a
corporal, and when we were scrubbing down and putting on
clean uniforms—doctors' orders, you know, so they wouldn't

have to wash us when we were hit—[*turns to* GOWDY] a bird said to me—it was old Smoke Plangetch, who was killed in 1913 in a Chippie joint in Yokohama—Smoke said to me: "You'd better swab down, you son of a sea-bitch, because I dreamed last night they wrote your name on a bullet." I said to him, "The bullet ain't been cast that can shoot Micky Quirt." He said, "If your name is on one, it will turn the corner and go upstairs to find you." Jeez! That afternoon when we made a landing and hit the beach, the spigs was on a hill five hundred yards off shore. We started up the hill—they weren't many of us dropping— and I came to a log I had to jump [QUIRT *illustrates this*] and I lost my balance and threw my hand up in the air. [QUIRT *extends his wrist.*] Look, right through the God damn fin, as pretty as a pinwheel. . . . Smoke saw it. "Oh, yeah, you wisenheimer son of a Chinese fart," he says to me, "your name was on that one and you had to reach up for it." [GOWDY *laughs.* QUIRT *is obviously embarrassed by having spoken of himself so much. He turns and recollects his business and goes over to* FLAGG. *Crosses to the foot of* FLAGG's *bunk.*] Rations detail in, sir. Lost the two Jameson boys in the ravine going down. Both badly hit. Lost Fleischman and Rosenthal in the dump. Both slight. Brought back all the ammunition and two sacks of bread, one of canned willie, French; I carried a sack of beet sugar on my back. Got a piece of shrapnel in it where they are shelling the cross-roads—stopped it square. In the next war, I'm going to wear a suit of beet sugar and stand forest fire watch in the Rocky Mountains. [*He turns, and then remembers and comes back.*] Oh, I brought up two of those thirty-day wonder lieutenants from a training camp. Sent up by divisional for instruction.

FLAGG. By God, I won't stand for it. They wipe their damned dirty feet on this company. They can give my men all their damned good jobs. They can keep us in the line all during the whole damned war. But I'll be damned if my sergeants have got time to teach army lieutenants how to button their pants in the dark.

QUIRT. They are in my hole now, sir. Pretty badly shaken up by the ravine. First time up, you know. Shall I send them to you, sir?

FLAGG. Send them to me, and for God's sake, don't call me sir any more tonight.

QUIRT [to GOWDY]. All right. You heard him. Hit the deck. You'll find 'em in my hole. [GOWDY goes.] Those Huns in the railway station again?

FLAGG. Try to cross the town square when there's a flare up, and you'll see.

QUIRT. You get a visit from brigade headquarters tonight. I saw their party in the ravine as we were going down to the dump.

FLAGG. The old man says we've got to drive them off the embankment. Huh! He can give me five general courts and I'll not waste another man at that business. It will take a brigade action to get them out for good.

QUIRT. Do you mind if I take a look around there now? I'd like to see this damned war some. For six days I've been a lousy bakery wagon—haven't seen a spiggoty yet, except stinking dead ones—I never see soldiers stink like these Heinies.

FLAGG. All right. Go get your blooming can blown off. But bury yourself, while you're about it. The burying detail is in for the night.

QUIRT. Gosh, I wish to hell I was home.

FLAGG. Go get one of those Alsatian lootnants then, and you'll get a leave.

QUIRT. I don't want to die yet, thanking you just the same. Well, here goes. [*Exit.*]

FLAGG. Well, keep your head down. I can't waste any grave-diggers on sergeants. [FLAGG *shrugs his shoulders and walks over to above* ALDRICH.] Sorry Moore blew up that way, Aldrich . . . you are a damned sight luckier than he is, but he doesn't know it. I'll have you out to-morrow night with the ration detail, and you'll be parking your body in a big white bed in another two days. Good luck. . . . You've been a damned good man. I wish you could get a ribbon for this town.

[*As* FLAGG *leaves,* GOWDY *enters with two lieutenants. They are just like tailor's dummies of a Burberry outfit, slicked to the notch and perky and eager. As they enter,* FLAGG *steps on his cigarette and stands facing them. The* LIEUTENANTS *come down and stand side by side.*]

FLAGG [*starts back in mock admiration and salaams deeply as they come forward*]. So *this* is the last of the old guard, eh? In the name of the holy sweet Jumping, are you gentlemen bound for a masked ball, that you come disguised as officers? Or do you wish to save the snipers the trouble of picking you off with a glass, that you wear signboards? [*He goes nearer them, inspecting their clothes.*] Can't you go without those trench coats even to the trenches? How long will you last in those boots? Take 'em off before you even part your hair in the morning. . . . [*He changes to a thundering staccato.*] My name is Flagg, gentlemen, and I'm the sinkhole and cesspool of this regiment, frowned on in the Y.M.C.A. huts and sneered at by the divisional Beau

Brummells. I am a lousy, good-for-nothing company commander. I corrupt youth and lead little boys astray into the black shadows between the lines of hell, killing more men than any other company commander in the regiment, and drawing all the dirty jobs in the world. I take chocolate soldiers and make dead heroes out of them. I did not send for you, Mister . . . [*he leans forward, and the first officer salutes and speaks: "Cunningham, sir"*] nor for you . . . [*"Lundstrom, sir," also salutes*]; and I confess I am in a quandary. Four days ago I should have been more hospitable, for I had four gunnery sergeants then. Now I have two, and can't spare them to teach little boys how to adjust their diapers. I've no doubt that one of you was an all-American halfback and the other the editor of the college paper, but we neither follow the ball nor the news here. We are all dirt, and we propose to die in order that corps headquarters may be decorated. I should be happy to receive suggestions as to what should be done with you. Ah, I have it! There are two German gunners over in the enemy railway station. Two bright young men might get them out and cut their throats before dawn; then no more could get in the station all day. Two bright young men, who know very little of anything just yet. I have two bright ones, but they are far too valuable. They are corporals with ten years' experience. [*The* LIEUTENANTS *are speechless. There is not a smile in the cellar.* CUNNINGHAM, *who is the bigger of the two, finally answers, in a slow southern drawl.*]

CUNNINGHAM. I'll do anything you will. Where is the railway station and the two bucks that have got you buffaloed?

FLAGG. Why, it's Frank Merriwell! All right, Frank.

You and me will be playing ball in hell by three o'clock this morning.

LUNDSTROM. Put me in too, sir.

FLAGG. Oh, no, no, no! We must have officers left. Rule of the game. Must have officers. Men would get right up and go home, and then there wouldn't be any war at all. Besides, three would be a crowd, and I hate crowds early in the morning around the railway station. They are so noisy, and they die so fast. [*He turns to* GOWDY.] Gowdy! Take Mr. Lundstrom to the fourth platoon sergeant, and tell him that here's his new officer. [RUNNER *and* LUNDSTROM *move to door.* FLAGG *is all business now.*] And by the way, Mr. Lundstrom, they filter through and bomb twice a week, small parties slipping down that ravine you'll find on your left. Watch it closely, or you'll all have your throats cut before you know it. And let that sergeant sleep for the next two days. Remember, he'll do no details until he's rested. Of course you can wake him for advice. That's all. Shove off. [RUNNER *and* LUNDSTROM *salute, and go out.* CUNNINGHAM *sits down.* QUIRT *enters with his helmet on, limping; steals forward quietly, and sits down on his bunk. There is a nice bloody mess on his right calf.* FLAGG *happens to turn, sees what's going on, sits up, watches* QUIRT. QUIRT *looks back, finally grins, then tries to open a first-aid pack.*]

FLAGG. What's the matter with you?

QUIRT. Got a can opener?

FLAGG. You crook!

QUIRT. I say, Captain, got a can opener?

FLAGG. Those things are supposed to be opened with the teeth.

Quirt. You don't say! Well, this'n' wasn't. This here can was evidently made for the Red Cross by the Columbia Red Salmon Company. Like as not instead of bandages I'll find the God damnedest mess of goldfish in it.

Flagg [*rises, crosses to* Quirt, *takes can away from him*]. Where were you? [*He comes over, strains at the tin. He is looking daggers.*] Where were you?

Quirt. Just looking around.

Flagg. Here. [*Hands him tin, opened.*]

Quirt. Thanks.

Flagg. Where were you, I said.

Quirt [*takes out bandage*]. In the vegetable garden, pulling turnips. [*Starts wiping leg.*]

Flagg. God damn you, Quirt, I believe you stuck your leg out. [*Goes back and sits on bunk.*]

Quirt. Like hell I did. If I'd wanted to stick my leg out don't you think I've had plenty of chances to do it before? No, sir, I stuck my head out and some bird in the church tower took a shot at me. There she is. In and out without touching the bone. Just let me squeeze the juice out and she'll be all right. Ain't she the prettiest little damn puncture you ever saw, Captain? Ain't she a beauty?

Flagg. I suppose you think you're going back to Cognac Pete's, huh?

Quirt. How'd you guess it? Yes, sir, back to my little skookum lady you tried to make me a present of. Am I happy? Am I happy? Oh, boy! Ask me, Captain, am I happy?

Flagg. You mean to say you aren't cured of Charmaine yet?

Quirt. Cured of Charmaine? No, sir, I ain't even getting better. Oh, Captain Flagg, ain't you proud of your-

self, ain't you a wizard? God, ain't I sorry to leave you all
alone here in this mess? Think of her sitting on my lap,
lighting my pipe in the kitchen, and you dodging machine
guns. I wonder I don't bust out crying. You know, I
wouldn't wonder if you got bumped off and never came back.
As a matter of fact, I hope you damn well get your head
blown off.

FLAGG. Yeah, you always did have a charming dispo-
sition.

QUIRT [*squeezing his wound gently*]. Oh, pretty baby,
papa doesn't mean to hurt you. Lookit, Captain. By God,
I wouldn't take a hundred dollars Mex. for that little
bumble-bee that flew in there.

FLAGG. Feel pretty cocky, don't you? Well, you can't
go out tonight. I guess you can work all right with that.
You'll wait here till Cunningham and I get back with that
Alsatian shavetail from the railroad embankment. Then I
get leave, the company gets a rest, and we go back together,
see?

QUIRT. Not much, I don't see. I've got a very important engagement back to Pete's place. Can't be postponed,
not even for the pleasure of your enjoyable company, such
as it is. I don't wait for nothing in the world but a medical
tag.

[*Enter* PHARMACIST'S MATE; *stands on steps, leans head
in door.*]

MATE. Heard your first sergeant was hit in that turnip
patch. [FLAGG *indicates* QUIRT. MATE *crosses to* QUIRT;
kneels.] Let's have a look. Um. Night soil in that patch,
and you, like a damned fool, crawl after they hit you, and
now you're full of that muck. Can you walk, Sergeant?

QUIRT [*lying back*]. Well, depends on what I see.

MATE [*helps up* QUIRT, *who carries helmet*]. Go to the sick bay at once for a shot of tetanus, and then get out of here. [*Takes his arm, and both cross.*] You can reach a collecting station before you're done.

QUIRT. Ain't this heart-breaking, Flagg? Well, duty calls. But my eyes fill with tears at the thought of leaving my old company commander. I don't know as I can go through with it.

FLAGG. Make it snappy, Quirt, or you'll find the door locked.

QUIRT. Yeah? What door?

FLAGG. Charmaine's.

QUIRT. Are you wounded, too, Mr. Flagg?

FLAGG. No, but inside ten minutes I'm going to be wounded or bumped off or have that God damned prisoner for the Brig.

QUIRT. Try to get killed, will you? To please me—just this once? [QUIRT *and the* MATE *go out.*]

FLAGG. Mr. Cunningham . . . I guess you thought I was joking when I proposed that little expedition to the railroad embankments?

CUNNINGHAM. I did not. When do we start? [*Coming to* FLAGG.]

FLAGG. Well, I was. I was kidding hell out of you. I'd no more let you go in there, boy, than I'd knife you in the back. The air is full of steel this side of that embankment, and a green man has about as much chance as a cootie on Fifth Avenue.

CUNNINGHAM. You going?

FLAGG. I've got official reasons for going, see? The Brig. wants a prisoner, and he also wants that nest wiped out. Also, I got private and personal reasons for wanting to catch up with that baboon that got the little present through his leg.

CUNNINGHAM. If you're going, that suits me. I ain't no green man. I can crawl on my belly.

FLAGG. Yeah?

CUNNINGHAM. I'm a locomotive engineer and I've been crawling under trains for fifteen years. Had several engines shot out from under me likewise. You think you can scare me with this here war? Christ! you ought to see a few railroad wrecks!

FLAGG. Well, Mr. Cunningham, I'm inclined to think you'll do.

CUNNINGHAM. You're God damn right, I'll do.

FLAGG. What do you say we black our faces and give a little party, now the guests will be asleep?

CUNNINGHAM. Sure. I like the cut of your jib, and you can lead me to it. Show me which one is the lootenant, so I won't hurt him.

FLAGG. You from Texas?

CUNNINGHAM. You hit it.

FLAGG. Now I get you. So we've got another damned Texan in this outfit, wanting to fight anybody that ain't from Texas.

CUNNINGHAM. Yep, and I ain't no God damn college boy, either.

FLAGG. Good stuff! Now throw away them fancy-dress clothes of yours and dip in here. [*He offers a can of lampblack.*]

CUNNINGHAM. Sure. [*Takes off overcoat.*] I was a locomotive engineer on the Louisiana Midland. Three wrecks in my division last year. Christ, but this war shore is a great relief to me. [*Both black their faces.*] I'm an engineer officer attached to infantry. My brother's still driving an engine back home. Had a letter last month from him. He says, "You dirty yellow sapsucker, quitting your job on the Louisiana Midland. I knew you always were a yellow dog, but I didn't think you'd go back on the road thataway."

FLAGG. Now if I only had a pretty little engine. [*Suddenly there is a scream upstairs, a shout in a burly strange tongue. "Heraus!" and three bombs explode.* FLAGG, *the* RUNNERS, *and all save* ALDRICH *dash for the door.*] Marines! Marines! Marines! [*The lieutenant who had been put to sleep stirs uneasily. After a brief tumult, the people of the cellar descend stairs,* FLAGG *holding a German officer by the collar. He takes him straight to the candle.*] Let me have a look at you, sweetheart, let me have a look! Boys, he's an Alsatian lieutenant! He couldn't wait for us to go after him, so he came over. [*He embraces his captive.*] Oh, sweetheart—you're the sweetest sight I've seen since Charmaine! Here, Kiper [*pushes him to* KIPER]—take care of him for me, and for God's sake don't scare him to death, because he's our ticket of leave!

LEWISOHN [*screams, outside*]. Captain Flagg . . .

FLAGG. Who's that?

LIPINSKY. It's little Lewisohn, sir.

[LEWISOHN *is carried in by* GOWDY *followed by* PHARMACIST'S MATE, *and he is crying monotonously for* CAPTAIN FLAGG.]

LEWISOHN. Captain Flagg. Captain Flagg. Stop the blood. Stop the blood.

FLAGG [*takes him from* GOWDY *and puts him on floor*]. I can't stop it, Lewisohn. I'm sorry. [*He examines wound in left side.*]

LEWISOHN. Oh, Captain Flagg, stop the blood.

FLAGG. Fix him with your needle, Mate. [MATE *gives him needle in arm.*]

LEWISOHN. Oh, Captain Flagg, can't you please, sir, stop the blood?

FLAGG [*puts hand behind* LEWISOHN'S *head and gently lowers him to floor*]. You'll be all right, boy. You'll be all right. You'll be all right.

[LEWISOHN *sighs and relaxes his body.*]

CURTAIN

ACT III

A tavern, known colloquially as COGNAC PETE'S. *Evening, two days later. The outside door is in the rear, small bar at the right, stairway left, an inside door at right. Windows rear.* FERGUSON *sits at long table smoking and playing solitaire, a bottle of Martel and a brandy pony at his elbow.* CHARMAINE *is in front of the table by the candles, sewing.* FERGUSON *is enjoying the luxury of talking to himself, for it is apparent that* CHARMAINE *is not following all he says.*

FERGUSON. I'm glad they're coming back here. [*He sips, between sentences.*] It's a good, quiet town . . . quiet . . . last time we were in a town where the M.P.'s and the mule skinners fought every night . . . glad they sent 'em back here. . . . *You* ought to be . . . Your father'll do a land office business when the outfit gets here. He better knock the bung in every barrel of red ink he's got. God, how they'll eat . . . what's left of 'em. When two hundred leave me behind with the stuff, I always get ready to mess two hundred when they return. Of course a hundred may not return . . . but they'll eat right through to the bottom of the kettle just the same. Now you take that big oakum-haired Swede named Swenson. I never see a Marine eat more than he did . . . I damn well hope Swenson gets back . . . I like to see him eat. There was a little Jew named Lewisohn that could out-eat him, weight for weight; but the Swede weighed twice as much. That

72

Swede could eat anything but a horse collar. [*He chuckles and* CHARMAINE *smiles.*] Well, I'll say we've kept each other company. We sure have, even if you can't speak a white man's lingo; that is, not to say *speak* it. Now if you'd been a Spanish girl we could have got together a little better . . . I lived with a Spanish girl at Cavite back in '99 . . . in those days I was salty as hell, a sea-going buckaroo.

CHARMAINE. *Est-ce-que* . . . you are lonely?

FERGUSON. It ain't so bad, staying behind this way. It ain't so bad. Twenty years now I've had 'em leave me. When I was younger I believed some of the liars who said they liked to fight . . . liked being under fire . . . but it always bored me to sit around and be sniped at. Somehow I never did get angry. And you've got to get angry when a bird's shooting at you if you're going to enjoy it. So I didn't have a good time. . . . Now you take Flagg there . . . there's the sort likes it. Flagg gets mad as hell if you don't even like him, let alone shoot at him. Flagg and me are different. Now Flagg——

CHARMAINE. Where is *le Capitaine?*

FERGUSON. Pretty near here, I suppose.

CHARMAINE. Near here?

FERGUSON. He'll be here presently, General.

CHARMAINE. *Le Capitaine Flagg*—he has been wounded ever?

FERGUSON. Naw! Flagg ain't never been wounded. Never will, neither, if you ask me. You can't hurt his kind. When you see a man like Flagg, it's curious, but they always have the pleasure of drinking themselves to death . . . funny thing . . . I never knew a man who could float a load of liquor, didn't hold all the cards besides. Now you take Flagg . . . he'll be here in fifteen minutes mebbe—

mebbe two hours—but just the same as ever . . . thirsty as hell, wishing he had forty geisha girls to play with.

CHARMAINE. Fifteen minutes . . .

FERGUSON [*with elaborate gestures*]. Le Capitany . . . ici . . . sank . . . min-use ici, sank min-use . . . Compree?

CHARMAINE. *Oui, oui, oui! Merci bien.* [*She runs upstairs.* FERGUSON *continues smoking, pouring a pony of brandy. Presently the door at rear opens slowly. Enter* SERGEANT QUIRT *in a major's army overcoat, with black braids and a leather-visored garrison cap. He is shaven, crafty-faced. Below the overcoat, which is bursting on his chest, may be seen rough army shoes, gray woolen socks pulled over the bottoms of striped outing-flannel pajamas. He looks exactly what he is, a slightly wounded soldier escaped from hospital in borrowed clothes.* FERGUSON *turns, and seeing him, comes to attention.* QUIRT *also has a bottle with about half a drink in it.*]

FERGUSON [*rising courteously*]. Good evening, Major.

QUIRT [*pours what remains in the bottle he carries into* FERGUSON's *glass; then, taking the full bottle, sets his empty one in its place*]. Sit down, Fergy, and use your eyes. Help me to get out of this rigging.

FERGUSON [*sitting; irritated*]. What are you doing in those gadgets, Quirt? Where's the outfit? Where you been to?

QUIRT. Listen. I ain't writing my memoirs of this war till it's over. All you need to know is, I got two M.P.'s on my trail, and I don't want to meet 'em in these. [*He removes his coat and is found to be in striped pajamas. A small red cross on the jumper pocket.*]

FERGUSON. You come from the lines in that outfit, Quirt? In night-drawers?

Quirt. I suppose you think I go 'round this way because I like it. [*He stows the overcoat and cap under the bench.*] Major, you're relieved. [*Takes slicker from peg on stair rail.*] Lend me your slicker, Fergy. I'll give it back if it thunders. [*He goes to chair at table, seizes the cognac, pours out two ponies and swallows them, looks at* Ferguson, *then pours a third drink; drinks it.*]

Ferguson. Of course you're paying for those, Quirt, even if you have gone cuckoo.

Quirt. All right, all right! Don't get on your ear about it. . . . And now you want to know where I've been.

Ferguson. Oh, no, if a soldier wants to campaign in a pair of night-drawers, it ain't none of my parade. It takes all kinds of sergeants to make an army.

Quirt [*drinking his third*]. You're too hard-hearted, Fergy. I ain't in my right mind. I was wounded, and now I've got aspasia. [*Mysteriously.*] My name is Field Marshal von Hindenburg, and I'm looking for a wagonload of pants that got lost in shipment.

Ferguson. Yeah?

Quirt. Yeah, sure. I wandered outta a hospital about five miles over at a place called Noisy. It was damned well named too, Fergy. Noisy was no name for it when I came outta the ether after I'd shipped in there with a piece of pants driven through a bullet hole in my leg.

Ferguson. Have to give you ether to take off your pants?

Quirt. No. They gave me ether so the stretcher bearers could steal a gold watch and eight hundred bucks off me. I certainly put up a squawk when I woke up and found 'em missing. But a hell of a lot of good it did me. I went looking for the bird that got them and ran into a guy in a bar-tender's coat in the operating room. He tried to pipe me down and I hung a shanty on the bimbo's eye [*enjoying the picture himself*] and when they washed him off he was a captain. So they locked me up, wound and all. And then I got aspasia, and here I am. You ain't seen me.

FERGUSON. No, I ain't seen you.

[*Distant voices shouting "Fergy!" "When do we eat?" "Chow," etc. At this sound, very faint,* QUIRT *rises quickly, starting for the stairs with a skip and jump.*] Keep your drawers on, Quirt. They ain't no M.P.'s. That's the outfit. I've got old Pete and his brother down at the bridge, keeping coffee and slum hot for 'em. Better go and give yourself up to Flagg as soon as he drives in. You'll be safe then. I'd like to see a set of doctors take Flagg's first sergeant off him when he's just out of the lines. It surely would be a pretty sight afterwards, them doctors working on each other like monkeys. [*The voices come nearer. The cry, long drawn out like a wolf's, comes from many throats: "Ch-o-o-o-w-w!"*] That's me. They're calling for me. Well, old Fergy's got their chow, and hot too. [*He goes.*]

[QUIRT *limps quickly to door after* FERGUSON *goes.*
    CHARMAINE *comes down the stairs at the same time.*]

QUIRT [*turning to find* CHARMAINE]. Hello, Pittsburg.

CHARMAINE [*with a small cry, comes toward him*]. You are wounded.

QUIRT. Sure I'm wounded. Ain't that enough to put me nine miles ahead of Flagg with you? I certainly beat him here.

CHARMAINE [*trying to put arms around his neck*]. Mais, mais . . . you are . . .

QUIRT [*restraining her*]. Don't embarrass me, darling,

because I ain't clothed and in my right mind. I just been waiting for Fergy to leave so I could steal a uniform from him. Where's his room? [CHARMAINE *points to door.*] Wait a minute, dearie, until I salvage a pair of breeches. [*He goes out.* CHARMAINE *goes to the outside door, where voices are now heard.* QUIRT *reappears.*] Damn it, he's locked his chest! Gimme a ice pick. [QUIRT *takes bottle from bar. There are steps and voices at the door, and* QUIRT *withdraws hastily to the right,* CHARMAINE *following. Enter* KIPER, GOWDY, *and* LIPINSKY. KIPER *spies the cognac bottle and holds it over his open gullet. The other two rush him. There is a tough scuffle.*]

KIPER. Lay off my bottle.

GOWDY. Say, don't drink it all!

[*All then sit behind the table and deliberately begin a tremendous racket.*]

KIPER. Hey! *Vin rouge!   Vin blanc!* You, Pete! *Venez ici.* Toot sweet!

LIPINSKY. Toot sweet—toot sweet—toot God damn sweet —jambon? *Des œufs! Fromages! Vin! Vin!*

GOWDY. Biere, biere, biere!

[FLAGG *enters. The three jump up and push back their chairs. When he yells "Clear out," the tumult instantly ceases. FLAGG is cold sober, still in his old clothes and dusty, but recently shaven, and possessed of rolled leggings and an old brown shirt.*]

FLAGG. Clear out, you yapping hounds, and tell the new platoon commander to billet every man down the moment he finishes mess. Tell him I don't want to see one of 'em around this tavern till that's done. [*Turns; crosses to bar.*] Tell them not to rag a man tonight. [*Takes bottle; turns to*

them.] As soon as they know their billets, let 'em out. Let
'em drink. Let 'em fight. Get out.

THE RUNNERS [*gently; somewhat discouraged*]. Ay, ay,
sir. [*They disappear.*]

[CHARMAINE *enters quietly and stands leaning in the
doorway. FLAGG pours a beaker and drinks it pleas-
antly, enjoyingly. Then he pours a second and walks
around to chair at table and sits down. CHARMAINE
has watched this from the doorway. He sees her at
last.*]

FLAGG [*arising and bowing grandiosely, holding aloft the
drink*]. Madame la comtesse de la Cognac!

CHARMAINE [*embarrassed*]. *Le grand Capitaine de ma
cœur.*

FLAGG. Yes, I'm the captain of your heart! Like hell
I am. Why don't you come and kiss me? None but the
brave, you know . . .

CHARMAINE. *Je ne comprends pas.*

FLAGG. Oh, no. You don't understand me. Well, I'm a
weary man, and I don't want any finnagelling from you.

CHARMAINE [*at door*]. You want me to kiss you?

FLAGG. Sure I want you to kiss me. Even though you
played the dirtiest sort of trick on me. [*The liquor is beginning to deaden him.*] A dirty trick on your poor old
Captain Flagg. [*Turns to her.*] If I weren't so kind and
gentle I'd go out in the orchard, cut a cherry switch, and
give you a tanning.

[*She crosses over, kisses him quickly, and draws back, a
charmed bird before a snake.*]

CHARMAINE. You're a terrible man, monsieur.

FLAGG. I ain't terrible to you, honey. Come sit by your
old man. [*She sits on the table and looks down into his*

eyes.]   Ain't I tired? (Jeez, but I'm off war for life.   It's all right with thirty or forty men in the hills who know their business.   But there's so many little boys along with me ain't got any business here at all.) [*He sighs and drinks the rest of the brandy.*]   Ah!   There ain't no strength in this stuff any more.   [*Hands her his glass, which she places on table. He gets up unsteadily.*]   Le's go walk by the canal.   I wanna get away from these new lieutenants.   Le's walk along that bicycle path.

CHARMAINE. *Non, non, non.   Demain soir.   Demain soir.*

FLAGG. Tomorrow? All right. I'm tired anyhow. Never been so tired before. Liquor just takes the pins out of my knees. Gimme a bottle to drink in bed. I don't want to think tonight.

CHARMAINE [*bringing him a bottle from the bar, smiling*]. *Ah, monsieur, vous est un grand soldat.*

FLAGG [*wandering to the door, suddenly apathetic*]. Nighty, sweetie. See you tomorrow. [*He goes out at rear.*]

QUIRT [*entering stealthily, in a farmer's smock which comes to his waist*]. So he's gone away. . . . What's the matter with the old boy? [*He attempts to kiss her. She shudders.*]

CHARMAINE [*drawing away from him*]. *Non, non, non! Merci.*

QUIRT. Why, what's the matter, Pittsburg? Don't you love me no more?

CHARMAINE. *Oui—mais——*

QUIRT. Of course I understand. Seeing him that way sort of cut you up, especially when I was wearing such a lousy outfit, you liking them all in uniforms. Just wait, baby. When I git that brass lock off Fergie's box and turn out in his blues on sick leave, you'll forget this Flagg person.

I understand. Sure. I been with soldiers' girls a lot, myself.

CHARMAINE. When you are beautiful, *mon sergeant*, then I love you—— [*She runs up steps.*]

QUIRT. Come back here! [*She disappears, laughing.*]

[KIPER *and* LIPINSKY *enter.*]

KIPER. Jeez, Sergeant, but you picked a funny outfit to be buried in.

QUIRT [*at foot of stairs—hostile*]. Who's thinking of burying me?

KIPER. I expect Flagg'll make me bury you. But he's going to lay you out himself.

QUIRT. Is he looking for me? How did he know I'm here?

LIPINSKY. We just heard Ferguson telling him. I ain't never heard him swear so much since I been with him. We came to ask you to run away some more.

QUIRT. You did, eh? Well, you can go down to the bridge and head him off. You can tell him he passed up visiting this place just before the outfit shoved last time. You can tell him if he comes up here I'll cut his gizzard out for him. You can tell him I'm engaged to be married, and I ain't got no duty for him around here.

[FLAGG *enters, drunk and swaggering.*]

FLAGG. Who's the hay-shaker? Well, if it ain't Sergeant Quirt! A regular family reunion. Quirt, how are you? When you coming back to the factory?

QUIRT. Flagg, you're out of this here detail. Your hands off my business after that dirty trick you put over on me. If I kill you there isn't a court can touch me for it in this man's army.

FLAGG. Quirt, you're drunk.

QUIRT. Both of us.

FLAGG. Yeah, both of us.

QUIRT. Well, then, Flagg, you're drunk. What are you going to do about it?

FLAGG. I'm gonna have a drink. [*Turns to bar and takes bottle; pours two drinks.*]

QUIRT. Both of us.

FLAGG. Yeah, both of us. [*They drink, first bowing to each other.*] Quirt, I got something I want to tell you.

QUIRT. The hell!

FLAGG. You want to hear it?

QUIRT. I ain't particular.

FLAGG. Well, this is it, Sergeant. You can go jump in the canal. I knew you'd head for Charmaine as soon as you got that bullet under your hide. You had half a day's start of me and you didn't beat me more than five minutes. You might just as well 'a' stayed on the bakery route. You ain't no more needed here than a third leg on a kangaroo. Have one on me. [FLAGG *pours for both.*]

QUIRT [*they bow*]. Delighted, I'm sure. [*They drink and replace glasses.*] You're a hell of an officer, Flagg [QUIRT *wipes right hand on smock*], and your views on me probably ain't worth a damn. On the other hand, it's only fair to warn you that I'm the sole survivor of seven catastrophes, any one of which was calculated to carry off every man-jack in the immediate neighborhood as was adjacent, and if there was to be a catastrophe of any dimensions in this here vicinity in the near future, I have expectations of survival exceeding your own. Have one on me. [QUIRT *pours drinks.*]

FLAGG. Thank you, Quirt, I will. [*They drink, and* FLAGG *drunkenly points finger at* QUIRT *until he can get his mind to working.*] Your method of expressing yourself, Quirt, is complicated by your tongue being as thick as your

God damn head. But if you mean trouble, let me point out
to you that among other things, you forgot to bring your
gun along. [QUIRT *feels for his absent weapon;* FLAGG
laughs heartily.] Ain't you a neat little fool, hoppergrass,
and will you drink?

QUIRT. I will. [FLAGG *pours. Both bow, then drink
again; but* QUIRT *has taken a sip before he realizes he hasn't
bowed.*]

FLAGG. Do you give up?

QUIRT. No.

FLAGG [*turns to bar and starts pouring*]. Have another.
[*As* FLAGG *starts to pour,* QUIRT *leaps like a flash on his
back.* KIPER *catches* QUIRT's *wrists from behind.* LI-
PINSKY *drags* FLAGG *away. When* QUIRT *jumps* FLAGG,
he takes the gun out of FLAGG's *holster with his right
hand; his left is in strangle-hold around* FLAGG's *neck.*
FLAGG *reaches back and holds* QUIRT *by back of neck.
They scuffle until separated.*]

KIPER [*holding* QUIRT]. What do you want done with
him, sir?

FLAGG [*to* LIPINSKY, *who is holding him*]. Let me go or
I'll knock you for a row of G.I. cans. Take the gun away
from him. [QUIRT *throws the automatic on the floor.* FLAGG
puts his foot on it.] Let go, all. [QUIRT *is turned loose.*]
Well, bo, had enough?

QUIRT. I'll tell you what I'll do with you. I'll go outside
with you and try two of them little toys at fifty yards.

FLAGG. And you, the best pistol shot in the corps, would
put one through my carburetor as easy as pitching a penny
in a well. Come again.

QUIRT. I'll take you on any way you can think of, you
baboon. I can out-shoot you and out-think you and out-

drink you. There ain't nothing I can't do better than you.

FLAGG. You're a liar, Quirt, and you know it. I could break you in two. You got my gun because you jumped me without warning. No soldier you ever soldiered with could head me when I got started . . . and by the way, Quirt, if you can out-drink me you ain't leading out very well tonight. You're talking thick and wild, Quirt, thick and wild. You'd better turn in somewhere and sleep it off.

QUIRT. Me? Sleep off a couple of drinks? I was living on cognac when all your buttons was safety pins.

FLAGG. Yeah, well, you can't carry it the way you used to, then. You're getting old, Quirt. Old and feeble. Yeah, you're getting old.

QUIRT. Not me. *You* may be an old man, Flagg. Or an old woman if it suits you better, but not me. Captains and generals, they pass along. I've seen hundreds of 'em. Better men than you, Flagg. They passed along. But top sergeants is eternal. They don't never die.

FLAGG. Well, if you don't want to die, you top sergeant, don't fool with me. I've seen top sergeants go damn fast— Now, listen, Quirt, are you going to jump in that canal or are you going to need six pall-bearers to take you there?

QUIRT. It'll take more than six pall-bearers to put me in one of these French canals. I don't like the taste of them.

[CHARMAINE *reënters*.]

FLAGG. Charmaine! Cognac!

[CHARMAINE *crosses behind table; gets bottle; pours drink for* QUIRT, *also for* FLAGG.]

CHARMAINE [*laying a hand on the* CAPTAIN'S *shoulder*]. Is it now—friends again?

FLAGG [*putting an arm about her*]. Best you ever saw,

Charmaine. We'll drink to it, Quirt. Flagg and Quirt forever—till you get bumped off. Flagg and Quirt, the tropical twins! There ain't room for both of 'em in the whole world! [Flagg *pats* Charmaine *on hip.*]

Quirt [*sets down his glass, hard*]. Damn you, Flagg!

Flagg [*setting down his glass*]. What's the matter, hoppergrass? Aren't you drinking?

Quirt. I got here first, Flagg.

Flagg. I know it. Nobody said you didn't.

Quirt [*rising*]. You take your hands off Charmaine.

Flagg. Any time you want my hands off Charmaine, you come and take 'em off.

Charmaine. No. No! You must be friends.

Flagg. With you around!

Quirt. It strikes me there's only room for one of us in this shanty tonight. Do you plan on going somewhere, or not?

Flagg. Did you ever see me leaving any place I didn't feel like leaving?

Charmaine [*touching the* Captain's *sleeve*]. Don't fight —please.

Flagg [*not looking at her—pushing her back*]. The hell you say! First time in six months I've had a good reason for fighting. The Germans don't want my woman. I been fighting them for eight dollars a day. . . . Go on back of the counter.

Charmaine. I—I love you both.

Quirt. You get to hell outa here, Flagg. Dig up a broad of your own.

Flagg. Sorry. Rejected.

Quirt. You ain't man enough to shoot me for her. Well,

here's what I'll do. I'll shoot you dice for her. [*Tosses out dice on table.*] High dice, aces low. [KIPER *and* LIPINSKY *take steps forward, interested.*]

FLAGG. Boys, is Quirt crooked with the bones? [LIPINSKY *goes back to lean on platform.*]

KIPER. He's got a pair ought to be in a circus. [QUIRT *gives* KIPER *a bad look.*]

FLAGG. Then we'll deal a hand at blackjack.

QUIRT [*picks up dice; puts them back in pocket, while* KIPER *goes back with* LIPINSKY]. And the guy that loses beats it for somewhere else.

FLAGG. What do you mean, beats it? We'll shoot, but my way. The man that wins gets a gun, and the man that loses gets a head start. Everybody wins, see? One gets the girl and the other gets a chance to stay in bed the rest of this war.

KIPER. Captain Flagg, I don't think you ought to do this.

FLAGG. Close your hatch. I'll try anything once, soldier. [*Briskly.*] Now for a game of blackjack for one automatic.

QUIRT. That's all right with me.

FLAGG. And the gun on the table between us. [*He picks it up.*]

KIPER [*as he and* LIPINSKY *seize* QUIRT'S *arms*]. Come quiet now, before he notices.

QUIRT [*writhing loose*]. Keep off me, you swine! [KIPER *and* LIPINSKY *fall back.*]

FLAGG [*having recovered gun, starts to straighten up*]. March out that door, both of you, and if you stick a neck in here before the game's over I promise to wreck you for life. Are you going, or do I demonstrate? [*They exit quickly.*]

Charmaine! Upstairs! [*She goes.* FLAGG *sits at table;* QUIRT *on table.* FLAGG *shuffles cards, and offering them to* QUIRT, *says "Cut."* QUIRT *fondles cards; says "Be good to me, babies, and I'll let moonlight into a captain." He cuts.* FLAGG *deals one to* QUIRT, *then one to himself; then one to* QUIRT, *and looks at the next one for himself.*]

QUIRT. What's that, a king?

FLAGG. How many you want? Make it snappy and knock off that guff. Here's looking down your grave. May you have many worms, Quirt.

QUIRT. Crawling, right out of your teeth, Flagg. Hit me.

FLAGG [*deals a card face up*]. A two-spot. Well, any more?

QUIRT. Hit me again.

FLAGG [*dealing one*]. Well, you got a king that time. Remember, if you hold six cards without going bust you can empty the automatic at me.

QUIRT. Hit me again.

FLAGG. A king, by God! [QUIRT, *with one sweep turns over the table, with candles and chairs, and dives through the door; runs off.*] You double-dealing Chinaman! [FLAGG *finds the gun in the darkness and fires shot just outside the door. He is heard reëntering.*] Show a light, somebody. Charmaine! [FLAGG *sets up the table.*]

CHARMAINE [*at the head of the stairs with a lamp*]. What is it? You have killed him? [*Goes up to door.*]

FLAGG. Killed hell! He knocked out the light and ran, the dirty hound! [CHARMAINE *looks out the door, shielding the lamp from the wind.*] Oh, he's gone.

CHARMAINE. Maybe you hit him. [*Puts lamp on table; then crosses to* FLAGG.]

FLAGG. Don't you worry. He was halfway to the river, the rate he was going, before I found the door. Don't you weep, sweetheart [*puts her on his left knee*]; you're weeping for a skunk that'd run out on a game of cards. It's you and me tonight, lady. Listen, Charmaine [*putting his arm around her*]; I love you like the devil. I always did. You love me, Charmaine?

CHARMAINE. Only you.

FLAGG. God, I'm dead—I'm going to sleep for three days. [FLAGG *rests head on her breast and sighs. Then* LIPINSKY *and* GOWDY *walk in.*]

LIPINSKY. Sorry to disturb you, sir.

FLAGG. My God, did you hear what I told you?

LIPINSKY. Got bad news, Captain Flagg.

FLAGG. Spit it out.

LIPINSKY. The outfit's going back. Battalion moving at once.

FLAGG. What? What?

LIPINSKY. We're ordered back. Ordered back in. Everybody's going back in. General movement.

FLAGG. Dammit, I'm on leave.

GOWDY. All leaves revoked, Captain Flagg.

FLAGG. Well, why couldn't you stay away from here? You knew where I was. Why in hell did you have to come and tell me?

GOWDY. Well, headquarters sent out, looking for you.

LIPINSKY. Kiper wouldn't come, Captain Flagg. He was for leaving you alone.

FLAGG. He was, was he? Well, Kiper's got sense. Look here, you never found me to give me the message, and I'm not going. Can you remember, or have I got to bury you to keep your mouth shut? What right have they got to offer a man leave and then revoke it? I gave them their prisoner! I've got their damn papers!

LIPINSKY. Well, you see, the company's going to shove off. What could we do?

FLAGG. You could have an attack of something, damn it to hell! You could fall and break your neck on the way here.

LIPINSKY. I was afraid not to let you know. You always wanted to know.

FLAGG. Well, you've got to do some tall lying to make up for it, because I'm not going. Tell them any story you think of, only I never got the news. I earned my leave, and it's signed, sealed, and delivered. That crowd at headquarters has got to live up to its end of the bargain. They can't take these men back in. I won't stand for it. [*Turns to* CHARMAINE.] Shall we stay here, Charmaine?

CHARMAINE. *Oui, ici.* [*They embrace.* FLAGG *rests head on her breast.*]

FLAGG [*after a pause, shakes himself a bit*]. No, I'll go. I may be drunk, but I know I'll go. There's something rotten about this profession of arms, some kind of damned religion connected with it that you can't shake. When they tell you to die, you have to do it, even if you're a better man than they are. Goodbye, Charmaine, put your money in real estate, and marry that cuckoo if you can. You'll never see me again. This town is a jinx for me. [*Again rests head on* CHARMAINE.] God Almighty, but I'm tired. [*He rises and crosses to where* FERGUSON *has entered.* CHARMAINE *sits in chair watching.*] Hello, Fergy. We're shoving off. Follow us, because we don't know where we're going. Nobody knows. [*He goes out, staggering, tired.* FERGUSON

follows him out. GOWDY *and* LIPINSKY *follow* FERGUSON.
CHARMAINE *buries her head in arms on table.*]

QUIRT [*comes in upper floor stairway*]. Hello, Pittsburg!

CHARMAINE. You are not KILLED?

QUIRT [*coming downstairs to bottom step*]. No. It's me
all right. Everybody gone?

CHARMAINE. Everybody.

QUIRT. Outfit's going in again, huh?

CHARMAINE. *Oui.*

QUIRT. Well, well! I been upstairs. Climbed up the
kitchen roof. Do you love your papa?

CHARMAINE. *Mais oui.*

QUIRT. Then you better kiss him goodbye. [*Pats her
face; then kisses her. Staggers up to door.*] What a lot of
God damn fools it takes to make a war! Hey, Flagg, wait
for baby! [CHARMAINE *watches from the table.*]

CURTAIN

FIRST FLIGHT

A Play in Three Acts

First Flight was presented in 1925, at the Plymouth Theatre, under the direction of Arthur Hopkins. The stage settings were designed by Joe Mielziner and the cast was as follows:

George Dozier	*Blaine Cordner*
A Hessian	*John Triesalt*
Hawk Peevey	*James P. Houston*
Lonny Tucker	*John Tucker Battle*
Major Singlefoot	*J. Merrill Holmes*
Nigger	*T. J. Glover*
Capt. Andy Jackson	*Rudolph Cameron*
Charity Clarkson	*Helen Chandler*
Hairy Lake	*Neill Neely*
Wes Bibb	*James Bowman*
1st Buckskin	*Jack B. Shea*
2nd Buckskin	*Joseph McInerney*
3rd Buckskin	*H. Ben Smith*
Sairy	*Virginia Morgan*
Rachel Donelson	*Ellalee Ruby*
Long John	*Jo Duckworth*
Cissy Clarkson	*Julia Gorman*
Mrs. Clarkson	*Caroline Newcomb*

FIRST FLIGHT

ACT I

Public Room in HAWK PEEVEY'S *tavern on the road to Nashville in the original state of North Carolina, in the last decade of the eighteenth century. Late afternoon. Late October. The sun shines low through a long window in the rear. A huge chimney staggers into the wall at the right. The main entrance at left; another at right. To the left, against the wall, a long, heavily built buvette. Some split-bottomed chairs around a circular central table and other chairs and rests scattered around. In the rear a cleated ladder, to the left. The room is white-washed, spacious, and, for the time and place, luxurious. When the curtain rises there are two men at the table, in the center. At the left side sits a* HESSIAN *ex-soldier, his head buried in his hands. He wears a salt-and-pepper skirted coat with knee smalls, worsted stockings, and shoes without buckles. He has a bullet-shaped head, close-shaven, and wears huge square-rimmed spectacles. Across from him, at right of the table, sits* GEORGE DOZIER, *a country lawyer, spare, lantern-jawed, forceful, and ominous. There are silver buckles on his shoes and his hair is tied in a rather distinguished cue with black ribbon. He holds a deck of cards in his fingers, riffling them.*

DOZIER. Peevey! [*He slaps down the cards and turns in his chair.*] Peevey! [HAWK PEEVEY *enters at right.*]

93

HAWK. Yo' obedient, Mister Dozier. [DOZIER *rises*.]

DOZIER. That nigger bed my horse down under his forequarters?

HAWK. Mr. Dozier, I looked in that stall and I swear the straw was deep enough for a horse to swim in. That nigger had remembered you, sir.

DOZIER. The last time here my mare was found standing with her forefeet on the bare ground at sunrise. A blooded mare, Peevey. At that time I spoke to the nigger.

HAWK. I hear you did, Mr. Dozier.

DOZIER. I hope it won't be necessary to whip the boy again.

HAWK. Pacify your mind, sir. I shall care for that nigger as if he was my own offspring.

DOZIER. It will be appreciated, Peevey. [*Moves back of table and sits.*]

HAWK. Yes, sir, pacify your mind.

[DOZIER, *his back turned, makes no answer.* HAWK, *somewhat embarrassed, goes out right.* DOZIER *riffles the cards. The* HESSIAN *opposite snores lightly.*]

DOZIER [*to sleeping form*]. Well. [*Again the snore.*] Well. [*He throws down the cards and rises, walking away from the* HESSIAN *in disgust.* LONNY TUCKER *enters quietly from left. He is a boy of twenty, dressed in linsey woolsey without fashion.*]

LONNY. Evenin'.

DOZIER [*turning*]. Evenin'. [*Somewhat constrained, for he and* DOZIER *have nothing to say to each other.* LONNY *sits at the table, facing the audience.* DOZIER *watches him.* LONNY *picks up the cards.*]

LONNY. You ain't been projecking around here lately, Mr. Dozier?

DOZIER. No, Mr. Tucker, I ain't.

LONNY. Lawyers are busy men.

DOZIER. Some are.

LONNY. You spend considerable time at Jonesboro—
you do?

DOZIER. Some. [*A pause.*]

LONNY. You seen Charity?

DOZIER. No, and you?

LONNY. [*A pause. Then* LONNY *continues casually.*]
I understand from Charity that her pappy is in favor of her
marrying you, Mr. Dozier.

DOZIER. Her father has done me the honor, sir.

LONNY. I can tell you right now, Mr. Dozier . . . you
won't be able to accept it.

DOZIER. Well, boy, we won't discuss that. We won't discuss it. [*Turns from* LONNY, *starts to shuffle cards.*]

LONNY. She's not going to marry you.

DOZIER. No?

LONNY. I have her promise.

DOZIER. We won't discuss it.

LONNY. I thought I might warn you, you won't have
her. You'll never have her.

[DOZIER *smiles without answering.* HAWK *comes in from
the right.*]

HAWK. Evening to you, Lonny.

LONNY. Evening, Hawk.

[HAWK *stretches out on a bench by the buvette.* LONNY
rises and goes toward the door, taking his cap.]

HAWK. You ain't leavin' already?

LONNY. I think I'll step along, Hawk. You tell the
Major I'm sorry I couldn't stay.

HAWK. He sholy will be aggrieved, Lonny.

LONNY.   You tell him you reckon I have to go. . . .

[MAJOR SINGLEFOOT *enters, left. He is sixty, tough, fluent, a dean of the frontier courts. He wears a costume of buff and blue, suggesting the Continental regulars, very spotty and soiled, yet with a lingering elegance.*]

MAJOR.   Good evening, gentlemen. Dozier, your servant. Mr. Tucker, put down your cap and begin on your gambling education. You come too near being a green man to run away.

LONNY.   I ain't runnin' away, Major.

MAJOR.   Then explain yourself. When I invite a friend to take part in a four-handed whist and he passes his word I take it very ill to have him make his excuses before the game starts, sir.

LONNY.   If I'd known Mr. Dozier was to make one, Major . . .

MAJOR.   Sho—sho—sit down. Mr. Dozier is a gentleman, sir, and a scholar, and his political opinions are ee-dentical with yours.

LONNY.   Mr. Dozier and I have a little bad blood between us, Major Singlefoot . . .

MAJOR.   Dozier, what's between you and this boy?

DOZIER.   A girl, Major. It's Charity.

MAJOR.   A girl! Dozier, would you spoil a round of whist over a girl?

DOZIER.   Not I, sir.

MAJOR.   Why then, sit down. Sit down, sir. You should know that women are a delusion, while whist is a science. [*They sit at the table,* DOZIER *and* LONNY *in their former places, the* MAJOR *with his back to the audience.*] Cards were invented, gentlemen, shortly after Adam was evicted

from the gyarden. They were invented by the male creature
to enable him to forget his troubles. It was about the same
time sugar began to turn to alcohol when subjected to the
proper environment. As I read history, gentlemen, our corn
was not grown until some time after, and the ancients were
not initiated into the mysteries of one hundred and thirty
proof Carolina dew. I hold it one of the glories of the ancients that despite this deficiency they were able to produce
some very remarkable military men. Hawk, how come you
ain't brought that demijohn? Git up and move around
some.

HAWK [*rising quickly*]. Lord, I thought I done brought
it. Podden me, gentry. [*He brings demijohn and places it
on floor above* MAJOR.] There, I reckon that'll hold you
down until moonrise . . . cep'n maybe the Major. I reckon
as how the Major has the finest taste for liquor of all the
men in this here free State of Franklin. Last year when he
stop here on the way to general sessions he drank more liquor
than has been drank by any other man ever stay here.

MAJOR. That's because there ain't any more gentry left,
Hawk. Nothing but new white folks swarming over the
Blue Ridge without a shirt-tail to their names. Takes a
hundred years of breeding to up-end a demijohn twenty-five
times neat.

LONNY. My grandpappy could drink any man in Fayette
County flat of his face in four hours, Major. He sholy ad-
mired liquor some.

MAJOR. Who was your grandpap, son?

LONNY. Nathaniel Tucker, sir.

MAJOR. Not old Nathaniel Tucker of the Second Carolina dragoons?

LONNY. Sho it was. Killed near Newbarn.

Major. Sho! Then you got blood in your veins, boy. What you staying in this hollow for? Cote House is the only place for a blooded man, same as the race track's the only place for a blooded horse.

Lonny. I'm going to read for the bar next year, sir. . . .

Dozier. The boy's in love, Major. He remains here for the same reason that I put up here. . . .

Lonny [*rising and flushing*]. I'll thank you to leave off ladies' names in taverns, Mister Dozier. They is some gentry left.

Dozier [*rising*]. Look here, young buckskin—

Lonny. I ain't a buckskin!

Major. Gentlemen, gentlemen, the court of love is adjourned. Throw this down into your haslets and praise the Lord that made corn grow on the Cumberland bottoms. [*He makes a wry face.*] Hawk, bring me a small noggin of rum to sweeten this here potation. And now, gentlemen, let us get down to the business of the evening, which is whist at a shilling a thousand. [*To* Tucker.] There'll be plenty of time to adjudicate matters at the shakedown tonight. Unless the custom of fighting at dances has lapsed since I was a young galoot. [*To* Dozier.] Proceed with the deal, sir. [*He looks at the sleeping* Hessian.] And wake up our bibbling friend from the settlements.

Dozier [*roughly to* Hessian, *shaking him*]. Wake up, stranger, and take your cards. Play.

Hessian [*coming to with a German accent*]. Blay? Blay? I blay anyting.

Major [*angry, rising*]. God Almighty of Gemini! A stinking Hessian! [*He rises.*] A hired foe of our glorious country!

Dozier. Oh, come, Major! I ain't filled with admiration, either. He's only selling whale-oil lamps. We had to get a fourth somewheres.

MAJOR. But this here varmint! I'd sooner play cards with George the Third than with this here pole-cat!

HESSIAN [*drops cards and looks at* MAJOR. *Dully.*] Bole-cat? Bole-cat?

MAJOR. Sho—a pole-cat, and a mighty strong one, right under my nose. I've a good mind to take my tickler [*he reaches for a collar holster at the back of his neck*] and take the scruff off you for presuming to set by me. [*He draws knife.*]

DOZIER. Come, Major! If you skin him he'll catch cold setting around in his side-meat and bones. And he's got to play cards, else we don't.

MAJOR [*anguished*]. Can't we get a fourth somewheres else?

HAWK [*back of bar*]. Ain't any other man in this tavern, gentlemen. Remember you two is late for court at Nashville yourselves.

MAJOR. Hell! I'll have to play with him, I guess, the damn Hessian skunk. [*He puts the knife back in his holster.*] But I warn you, varmint, I'm ready to start a dogfight without the slightest provocation.

DOZIER. Shucks, Major, he fought against the Continental Congress, and you'll be fighting against it yo'self in a short time, if it's true what I heard over east.

MAJOR. What did you hear, sir?

DOZIER. Back on the settlements they is talk they've included the Free State of Franklin in the western district of North Carolina, and they're sending out a state's attorney to represent the State of North Carolina at Nashville.

MAJOR. What is your plan, Mister Dozier?

DOZIER. Major, I reckon we'll natcherly have to eject this state's attorney.

MAJOR. I reckon I hope so, Mister Dozier. The Free State of Franklin is a sovereign power, separate and distinct from the State of North Carolina, and so far unassimilated into the union of states. Do you hold with me, gentlemen?

DOZIER. I think you can rely on us, sir.

MAJOR. I go further, gentlemen. The Free State of Franklin is not only separate and distinct from every other state, it is also prepared to negotiate with the representatives of other states recognizing its independence, and to all other states not recognizing its aforesaid independence, it is prepared to issue defiance and defend itself by force of arms from foreign aggression. [*Decisively to* TUCKER, *after pause.*] Mr. Tucker, I play cards with no man whose views on that subject fail to accord with my own. Are you with us, sir?

LONNY. Certainly, sir.

MAJOR [*to the* HESSIAN]. And you, sir? [*A pause.*]

DOZIER. It's quite possible the gentleman is unaware of the issue, Major. However, he has already fought in one war against the colonies, and it's likely he'd be willing to do it again. The point is, sir [*to the* HESSIAN] would you fight to maintain the Free State of Franklin?

HESSIAN. Fight? I fight anything.

DOZIER. I reckon that'll have to do, Major.

MAJOR. It is my plan to publish this approaching state's attorney, publish him on the threshold o' the courthouse at Nashville, and to issue him cartel and defiance, offering him the satisfaction that a gentleman o' one political faith affo'ds a gentleman holding an opposite one.

DOZIER. Major, I had planned to reserve the privilege fo' myself. I had planned to do it befo' he gits to Nashville.

MAJOR. It may be that they are sending a man whose prudence exceeds his sense o' honor. I figger it will take a heap o' contumely to bring him to the straights o' the code duello.

DOZIER. You are too polite, Major. I reckon I'll either kill him, or scare him to death, befo' then. Not being licensed to practice before the Carolina bar, I don't think he'd be obliged to meet me with pistols if he ever gits to Nashville. . . . Moreover, if he gits there the Free State will be done.

MAJOR. I reckon, then, he never will git there. [*Seating himself; he fingers his knife-holster.*] So they delegate us a prosecuting attorney for the western district of North Carolina, do they? Gentlemen, it will be a pleasure to see him fleeing these parts with his hair flattened in the wind and his saddle bags scattering legal information all along the Nolhichucky Trace.

HESSIAN [*interested*]. Vot is it you say?

MAJOR. I say no treason, sir, no treason.

HESSIAN [*rising*]. I have no treason.

MAJOR. Set still, Adolph, set still. And play.

HESSIAN. I set still.

DOZIER [*pushing cards forward*]. It's your play, Major.

MAJOR. My honor, sir. [*They cut. The* MAJOR *deals, and the* HESSIAN *drops some of his cards, slopping over on the* MAJOR *as he stoops to pick them up.*]

MAJOR [*settling down his mug angrily*]. Stranger, lower your elbow or I'll have the haslet out of you real soon. [HESSIAN *lowers elbow.*]

HAWK. Don't bother his haslet, Major. I spent a sight of time last Fourth of July cleaning up folks' haslets that was left around. We had thirty-four fighters to the cross-roads for the speakin' besides the speakers.

MAJOR. If he fools with me I'll have his liver out and make him clean up after it. [*He turns to* HAWK.] Give me a plug of navy and bring a wide gobboon. I'm a tolerably inaccurate spitter after six potations.

LONNY. We are waiting for you to play, Major, please, sir. [*They play one-half through hand.*]

MAJOR [*playing*]. Beat that, varmint.

HESSIAN [*playing*]. Dray of Tiamonds. [*They finish hand.*]

MAJOR. Hawk, is there big planning for the soirée tonight at Wes Bibbs' barn?

LONNY. I'm gonna be there, Major.

DOZIER. I'm gonna be there too.

MAJOR. Which one of you gentlemen is escorting Miss Charity?

LONNY. I am, sir.

DOZIER. You think so, boy.

LONNY. I am!

MAJOR. Gentlemen, gentlemen, you know you two remind me of a story I heard from a feller who stood up with Dan'l Boone at the Colonel's wedding. He knew Dan'l when Dan'l was courting his bride-to-be. I never hearn the beat of it. 'Pears like Dan'l come to the settlement just like you two [*pointing to* DOZIER *and* LONNY] come here tonight after the same girl, to attend a harvest soirée and ask her ma for her hand. Dan'l wasn't so well known at this settlement where he come, being only a tolerable young galoot about seven feet high, which wasn't even middling tall for the buckskins along the Tennessee River in them days. Of course he'd been biting the heads off b'ars and catamounts in his own hollow [HESSIAN *raises elbow*], but his reputation for such was purely local. [*The* HESSIAN *deals, using a high elbow in the* MAJOR's *face.*]   Stranger, lower your elbow, else I'll claw your jugular. [*He lowers elbow.*]   So Dan'l hearn tell of the puttiest gal in the Tennessee country, daughter of a widow woman who owned her own cabin and who 'lowed that the galoot who got her darter would just naturally be powerful enough provider to cut a winter's supply of firewood with his eye teeth. Well, sirs, Dan'l always was powerful minded to start out and see anything he knowed was there, and he set out for this here gal. He started off loping along to where this paragon of Venus lived. . . . She was sixteen years old and was fat as a butter ball and pink as a haw bush in spring. Dan'l started loping along chomping his eye teeth and wishing to God he was bigger for his size. Pretty soon, he come to the clearing. Well, sirs, this clearing was as plumb full of suitors as Penelope's house in the Odyssey. They was two brothers from South Carolina nine feet tall, each one wearing a live racoon for a cap and not speaking to nobody under their size. Now Dan'l hadn't been unmindful of the first impression women folks gets of their men, and he was leading a three-hundred-pound panther by a string as a sort of little present for this gal. But his spirits sank when he see the sight of powerful men in the yard before the door. They was a red-headed fellow sixteen hands high setting on the stoop talking to the darter and letting a pet rattlesnake suck on his thumb. [DOZIER *and* LONNY *laugh; the* MAJOR *takes a chew of tobacco and a drink on top of it.*]   So Dan'l slunk around the house to set and chew grass for a spell and think up something, and God Almighty, he beheld two Georgia crackers entered in the race. They were cutting firewood like beavers, and one of them had lost his teeth fighting his way north and he was gumming the damned oak wood into three foot lengths. Dan'l was down-hearted for a minute or two. . . . [*He takes a drink.*]

MAJOR [*discharging his quid. To* HESSIAN, *reaching wrathfully toward his collar*]. Stranger, you're going to lose that elbow.

HAWK [*who has wandered to the window*]. One moment, gentlemen. There's a man on horseback coming west, followed by a nigger on a mule and leading a bay mare.

MAJOR [*to* HESSIAN]. Would you condescend to inform me, sir, whether your interior framework is so constructed that you cannot fold your flippers down to your ribs or whether it will be necessary to operate, sir.

NIGGER [*to* HAWK]. Cap'n Jackson, suh, say if he mek Tooly Hill by nightfall.

HAWK. Nigger, tell him it's seven miles and a hard ride and a harder bed in the blockhouse which he will git to, if the redskins let him get to it. Tell him we don't ride no further without scouts and hunters.

NIGGER. Den Cap'n Jackson, he stay here den, suh. He got racing mare, spo'ting dog and two fighting chickens to board.

HAWK [*reaching for his cap*]. I'm coming right out.

MAJOR [*to* NIGGER, *who starts to go*]. One minute, nigger, who is your master? A Port Royal Jackson?

NIGGER [*pausing in door*]. Naw, sir. We's Salisbury Jacksons.

MAJOR. Salisbury Jacksons? I never heard tell of Jacksons in Salisbury.

NIGGER. Well, you'se gwine to now, Marse General. Us

is the biggest hearn-tell-uns in No'th Ca'lina. Us is de one and only Cap'n Jackson. De one *an'* only.

MAJOR [*as* NIGGER *goes out and* HAWK *starts to follow*]. Hawk, before you leave to attend on the arrival of this unique Jackson and his sporting menagerie, would you step around and bring me another noggin of rum? [HAWK *brings the rum.*] The importation of aristocracy is a rare occasion, but a Salisbury Jackson is not a Port Royal Jackson, and in the opinion of this here court you need not fluster yourself.

HAWK　No, sir, Major. I 'low I won't allow myself to be flustered. [*He goes out, right.*]

LONNY. Now about that story, Major.

MAJOR. Sho, now, I was embarked on a narrative. I was indeed. I had merely paused, sir, until it became fairly certain that we should have no further interruptions. [*The* NIGGER *enters left, carrying saddle and saddle-bags, which he sets down near the rear wall. He goes out left.* HAWK *enters immediately, carrying a long black duelling case and followed by* ANDY JACKSON, *about twenty years old, slight, tall, fiery, dressed in light blue, rather soiled, but smart, his red hair tied in a queue with a small black string.*]

HAWK. I'll set it right here, Cap'n. And what can I get for you?

JACKSON [*hardly glancing at the card table*]. Give me a glass of whiskey, host. A double glass of your finest.

HAWK. Yessir, Cap'n. [*He serves the whiskey.*]

DOZIER [*to* LONNY, *who has drawn in a hand*]. Are we to understand by that action, Mr. Tucker, that you labor under the impression that your nine of clubs was sufficient to capture that last trick which you have under your hand?

LONNY. Oh, I beg pardon, gentlemen, my mistake! [*He pushes the hand back.* DOZIER *takes it.*]

JACKSON. What village is this, host?

HAWK. Some say it's Peevey Hill on the hill, Cap'n, and some say it's Peevey Bottom on the bottom. It don't make no difference to me. My *name's* Peevey.

JACKSON [*seizing his glass*]. You are near Nashville?

HAWK. A hundred thirty miles, as the crow flies, Cap'n, and some extra, up and down, dodging the Injuns.

JACKSON. It's rather dull here, no doubt, by contrast with social life at Nashville.

HAWK. Lord! a sight dull, a sight dull. A body don't get no entertainment here to compare, sir. Now Nashville, there's a town that's gay, sir. A sight of people there. Eight hundred if there's a man, besides the gamblers.

MAJOR [*flipping down a card*]. Now, as I was saying, gentlemen, in regard to Dan'l, he was considerable tuckered and set still for quite a spell, ruminating in his mind. And the longer he set there the tougher that there oak wood looked to him. [HESSIAN *raises elbow.*] It was an entire winter's supply for a seven-foot opening. [*Pause. To* HESSIAN.] God damn you, keep your elbow out of my eye! But Dan'l made up his mind he'd have to learn to chew it, because he wasn't a man to give up easy, and so he sauntered over, and set his teeth into a joint of dogwood just to try it, and the very first gnaw convinced him he'd have to cogitate on something else to do. So he edged away, casual like. Nevertheless those two Georgia Crackers bust out laughing fit to kill themselves. At that Dan'l's temper kind of give way and he ventured to them Crackers that they would probably live only a short time to regret their actions if they was unable to moderate their amusement within a very brief interval. Well, sirs, they failed to moderate in time, and Dan'l waded into them with his bare hands and began to start a little flurry in the back yard. Now they wasn't critters themselves, and right soon you'd 'a' thought from the trampling and confusion that maybe a thousand men had got into trouble with each other in that there rear acreage. The widow woman and her darter come running around the corner of the house and what they see was a pillar of dust a half mile high going round like a cyclone, all mixed up with firewood and bare feet and occasional breech-clouts busted loose from the human form. Well, sirs, it was some time before it quieted down in that region, what with the b'ar dogs barking and the turkeys running and all like that, and when the dust begun to settle, the onlookers caught sight of one of them crackers ninety foot up on a dead limb of a rhododendron tree hanging by a endpiece of his shirt. The other cracker was swimming back toward them from half-way across the Tennessee River, which he had been fortunate enough to descend into. [LONNY *and* DOZIER *laugh.*] There! eighteen cords of firewood tromped plumb into kindling, and Dan'l was standing there, still holding his panther by his string. He was nigh onto a foot taller than he was when he arrived, having growed that much from the exercise. There is them that say he got his full growth on that occasion and never did grow no more. [*He drinks.*]

LONNY. I reckon he got the lady, sir.

MAJOR. She has since borne him fourteen men-children, sir. [*The door at the right opens and* CHARITY CLARKSON *slips in, perfectly at ease in the company of so many men. She is a slight girl of fifteen dressed in linsy-woolsy.*] By God, we were men in them days.

DOZIER [*seeing* CHARITY *and rising in his place*]. A pleasure to see ye, Miss Charity. [*All rise except* HESSIAN.]

CHARITY. My pleasure, Mr. Dozier.

LONNY [*turning toward* CHARITY. *Rising, flustered*]. Evening, Charity.

CHARITY. Evening, Lonny. [DOZIER *resumes his seat*.]

MAJOR. I beg your pardon, ma'am, for indulging in the sin of blasphemy in your presence.

CHARITY. Lawd! Major Singlefoot, I don't mind none. It ain't a sight to pappy when he works half the night borning a calf, and it comes a bull.

MAJOR. Let us hope that is not because your ears have become accustomed to the rude talk of vigorous men, Miss Charity, but because your kind heart finds special clemency for my transgression, ma'am.

[LONNY *sits down*.]

CHARITY [*ending the matter*]. Major, how you do run on.

HAWK. Is your mammy sent you for that sugar loaf, Miss Charity?

CHARITY. Yes, Mr. Peevey, she says she can't pay but for half of it today. [*She shows a shilling*.]

HAWK. [*The card game sits*.] Lord, that's all right, child. [*He is breaking up something behind the bar*.] You tell her I'll just let her have the half of it today, and keep the rest for her.

CHARITY. But she'll need it all, Mr. Peevey, if she gets my snack ready for the soirée tonight.

JACKSON [*to* HAWK, *ominously*]. Surely, host, you cannot think of sending half.

HAWK. Cap'n, I sho' couldn't. Cap'n, I just couldn't.

JACKSON. A loaf is a powerful lot of sugar for one who seems sweet enough in her natural self.

CHARITY [*curtsying*]. You seem to have caught your tongue from the Major, Cap'n.

DOZIER [*rising, pushing his chair*]. I do not know you, sir. . . .

JACKSON. Captain Jackson, sir, of North Carolina.

DOZIER. I repeat, I do not know you, sir, nor do I care for your impudence.

JACKSON [*turning back on* DOZIER]. It affords me no regrets, sir.

DOZIER. Miss Charity, I hope it is not your custom to meet the tavern loungers as they arrive?

LONNY [*angry, rising*]. Mister Dozier!

DOZIER [*to* CHARITY]. It would appear that when there are errands to be run to the tavern yo' mother might find a child to run them, Miss Charity.

CHARITY [*jolted and frightened*]. I came to get a sugar loaf, Mr. Dozier. Mammy wanted to surprise you with a sugar cake when you called for me tonight.

LONNY [*rising*]. Charity, are you going to the soirée with him, after all?

CHARITY. Yes, Lonny.

LONNY. You promised me.

CHARITY. I know I did. [*A pause.* LONNY *and* DOZIER *look at each other.*]

MAJOR. Sit down, gentlemen, sit down. I ain't set at such a restless card table since the flea season. [DOZIER *and* LONNY *seat themselves,* DOZIER *first.*]

HAWK [*still busy under the bar*]. Ef you will wait, Miss Charity, I'll git a paper to wrap up the sugar.

JACKSON [*sipping whiskey*]. You say you find it dull here, Mr. Peevey?

HAWK. A sight dull, Cap'n, a sight dull.

JACKSON. The manners here are mighty bad, no more than one hundred thirty miles from the metropolis of western North Carolina, Mr. Peevey. Most disappointing, I vow. [*The table stops playing and listens.*]

HAWK [*low, to* CAP'N]. Bless your stars, Cap'n, don't say North Carolina. It ain't done around here. A body might get kilt for that. We are the Free State of Franklin. We ain't in the union. We's a sovrain power.

JACKSON. You don't say, sir, you don't say!

HAWK. Anybody'd know you was a stranger round here, or you would sho'ly know that, Cap'n. Now, Miss Charity, if you'll wait just one moment. [*He climbs to the loft. There is a brief silence, a hand playing out rapidly at the table.* HAWK *is half-way down the ladder as the* HESSIAN *starts to deal, his elbow in the* MAJOR's *eye. The* MAJOR *roars, draws his knife and wounds him slightly. The* HESSIAN *screams, ducks to the floor, and grovels.* CHARITY *shrinks to the left door.*]

HAWK [*dropping his paper and running to the* HESSIAN]. Gentlemen, gentlemen!

MAJOR. By God, you'd better grovel.

HAWK. Aw, why didn't you keep out of the Major's way? [*He lifts the* HESSIAN, *walks him to right door and pushes him out.*] You ain't fitten company for gentlemen. [*They go out. Pause.*]

LONNY. Charity, may I fetch you home on my pillion?

[*Enter* PEEVEY, *stops at lower corner of bar.*]

CHARITY. No, no! Mr. Peevey, could I have my sugar?

Hawk. I'm getting it, Miss Charity. I'm getting it. [*He picks up paper and goes behind counter.*]

Major. Ma'am, for the second time I submit my deepest apologies. I am most extravagantly sorry.

Charity. Lawd, fightin' ain't no offense, Major! But ain't the man bleeding now?

Major. Ma'am, you don't want to worry about him the least in the world. He ain't hardly hurt at all, to speak of. It saves him the leech's fee. [*To* Jackson.] Cap'n Jackson, I believe you said, sir.

Jackson [*bowing*]. Your devoted, sir.

Major. I am Major Singlefoot, formerly of South Carolina, now of the Free State of Franklin, Cap'n Jackson. This is Mister Tucker of hereabouts. And this gentleman is George Dozier, Esquire, one of the leading legal lights o' this sovereign region. It happens that an untoward accident has deprived us of our fourth at cards, Cap'n Jackson. Air you disposed to join us at this juncture, sir?

Jackson. Why, sir, I had promised myself that I would not tetch cards until I reached Nashville. It falls out most unlucky, I am sure.

Major. And you will not reconsider?

Jackson. I fear not, sir.

Major [*flustered, a little sullen*]. Indeed, sir.

Dozier [*sits back of table*]. Oh, come, Major, we can have our game without picking up strangers from the road! Mister Peevey, you have a little whist, I believe.

Hawk [*back of bar*]. Mister Dozier, the host don't never submerge himself that-a-way. Not that I ain't itchin' to sit in, gentlemen, only I am obliged to make that there rule, having gone completely bankrupt back in the settlements no less than two times. I just naturally has to refrain, sir.

JACKSON. I will join with you, after all.

MAJOR [*pleased*]. Sit down, Cap'n, sit down.

JACKSON. And will you liquor with me, gentlemen?

MAJOR. Instantly, sir.

LONNY. With pleasure, sir.

JACKSON [*to* DOZIER]. And you, sir, how do you feel about it?

DOZIER [*snarling and snapping his fingers*]. I don't feel that about it, not that! Play or not. I can care for myself.

JACKSON. Thank you, sir. [*He sits in the* HESSIAN'S *place, takes up the cards to deal, and sticks his arm right into the* MAJOR'S *eye.* HAWK *brings another jug.*]

MAJOR. Will you deal, Cap'n? [*After pause.*] Cap'n, are you aware that you are courting death by your antics?

JACKSON. To what antics do you refer, sir?

MAJOR. To your elbow, sir, your elbow.

JACKSON. As to my elbow, you shall have to put up with it, sir. You shall have to put up with it as best you can.

MAJOR [*rising.* DOZIER *and* LONNY *rise*]. You are a Jackson from Salisbury, I believe, sir?

JACKSON. Your memory is excellent for names, Major. Captain Jackson, sir, of Salisbury.

MAJOR [*reaching for his knife*]. I was not aware that there were Jacksons in Salisbury, sir, but it is easy to see, sir, that if there are Jacksons in Salisbury, they lack manners.

JACKSON. A Jackson from Salisbury's too much of a gentleman to use a knife, sir. I believe they use other and mo' courtly weapons.

MAJOR. Meaning, sir. . . ?

JACKSON [*rising*]. That I am ready, sir, to give any

gentleman satisfaction [*to* DOZIER] who cares to meet me.

MAJOR [*rising*]. Hawk, get them pistols out of my saddle-bags and load 'em with ball.

JACKSON. I have a pair ready loaded in my case, sir.

LONNY. Gentlemen, gentlemen, this is entirely unnecessary. [*Strolls upstage.*]

HAWK. Yes, gentlemen, for God's sake don't start no killing on a night like this. If you start killing one another it'll spread till there won't be no dance at all.

MAJOR [*to* JACKSON]. It is one of the peculiarities of our neighborhood, sir, that such is very probably the case.

HAWK. It would sho'ly be inconvenient, gentlemen.

MAJOR. But I should be loath for to give any man cause to believe I was in the habit of postponing such engagements, sir. I positively hasten them, sir.

HAWK. Furthermore, gentlemen, it's after sundown and one of you would sho'ly be handicapped in your back lighting.

MAJOR. Mister Peevey, you will kindly remove yourself? Captain Jackson, there will be a harvest moon. I am at your service either at moonrise or at sunrise. My hesitation in this affair is due solely to a wish not to interfere with later festivities of the evening.

JACKSON [*bowing to* CHARITY]. I, too, should grieve if this young female lost her jig.

MAJOR. Why, then, that being the case, I'd as lief kill you at sunrise as at moonrise. 'Pears to me like you are spoiling for a fight right now, but if you'll keep until dawn I can bide my time to teach you manners in the Free State of Franklin.

JACKSON. Then shall we say sunrise, sir?

MAJOR. Sunrise, sir, and most happy, sir.

Dozier [*pause*]. Major, I shall be glad to serve you in this matter.

Major. Thank you, Mister Dozier.

Jackson. And will you act for me, sir?

Lonny. Certainly, sir.

Dozier [*to* Lonny]. Look here, boy. You don't want to serve with every blackguard that traipses into a tavern trying to get a reputation on his marksmanship.

Jackson. Sir, I hope you will not be swerved from an act of chivalrous generosity by the advice of some blackleg lawyer of the trumpery State of Franklin.

Dozier. You must fight me for this.

Jackson [*turning to* Dozier]. Sir, I had a mind to kill you when you rebuked this young lady so rudely.

Dozier. We need not wait five minutes longer.

Major. One moment, Mister Dozier, sir. I believe I have the prior claim on the young blood's attention. He is not to fight me till dawn, sir, and you must postpone further adjudication till a clean sunrise.

Jackson [*to* Dozier]. You are to be the young lady's escort, I believe, and even the pleasure of spitting your black heart is not first in this affair.

Major [*half amused, half grim*]. No doubt you aim to dodge my fire, son, since you figure on surviving to meet another.

Jackson. Sir, you are a veteran and a duelist; I should take it most courteous of you if you could be prevailed upon to yield this gentleman first place on my list. For I must kill him, even though I stand dying from your wound.

Major [*drinking and reflecting*]. Well, now, sir, I got to think it over some. I'd admire to reserve for myself the pleasure of challenging the new prosecuting attorney the

Governor of North Carolina is sending out here to the Free
State of Franklin, and it's possible if I was first on your
list I might not be able to kill him the hour of his arrival.
Yes, sir, thinking it over, I don't want to be no hog. If
Mister Dozier agrees to give me first shot at the prosecuting
attorney I'm free to say he can have first shot at you, sir.

DOZIER. Done, sir.

JACKSON. Sir, I am your most obedient, but I fear the
affair cannot be so simply arranged, as I happen to be the
newly empowered prosecuting attorney for the western district of North Carolina. [*They step back from him.*]

DOZIER. No!

MAJOR. Did I hear you rightly, sir? Did you say *you*
are the new state's attorney?

JACKSON. I am, sir.

MAJOR [*raising his glass*]. Providence is indeed gracious
to me. Mister Dozier, I withdraw my resignation. I shall
insist on meeting the Cap'n first.

DOZIER. You have the right.

MAJOR. And I may tell you, Cap'n Jackson, that my
feelings toward you have undergone a sudden and I may
say a revolutionary change. Before this announcement was
read into the record, sir, I was inclined to admire your carriage and even to regret that so young a man was so unlikely to finish his first journey to Nashville. I was inclined
to wish you a rapid recovery from your two wounds, and
subsequent to that a long and more cautious career. But
in your character of the new state's attorney, sir, and a
representative of a foreign government, I shall find it necessary to kill you, sir, and it is my hope and belief that I
shall do the same for every prosecuting attorney the State
of North Carolina sends into this free and sovereign region.

It is my intention to lay them out one by one, sir, as fast
as they are sent, sir, until the State of North Carolina gets
completely tired of sending prosecuting attorneys in this
direction, sir.

JACKSON. Your sentiments, sir, and those of your friends
are well known in the state I represent; and it may be that
the office I hold has gone begging for some time on account
of a certain timidity felt by some barristers more learned
than patriotic. That timidity, sir, I did not share. I do
not share it now. I abhor your sentiments, sir, but I admire
you, sir, and I am only sorry that your political views must
bring about your untimely end.

MAJOR. I understand you, sir. Your devoted. [*They
bow.*] Mr. Dozier, shall we stroll up to the corners and take
squinting practice a few times? Your silhouette is a trifle
thicker than the Cap'n's, but 'twill serve. [DOZIER *and the*
MAJOR *take their saddle-bags and go out, left.*]

HAWK. Miss Charity, your sugar is ready. Sorry you
had to wait. [*He hands her the package.*]

CHARITY. It was a treat, Mister Peevey. I do love to see
a quarrel.

LONNY. It's getting late, Charity. May I walk with
you?

CHARITY [*opening right door*]. It's only a mile.

JACKSON. Mister Tucker, I hope you will convey to Miss
Charity my regret that this episode should have occasioned
her annoyance.

LONNY. Cap'n Jackson wishes to say . . .

CHARITY [*cutting in*]. It ain't no matter at all, Captain
Jackson. Please don't hurt the gentlemen none. [*Lingering. To* JACKSON.] Good night . . . sir.

JACKSON. Not good night, ma'am. Surely I may hope for a taste of the sugar cake at the soirée?

CHARITY [*gravely.*] If you air mean enough to come you may surely have some, sir, and very welcome. [*She goes out. The* MAJOR *opens the left door and looks in.*]

MAJOR. Hawk, that there varmint of a Hessian is sleeping like a wooden image under your signpost, and I reckon you better lay him in the barn before he ruins your trade.

HAWK. Yes, sir. Thank you, Major. [*The* MAJOR *disappears.*] Mister Tucker, would you give me a hand with him?

LONNY. Surely. Captain Jackson, if I am to act for you, we shall want a few minutes' conversation, I believe.

JACKSON. If you should like to reconsider acting for me, Mister Tucker, why, I should wish to leave you entirely free.

LONNY. I am bound, Captain. Moreover, I'll be happy.

JACKSON. You place me under deep obligation, Mister Tucker. I await your leisure. [*They bow.* LONNY *and* HAWK *go out left.* JACKSON, *left alone, opens the dueling case and begins methodically to adjust a flint. The door at the left opens slowly, and* CHARITY *looks in. She still carries her package of sugar.* JACKSON, *seeing her, rises. For a moment they do not speak.*]

CHARITY. Mister Peevey is— Mister Peevey has gone out, Captain?

JACKSON. They have stepped out for a minute, ma'am. Would you wish me to call Mister Peevey?

CHARITY. It was only— No, I'd rather not. [*She closes the door behind her. She comes a step forward.*] I wanted to warn you . . . if you don't mind, sir . . .

JACKSON. You tetch me, ma'am.

CHARITY. You don't know us here none, Captain. We are buckskin in the Free State, and you don't know us. The Major is always dueling, and so is Mister Dozier. Mister Dozier is the worst. They have killed a sight of men, Captain. They are clost-shootin' men, Captain.

JACKSON. Yes, ma'am, I'm sure they are.

CHARITY. They mean to kill you, I'm sure of that. You are mighty young and pretty to be kilt here, so far from your pappy's house.

JACKSON [*bowing*]. You will never know how grateful I am, ma'am.

CHARITY [*with terror and admiration*]. You ain't running away, really, Cap'n? Ain't it true about red-headed men? So little and no beard at all, and picking fights a'ready like a bear dog. Picking 'em with anybody at all.

JACKSON [*gallantly*]. Only, ma'am, with those who do not seem to serve you well. With that Dozier, for example.

CHARITY [*anxious*]. Cap'n, I'd admire to see you fight him, I would that. But they's two on your back. You'd better hit the trace.

JACKSON [*pompously*]. Shortly after sunrise, ma'am.

CHARITY [*dropping the latch and returning slowly*]. You don't mean to . . . to fight the Major and . . . Mister Dozier?

JACKSON [*terribly swanky*]. I'm much more likely to do the inflicting, ma'am. If you knew me better you would warn Mister Dozier against me. I've seen trouble some.

CHARITY. You air mighty young and foolish. . . .

JACKSON. I'm old enough to be a cap'n, ma'am. I was through the war, and a prisoner to the redcoats at fourteen. I've seen a sight of men die. . . .

CHARITY. Lonny is twenty.

JACKSON. Indeed, ma'am. It is none too young to enjoy your society.

CHARITY. Air you too old, Cap'n?

JACKSON. Almost, ma'am, unless you are as charitable as yo' name.

CHARITY. Lonny is a fool boy, Cap'n.

JACKSON. He don't know the hell that's in men, ma'am. He has never had to fight for his place and eat the crumbs from the table o' the gentry. And yet you love him a sight, I'll be bound, ma'am.

CHARITY [avoiding]. Pappy's marrying me to Mister Dozier, Cap'n, when he comes home.

JACKSON. No, he's not, ma'am.

CHARITY. You aim to shoot Mister Dozier?

JACKSON. Not if you'd rather he killed me, ma'am.

CHARITY. I wouldn't.

JACKSON. Then he won't.

CHARITY. Please don't kill him, Cap'n. It ain't Christian. You're too young and pretty to go around killing men. Please hide until morning, and then hit the trace, Cap'n.

JACKSON. But I must dance a reel with you about moon-down.

CHARITY. Do you mean it, Cap'n?

JACKSON. Will you give me that blossom in yo' smock as a gage?

CHARITY [taking a laurel blossom]. Law, Cap'n, a body would think you meant to come! [She hears voices and turns from him. Looks enigmatically at him, curiously, without smiling. She goes out. JACKSON puts the blossom in his pocket carelessly and begins methodically to adjust a flint in his pistol. HAWK enters.]

HAWK [comes up and observes the pistols]. Cap'n, you

are smart to carry them things around, if you aim to represent the old North State here. You'll need 'em a sight o' times befo' you are done.

JACKSON [*playing with pistols all the time*]. A bold front's half the battle. I'll only need them once or twice.

HAWK. You reely aim to meet these two?

JACKSON. How can I avoid it?

HAWK. Lots o' ways, Cap'n. Go on back to Jonesboro.

JACKSON. Sir, I am on my way to Nashville.

HAWK. No offense, sir. I'm for you. I ain't for this here Free State. A tavern keeper knows that unless gentry run a thing, it don't run. And George Dozier's no gentry.

JACKSON. Does he aim to run his own state?

HAWK. That he does. He and the Major. He'll end by running the Major, too. Cap'n, you may as well know how things stand. There'll be a sight o' enemies here, and you'll be lucky to leave while you can. You better go back and bring mo' on your side befo' you tackle George Dozier in his own neck o' the woods. Mind you, I ain't ag'in you. I'm for you. I kain't run this tavern without yo' kind o' patrons.

JACKSON [*looking at pistols*]. If you are for me, show me the way to the dancing tonight.

HAWK. Cap'n, I'd rather drop you into a barrel full of hot spittin' wildcats. They'll be buckskins there from four rivers and three mountain ranges. They'll be carryin' a thirst they been nursin' all summer long, and if they see you, Cap'n, you won't have to bother about no duelin' in the morning.

JACKSON. Peevey, all I ask of them buckskins is that they wait until I have one reel with Miss Charity.

HAWK. And now, Cap'n, is it your desire to squint down your barrels a few times? I kin light candles if you care to keep your skill with them a secret. I can tell you those two gentlemen are the clostest-shooting gentlemen in the Free State of Franklin.

JACKSON. Bring the candles, host. I'll try two shots.

HAWK [*reaching under the bar*]. Lord, it's real unnatural.

JACKSON [*turning below table*]. What is, sir?

HAWK. These two tapers. One fat and one lean, like your opponents.

JACKSON. Place them in the window, host. [HAWK *steps on bench, places candles, lights them, and goes behind bar.*] Is there likely to be any one passing outside?

HAWK. Lord, no! It's a log wall behind. You can't hurt it none.

JACKSON [*showing* HAWK *two pistols*]. Major, I shall only dust your coat. [*He fires, and the fat candle flickers, but still flames.*] Mister Dozier, here's where I extinguish the leading legal light of the Free State of Franklin. [*The thin candle is out instantly.*]

CURTAIN

ACT II

Time: moonrise. 2 A.M. *Cleared ground in front of* WES
BIBB'S *new log barn, which curtains the back-stage,
with small door right which is wide open. Through the
chinks may be discerned the color and movement of
dancers, also the woodsmoke from fat-pine torches.
The stage is bare, save for three stumps. To right a
dried cornfield, and at one point stalks trussed into a
seat. To left is a forest, unbroken save for a helter-
skelter path leading off. Moonlight through forest.
For a few minutes the only movement is the shadows of
dancers, and the squeak of one very bad fiddle is heard.
The shouts of the fiddler are audible, and so is the stamp
of dancers' feet and the occasional whoops of the more
antic dancers. His calls, about thirty seconds apart,
are as follows:*

Eight hands up and go forward,
Half and back;
Partners: Sash-i-ate.

Gentlemen stand and ladies swing;
In the center; own partners,
And half sash-i-ate.

All hands up and go to the left;
Hit the floor;
Corner turn; and sash-i-ate.

122

First couple cage the bird with three arms around;
Bird hop out and hoot-owl in;
Three arms around and hootin' again.

*As the music dies momentarily (and it will be resumed
again whenever the barn is filled with people to the ac-
companying, though softer calls of the fiddler) three
men burst steaming from the side doorway and come
quickly to the array of jugs and horns upon stumps and
crude settles near the piled cornstalks. They are
MAJOR SINGLEFOOT, as of Act I precisely; WES BIBB, a
big, bearded giant of a pioneer farmer in linsy-woolsy,
boots, and antique wig; and HAIRY LAKE, a picture of
the frontiersman of the late eighteenth century, in full
buckskin, worn soft and dark and fitting, with a fine
coonskin cap, and dark moccasins casing the ends of his
buckskin breeches, leather girdle with knife and toma-
hawk on right side, powder-horn and shot-bag on left.
He carries (and will carry when he moves) a long, flintlock rifle of small bore. Nothing about him gleams.
His hair is hacked off as it hits his shoulders, and he has
a marvelous hacked beard. He is about forty, and a
giant. He is never still and continually wears the in-
quisitive nose and poised ear of a fine hound. WES and
the MAJOR flop down instantly, but HAIRY moves to the
jugs.*

HAIRY [*grasping a jug*]. Your jug, Wes?
WES. My jug, Hairy.
HAIRY [*having already poured three, hands one to WES
and offers the other to the MAJOR.*]
[*Music fades and dancers exit to left. Faint laughter.*]

Major [*nobly protesting*]. Gentlemen, gentlemen, with that last noggin emptied, I had quit the field.

Hairy [*anxious*]. Hell, Major, air yo' bowels weakening? So soon, Major?

Wes. Why, Major, you ain't half under! No, not half.

Major. But, gentlemen, I'm to kill another gentleman at sunrise . . . and any more than a half gallon o' distillate is a powerful burden upon a marksman.

Hairy. But I trailed forty miles to have a shivaree with ye. . . .

Wes. He did. Sho. He did.

Hairy. And thirty miles of it on the Nolichucky trace.

Wes. He did. Sho. He did.

Hairy. Met redskins twice.

Wes. He did. Sho. He did.

Major [*sighing*]. I have to hoist one more with ye, Hairy. [*Laugh, off left.*]

Wes. You will. Sho. You will.

Major. But it will founder me, as surely as the devil made little Injuns. I'll have to, though, in memory of King's Mountain.

Wes. And who'll we drink to, Major?

Major. Sho now, we'll drink to the Father o' his country, victor o' Yorktown, woodman, hunter, and military marvel o' the ages. His excellency, General George Washington, President of the United States. [*All drink. Pause.*]

Hairy. Hit air a pleasure to drink to a man, Major, when you name him with such a ruffle.

Wes. The Major are a mocking-bird, sho.

Hairy. But it air unfair to General Greene, not to have the Major name him.

Wes. We'll drink to him, sho!

MAJOR. General Greene were a ree-markable soldier, my friends.

HAIRY. And deservin' of a ruffle, Major. I have clasped his hand on the field, sir.

MAJOR. I believe he felicitated you on yo' marksmanship, after the battle.

WES. Sho. Fill 'em up again, Hairy.

MAJOR [*as* HAIRY *sets about the jug*]. I must decline, gentlemen, though not from disrespect, fo' I served with distinction in General Greene's long rifles in the same engagement.

HAIRY. God a'mighty, an' you won't drink to him!

MAJOR. Well, we might wet the bottom of our throats to him, a sort o' salutin' piece, you might say.

HAIRY [*passing them around*]. Name 'im, Major, name 'im. [*He holds his head with appreciative gusto as the* MAJOR *proposes the toast.*]

MAJOR. To a soldier who never left the enemy upon the field, who purged the South o' the Tories and hirelings of that despot George the Third, who endured the hardships of his troops with the joy that a babe knows when sleeping on his mother's breast—to that scourge o' traitors and peer o' freemen——

HAIRY. Name him, name him!

MAJOR. General Nathanael Greene of Savannah. [*They drink.*]

HAIRY. Hear! [*All drink.*] Why, Major, when you set here and name 'em, I feel as if I could stand to and bibble a horn to every man in the armies o' the Congress.

WES. We could. Sho. We could.

MAJOR. I have always deemed it unwise, my friends, to drink more than one toast; for the heart grows larger under the mellowing influence o' the corn, a host of our glorious heroes comes to mind. . . .

Wes. Who are it now, Major?

Hairy [*moving to the jugs again*]. Name 'im, name 'im.

Major [*continuing his revery*]. And so the heart is more capacious than the bowels. . . . How could we drink to that pearl of the live-oaks, General Marion, the swamp-fox, and yet disregard the claims o' the brilliant and dashing Pulaski? . . . Or how could we pass over the name of Lafayette, young markee of France, Major-General o' continental line at the tender age of nineteen, and son in arms to our illustrious commander? . . . Or to Lighthorse Harry Lee, prince o' horsemen from the Old Dominion, and sweet flower o' Virginia's gentry?

Hairy [*passing the cup*]. Lord, Major, but ye excite me [*Music starts. People begin to filter into the barn, dancing.*] and my head gets to drummin'. . . . Name one, fo' God's sake, name one!

Major. I give you one, my friends. [*He stands up.*] We drink to a man next to General Washington in the gratitude of our country; a man whose melodious name quiets children at their mother's knee, who has dared the trackless wilderness, known the rivers, fields and streams, who has slain where none others ever chanced to look upon, peerless rifleman and hunter, as gentle as a dove, brave as a lion, hardy as the eagle o' the crags . . . moreover, a man who's a close personal friend o' mine . . .

Hairy [*screaming*]. Name 'im! Name 'im!

Major. Colonel Daniel Boone o' Boonesboro. [*Bottoms up desperately.*]

[*As they finish the toast, Dozier and Charity come out. He is holding her arm.*]

MAJOR [*seeing them and evidently clearing the ground*]. After which name, gentlemen, it were sacrilege to wet our pipes again. Having toasted glory, shall we repair to the hall and pay our devoir to beauty? [*Long pause.*]

WES. We will. Sho. We will. [*Exit the three.*]

DOZIER. Charity, want to dance?

CHARITY. I am dancin'.

DOZIER. Next time I go to Nashville, Charity, you'll be going there with me.

CHARITY. There's a sight o' people there, Dozier.

DOZIER. But none like you, Charity. You will surely queen it in Nashville.

CHARITY. I reckon you're a mighty big man at Nashville.

DOZIER. I'm going to be bigger, Charity. I'm going to run the country in my time.

CHARITY. If you figure on running things . . . you won't be dueling that little gentleman from the tavern.

DOZIER. And why not? I aim to kill him if he comes round here.

CHARITY. I'd hate to marry a man with blood on his hands.

DOZIER. Where will you find a man any good without?

CHARITY. I allow I ain't looking fo' a man jes' now anyway.

DOZIER. I allow there's one looking fo' you.

CHARITY. Mister Dozier, it ain't me you want fo' Nashville. . . .

DOZIER. I want you anywhere, Charity. I want you fo' myself. I've told your pappy, before he went into the woods last spring, that I could do more fo' ye than any other man in this country. He allowed that I could.

CHARITY. I ain't said yet that I'd follow what pappy told me to. I ain't said I'd marry ye.

Dozier. But you will?

Charity. I ain't fo' marrying a man who runs around killing everybody that gits in his way.

Dozier. It's a killing country. I've had to do it. . . . I'm starting to Nashville in the morning, Charity. Tell me yes now, so's I can build a house there fo' ye.

Charity. I don't know my mind, Mister Dozier.

Dozier. I can wait a while, Charity, but I'll be bound to have ye.

Charity. If you say you'll be bound to have me, like that, I'll tell you that you ain't sure you'll have me.

Dozier. You wouldn't quarrel with me, Charity? Nobody's offered ye more than I.

Charity. Yes, I would quarrel with you, and quarrel hot. And I ain't any little lost gentleman in a tavern for you and your friend to bait with pistols.

Dozier. Are you siding with him?

Charity. I don't say I'm siding with anybody. Only, I don't like your ways. And you can't come courting me like you go into a tavern, killing everybody that gits in your way. You can stay here a spell and cool off. And make up yo' mind whether you came here for me or fo' fighting. [*She turns and runs into the barn.*]

[Hairy *and three buckskins come out dressed alike with long rifles.*]

First Buck. If this here country gets any thicker in lawyers and thieves, I'm a-going out to whar he is.

Second Buck. The way I see it, leaving right now is a sort o' treason. If we all take to the woods now, they'll git this country sho.

Third Buck. I aim to stay here a spell with my long rifle, and shoot it out.

HAIRY. Boys, if this Free State fails again, I aim to join Colonel Boone.

SECOND BUCK. Ye'd never find him.

HAIRY. That I would.

THIRD BUCK. Whar?

HAIRY. He's in the Dakota country, ain't he? I guess a body could go there and pick up his sign. [*He sights his rifle.*]

DOZIER. You kain't, Hairy, until after yo' trial.

[MAJOR *comes out and joins them.*]

HAIRY. Trial, trial, always a trial! Mister Dozier, I don't think I'll go to my trial.

[WES *comes out.*]

MAJOR [*coming up*]. But it's the law, Hairy, the law!

WES. It's lawful, Hairy, sho it's lawful.

HAIRY. Oh, it's law, law, law, law! That's all a body hears. I told my triers at the first trial I was plumb wore out with it. Here this country is so big and pretty. . . . I can mind when there weren't three white men in hit . . . now a body cain't go into the wilderness a month without meetin' a white man and all of them talkin' law, law, law.

MAJOR [*sententious*]. A reverence for the common law is the chief characteristic of our race, Hairy.

HAIRY. Common law? Now who's banting common law, major? Hit's this here cote house law. I won't put up with it. Since these here prosecutors tuck hold here—come jabberin' law, law, law—a body cain't put a knife under a rascal's ribs. I told my first triers I was wore out with it. One o' my triers said to me, "Why, Hairy, ef you thought the traitor had given you a faulty firelock, why didn't you have the law on him?" Do you hear that? I said to him, "I ain't a puke and a sneak like that fellow Blackstone they're jabbering about. Do you think I want it throwed up to my grandson when he grows up that his grandpappy had the law on a man?"

Major. But, Hairy . . .

Hairy. Major, allow me to pester ye. Throw away yo' cote house mind and answer in common law.

Major. Common indeed, sir.

Hairy. What air yo' opinion o' Colonel Boone's jedgment in the matter? He have slain his millions. Would he set to heel an' allow a passel o' lawyers to try him fo' ticklin' a rascal's ribs?

Major. Hairy, his actions are precedents for heroes, not points for indictment.

Hairy. Would he let a body o' lawyers make rules on his physical manners in a shindy with a gentleman of sharp practice?

Major. Hairy, he is a man o' his own will in physical matters.

Hairy. Then I 'low if Colonel Boone ever returns, he will not abide the old North State.

Major. The evidence is in your favor.

Hairy. Now, then, is this trial o' mine under the Free State o' Franklin or under No'th Carolina?

Major. It is brought under the jurisdiction of the State of North Carolina, sir, the Free State of Franklin bein' temporarily in abeyance.

Hairy. Major, that's one reason why I trailed in here tonight . . . first because I wanted you should memorize the time you and me fit the redcoats at King's Mountain by holdin' a shivaree . . . but also to tell you not to defend me against the State of No'th Carolina at the cote at Nashville because I don't pretend to go to that trial myself. I don't think I could sit through all that law talk again. I don't believe Daniel Boone could sit through it.

MAJOR. Would you go to your trial if it was the Free State brought it?

HAIRY. If the Free State brought a man to trial for defending himself again' a fraud, hit wouldn't be no free state. I know the Free State, sir. I was there when hit begun, and hit wouldn't do it, sir. It wouldn't do it.

WES. Hear, hear! Fill 'em up again, Hairy.

MAJOR. Gentlemen, I must decline.

HAIRY. Hell, Major, you ain't put out with me?

MAJOR. No, Hairy, your reasoning is logical and correct. I cain't controvert it. But I feel the corn stealin' over me, gentlemen. If I should take one mo' drink I would default in an affair o' honor.

HAIRY. Why, Major, we ain't trolled a stave yet, not a stave. [*He is filling them up again.*]

> Git my fiddle tuned up good,
> Best old fiddle in the neighborhood;
> My home ain't here, nohow, nohow.

[*The buckskins join in the songs.* HAIRY *passes the horn.*]

WES. Who we drink to, Major?

HAIRY. We won't drink *to*. We'll drink *again'* somebody. [*He raises his mug.*] God damn King George of England!

> Dance, dance, bucks and gals,
> I just come here to the party.
> I ain't no hand for to raise a row
> I'm hell when a row gets started.

[*He leads another stave.*]

ALL [*in chorus*]. My home ain't here nohow, nohow.

HAIRY. Shall I fill 'em up again, Wes?

WES. How's my jug now, Hairy?

HAIRY. Heavy, Wes, heavy.

WES. Fill 'em up again, and God damn King George of England.

HAIRY [*singing*]. You swing Sal, I swing Sue;
       They won't be a nigger in a mile or two.

ALL [*in chorus*]. My home ain't here nohow, nohow.
[*They drink.*]

MAJOR [*sipping lightly*]. In three hours I am to hazard a noble reputation on the field of honor to sever one tentacle o' that octopus we all abhor, North Carolina.

HAIRY. Hell, Major, I kin drop him for you any time a-tall. [*Hand caresses knife.*] There's one thing the law ain't changed.

WES. Peevey Hill air only two years old, but it has a fine reputation, Major. No stranger ever come here and win a fight.

MAJOR. My dear friends, to interfere in an affair o' honor is to stain honor and defeat justice.

[*A number of buckskins come crashing out the door,
    followed by the crowd.*]

FIRST BUCK. God damn you, get away from her.

LONG JOHN. You take me away.

FIRST BUCK. I'll take you.

MAJOR [*arising with alacrity*]. Here! Here! [*To* BUCK-SKIN *near by.*] What's the row about, son?

THE BUCKSKIN. About dancin' with Sairy, sir. There's a mighty fine place for fightin' down by the creek bed. Everybody can sit by the bank and see them gouge.

MAJOR. Take 'em down to the creek bed and everybody'll set on the bank and see 'em gouge. [*Cries of* Leggo! *and* Holt still! *The procession moves off. The stage is now quiet in the moonlight as the voices fade.* LONNY *and* CHARITY *steal back for a tryst. They sit on the corn-stalks, silent a moment.*]

CHARITY. Let's not, Lonny. I don't want to see that gouging.

LONNY. I'd rather stay here with you, anyway, Charity.

LONNY [*putting an arm around her*]. When I git my law license to practice I'm going to take you away to Fayettesville.

CHARITY. Pappy will have me married long before you kin git that, Lonny. Takes two months' study to git a law license in the Free State and mo' than that in the old North State.

LONNY. But you got to hold out again him.

CHARITY. Ain't I held out nearly a whole year?

LONNY. Hold out another one. You kin.

CHARITY. An' then I'd be 'most seventeen. He'd be afeared I'd turn into an old maid.

LONNY. Hold out jus' two months, Charity, and I'll carry you away. Just two mo' moons like this.

CHARITY. But Dozier's here, and he's here to take me. He'll have me sho, before the old moon comes.

LONNY [*grimly*]. He's got to git by Captain Jackson.

CHARITY. Captain Jackson will be down the river by sunrise, that little fellow will. All prance and preen and no fightin' a-tall.

LONNY. That he won't. He'll be here just before moondown. He said so.

CHARITY. You are trusting, Lonny. Gentlemen like him

don't fight about women like me. They either takes us [*she sighs*]—or they leave us.

LONNY. Sometimes they take you and leave you too.

CHARITY. They won't me.

LONNY. That they won't. I'll take you, though.

CHARITY. How will you?

LONNY. I'll fight Dozier fo' you, if the Cap'n runs away.

CHARITY [*brushing the hair from his forehead*]. Poor boy. He'd kill you. You kain't duel.

LONNY. I kin duel. Cap'n Jackson has already learned me how to start one.

CHARITY. And now he'll teach you how to run away from one.

LONNY. That he won't!

CHARITY. It ain't no use, Lonny.

LONNY. Kiss me once, Charity. I'd die for you, Charity.

CHARITY. It ain't no use.

LONNY. Once.

CHARITY. Once.

[*He kisses her. She remains cold.*]

LONNY. You didn't kiss me back.

CHARITY. I ain't never kissed back to a man.

LONNY [*trying again*]. I'll teach you.

CHARITY [*springing up*]. Look you here, Lonny Tucker. . . . [*She springs up literally to confront* JACKSON, *who seems to have stepped out of enchantment. He is in a Continental uniform of buff and blue, remarkably splendid on the moonlit stage.*]

JACKSON. Good evening, ma'am. I trust I'm not too late for the fiddling.

HAWK [*who follows* JACKSON *in and moves toward the jugs*]. Where be they all, Miss Charity?

CHARITY. Law, Captain, you scared me. They're all down by the creek bed to a fight, Mister Peevey.

JACKSON. Whetting their appetites, doubtless, ma'am, for the prize main of the evening.

CHARITY. And what will that be, sir?

JACKSON. Why, ma'am, I believe you were there when the birds were paired. A red bantam cockerel against a South Carolina shawl neck, and later ag'in a Free State bluffer.

CHARITY. Be you the bantam, Captain?

JACKSON. None other, ma'am.

LONNY [coming up for the first time]. Cap'n, be warned. George Dozier's got pistols on him, ain't tasted spirits this evening, and that there Rachel Donelson from Nashville's been taunting him all night. She ain't been dancing with him, not a reel, sir—telling him fie and foe, and how she's saving her powers for that red-headed cap'n who ain't afraid of the whole neighborhood.

HAWK [drinking pleasantly]. Has she now? Bless her heart.

JACKSON. Ma'am, I trust I may bear such a provoking honor modestly. [He grins.] And I'd a sight rather have a measure with you, ma'am.

CHARITY. Oh, no, Cap'n, you know you'd admire to see the widow Rachel first. . . . Lonny, will you mind fetching her here?

LONNY. It will be a sight of trouble tearing Rachel away from a menfolk's fight, Charity, but I reckon on this occasion she'll come. [He starts off.] And, Cap'n [he turns and bows], arrangements have been made for sunrise, sir.

JACKSON [bowing to LONNY]. I thank you, sir. [LONNY goes out.] And, ma'am, I hate to think you are refusing a measure with me.

CHARITY. Will you go help Lonny, Mister Peevey?

HAWK [*taking in the situation*]. I will, ma'am, I will. [*Exit.*]

CHARITY. Captain, I got them away so's to ask you to hit the trace now.

JACKSON. What trace, ma'am?

CHARITY. Along the river. They's a raft going down to Nashville at sunrise, and you can tail it before you reach dangerous country.

JACKSON. Why, ma'am, air you tired of me?

CHARITY. How can I be tired of you, Cap'n, when I have hardly seen you yet? I don't know you. I don't even want to know you. And I don't want to see you go fighting about me.

JACKSON. But it will be a pleasure, ma'am.

CHARITY. To be kilt by George Dozier?

JACKSON. Since you don't know me, ma'am, it won't trouble you none.

CHARITY. But I'd know you then, sir. . . . All my life I'd see you lying dead in that pretty blue coat, all account you came to dance with me. If Dozier finds you here, Cap'n, it won't be a duel. It'll be a murder.

JACKSON. But I don't aim to die soon, ma'am.

CHARITY. But you will die. You'll be killed befo' you finish yo' dance. You'll have to go. Please go. If you killed George Dozier, it'd be unchristian ever to see you again.

JACKSON. Would you mourn for him, I wonder?

CHARITY. It'd be my duty to mourn fo' him.

JACKSON. Maybe I wouldn't kill him dead, ma'am.

CHARITY. Please go, Cap'n. I'm a sight from being helpless. I ain't afeared.

JACKSON. Who protects you, child, that you aren't afraid? Where's your father?

CHARITY. He's a long hunter, Cap'n. He's on a party west since the spring.

JACKSON. And he's marrying you to Dozier?

CHARITY. As soon as he gits back.

JACKSON. He admires yo' intended?

CHARITY. That he don't, Cap'n. Only he wants me safe.

JACKSON. You aim to marry him?

CHARITY. I reckon I must.

JACKSON. He might mistreat you, ma'am.

CHARITY. That he won't.

JACKSON [fiercely]. No, I allow he won't, either.

CHARITY. Cap'n, you won't be favoring me none by fighting.

JACKSON. Ma'am, I trust I will. . . . I'm going to, sure.

CHARITY. There'd be a sight o' trouble.

JACKSON. Ma'am, you won't be touched by my actions. . . . You are a flower. . . . And I reckon Mister Dozier won't pluck you soon. . . . And you won't have to see me again. . . . I don't figure on lasting long. . . . I was born for trouble.

CHARITY. Yo' kind is so kind they is spared, Cap'n. You were born for glory. Please hit the trail now. And when you're passing you can lay to just beyond the last house up the trace—hit's pappy's place.

JACKSON. Yes, Peevey showed it to me, ma'am, as we came by. And would that outside ladder lead to your chamber, ma'am?

CHARITY. It does, Cap'n, right to it. After you've passed pappy's place, you kin join the hunters when they go through. But don't go in the wilderness beyond. You'd

be lost in that coat if there were Injuns on your trail.
They'd want that, sho. . . .

JACKSON. Will you see me, if I come by?

CHARITY. Nobody ever passes that I don't see him.

JACKSON. And would you be so unkind as to refuse me
one word when I pass there—for the last time?

CHARITY. Not if you will go now. It would be better
there than here.

JACKSON. But surely you can see I couldn't go now. Not
without dancing once with you.

CHARITY. You'd never leave here alive if you did, Cap'n.

JACKSON. Indeed, ma'am, I might never want to. I might
want to stay here all my life.

CHARITY. Here?

JACKSON. What's to hinder?

CHARITY. Why stay here, Cap'n?

JACKSON. Wouldn't you know, ma'am, even now?

[*There are returning voices.*]

CHARITY. I would not.

JACKSON. Then I can tell you, ma'am.

CHARITY. Not here—I can hear them coming back.
Please go, Cap'n. You kin come by at dawn. I'll come to
the window and hear. You'll see my light in the loft. And
then you'll go down by the trail with yo' horses and yo'
nigger. Please go, Cap'n.

[*The voices come nearer.*]

JACKSON. If I can sit my horse, ma'am, you will surely
see me.

CHARITY. They're nearly here.

JACKSON. There was something I wanted to tell you, and
I can tell you now. [*She is half eager.*] Just now, Charity,

I heard you say to that boy you ain't never kissed back to a man. . . .

CHARITY. Please go.

JACKSON. Kiss me, Charity. [*He puts his arms about her and kisses her beautifully, with quick tenderness, and she responds.*] I can't go now, Charity.

CHARITY. Then God keep us both, Cap'n. [*They spring apart as* HAWK, LONNY *and* RACHEL *come on.*]

HAWK. They're coming back. Long John bellowed calf-rope in time to save his ear and they're shakin' hands on it. [*To* RACHEL *and* JACKSON.] Cap'n Jackson, allow me to present Miz Donelson, who is pleased to meet you.

JACKSON [*cocky again*]. Honored, ma'am, honored.

RACHEL. Cap'n, I believe you scairt George Dozier into not drinking. He's tee-total. God A'mighty, but I'm a proud to know ye for it!

JACKSON. Why, Miz Donelson, 'tis unseemly for me to deprive a gentleman o' his liquor when he's so near t'other side o' Jordan as he is tonight.

RACHEL. Air you allowing him to deprive you of yo' refreshments, sir, or would you share with me? It'd please me mightily fo' him to find you drinking with a body he'd refused.

JACKSON. 'Twould be ungallant to refuse you anything a-tall, ma'am, up to and over a quart o' the fiery stuff. Will you serve yo'self a small, ladylike potation, ma'am, and give me the jug?

RACHEL [*pouring, as* CHARITY *looks on hostilely*]. Do you dance the Virginia reel, Cap'n?

JACKSON. Like an elephant, ma'am, an elephant.

RACHEL. La, Cap'n, you are that modest.

JACKSON. Indeed, ma'am, I'm that conceited. Miss

Charity's promised me the first reel—and may I pledge this to the second one with you?

RACHEL.   Why, Cap'n, you should stay and dance out the night!

JACKSON.   Ma'am, you are most kind.   [*Pause.   The hubbub comes nearer, and several boys and girls break in, rushing the fiddler into the barn, unconscious of the tableau by the corn-stalks.   The major portion of the crowd, with* DOZIER *to the fore, the* MAJOR *and* HAIRY *near by, halts at sight of* JACKSON.   JACKSON, *finishing his mug, and conscious of the limelight, moves to* CHARITY's *side as the fiddler is heard scraping his preliminary chords.*]   I find you unattended, ma'am.   Might I claim the honor o' the next dance?

CHARITY [*enjoying the tension despite her fears*].   La, Cap'n, would you now?

JACKSON.   Nothing could prevent me, ma'am.   [*He places her arm in his and looks toward the crowd.*]   Not all the cheap-jack lawyers in this here and now State of North Carolina.   [DOZIER *takes a step forward.   CHARITY's head goes back proudly, but she interposes her body between* JACKSON *and* DOZIER *as the latter approaches, hands caressing the waist of his coat.*]

CHARITY.   Cap'n, I surely would hate to fetch trouble to you.

JACKSON [*interposing in turn, between* DOZIER *and* CHARITY].   That too would be a pleasure.   I was born fo' trouble, ma'am.   Shall we go inside and dance a spell while trouble gathers outside?

CHARITY.   Yes, Cap'n, we will indeed.

DOZIER.   I believe you realize, sir, that your presence here is an insult to the company and that your attentions to this lady are a personal affront to me.

JACKSON. Mister Dozier, I should be loath to think you spoke for this community, fo' my feelings toward it are affable and friendly. As for you personally, sir, I am happily relieved by custom from further converse with you before the appointed hour.

DOZIER. Custom or no custom, I have something to say to you now! And you shield yo'self, sir!

JACKSON. Ma'am, would you be so kind as to release me?

CHARITY. No, Cap'n, I would not.

JACKSON. You place me in an awkward position, ma'am. Yo' hand on my arm is withholding Mister Dozier from reaching for his pistols. [*Music.*]

CHARITY. I reckon Mister Dozier will have to wait, Cap'n Jackson, for the fiddlin' is under way.

JACKSON [*to* DOZIER]. You apprehend my situation, sir. [*He bows.*] However, I shall be here quite a spell, sir. [*He enters the barn with* CHARITY, HAWK *following to cover up the rear.*]

DOZIER [*moving forward after them*]. By God . . .

RACHEL [*crossing the stage and confronting him*]. See here, George Dozier, if you spoil the little thing's jig with that gentleman I'll swear I'll have you tarred and feathered when you come to Nashville.

LONNY. You won't have to, Miz Donelson. I aim to feather him myself.

DOZIER. One at a time, sir, and I'll handle you all. [*He continues toward the barn.*]

MAJOR. Season yourself, Mister Dozier. 'Pears to me like you forget my preference in this matter, which can keep till after this festive occasion. [DOZIER *enters the barn, followed by what part of the crowd is left, save the* MAJOR, HAIRY, *and* RACHEL. HAWK *runs out from the barn.*]

Hawk. God A'mighty, gentlemen, you should see the Cap'n dance! He can jump higher'n a show-dog.

Major. Hairy, shall we repair inside and observe the antics of this yere short-lived marvel?

Hairy. I aim to see him, sir. [*They enter the barn.*]

Rachel [*to* Hawk, *as he moves to the jugs as their backs are turned*]. I thank you for introducing a body like him to our neighborhood, Mister Peevey.

Hawk. That you do, Miz Donelson, and he will be a sight popular with you, I'm sure.

Rachel. I surely envy the other ladies o' Nashville when he gits there, Mister Peevey.

Hawk. But not the gentlemen none! Lawd, he'll shoot 'em all, Miz Donelson. All, ma'am.

Rachel. Is he really warlike, now?

Hawk. Man, he come to my doggery at sundown with a racing mare, a sporting dog, and two fighting chickens. He drank a double-glass o' the finest, set in at whist, quarreled with two hard-roweling gentlemen, is dancing at dawn, and will shoot the two of 'em at sunrise. . . . Would that be peaceable or warlike, ma'am?

Rachel. I'd admire to see him slap every created man in the face, Mister Peevey.

Hawk. You will, ma'am, before cote's in session a week. [*He wipes his moustache on his sleeve with an air of relish.*] And now, ma'am, will you go inside with me and jig about some to settle my liquor?

Rachel. We'd better hurry, Mister Peevey, else 'twill take holt so you can't dance. [Major *and* Hairy *stroll out, followed by* Wes.] Air you quitting so soon, Mr. Lake? I ain't never seen you dance.

Hairy. And you won't, Miz Donelson. [*He sits in a*

study, the MAJOR *and* WES *taking places by him, both groaning slightly, and unsteady.*] He air mighty small, Major, mighty small for a body to take aim on.

MAJOR. An infant, sir, an infant.

HAIRY. But his wardrobe makes up for hit. Like the sheen on a turkey's wing, and 'twill guide the bullet to the mark.

WES. To the mark, sho.

MAJOR. I'd a sight rather he had darker clothing, gentlemen, and a larger body. . . . My liquor's tuck hold of my shooting arm like a snapping-turtle.

HAIRY. Major, if you was only to say the word I could drop him fo' you without a mite o' trouble, not a mite.

MAJOR. Hairy, yo' words pain me inexpressibly—inexpressibly, sir. Do you want I should die dishonored?

[LONG JOHN, *a long, utterly dirty and disheveled buckskin, comes painfully and sadly from the forest, limping.*]

MAJOR [*quickly*]. Move over, Hairy, and let Long John set. He's mortifying from having lost the fight.

HAIRY. Sho. I lost one once.

MAJOR [*as* LONG JOHN *sits*]. Don't feel so downcast, Long John. It's the carriage o' the man in action, and not the infliction o' his will upon the opponent, that makes our race so glorious.

LONG JOHN [*de profundis*]. I kain't help it, Major, I kain't help it. [*He is weeping a little.*]

WES. Sho. What's losing a fight? I've lost every one I ever had, and look at me.

HAIRY. Let's drink to him, gentlemen, let's drink to him. [*He's up and pouring four.*]

MAJOR. Just wet the bottom o' mine, Hairy, I'm foun-

dered in fathoms. . . . Long John, did I never tell you
about the time that Colonel Boone fit the gouging match
with three Iroquoy Indians, and lost it, thus becoming a
full member o' the tribe?—Thank you, Hairy. [*Drinks.*]
Colonel Boone was trying to find the headwaters o' the Elk
River, and had had right smart annoyance from the Iroquoy.
. . . He hadn't been exactly lost; but he confessed later he
had been bewildered fo' fo' days. . . . [*Drinks.*]   Daniel
hadn't fetched his rifle along.   Hit were a beautiful weapon,
all carved and fretted with kickshaws and designs, brought
on from London by Lord Dunmore and presented to Daniel
as a token o' royal esteem. . . . Daniel was proud of it,
and he jus' wouldn't take it along in river work fo' fear o'
rusting it. . . . It certainly gave the advantage to three
thousand Injuns for Colonel Boone to be armed only with
his knife and hatchet. [*Drinks.*]   But the important thing,
gentlemen, was that the Indians didn't know that he hadn't
fetched it along.   It certainly gave the advantage to Daniel.
[*Drinks.*]   Well, at daybreak the Injuns divided into three
savage war parties, a thousand painted heathen in each
force.   So Colonel Boone took up a position on a bluff over-
looking the headwaters o' the Kaintuck River, and left Injun
signs all 'long that he had done bloodied the wampum and
was in one o' his tantrums.   No sooner had the Iroquoy
picked up the wampum belt than they called a council o'
war.   Well, the upshot was that they decided, in response to
the lamentations o' their widows an' old men, to offer Colonel
Boone a limited proposition o' war.   Three Injuns, which
seemed fair enough to their chiefs, would fight Colonel Boone
simultaneously, any weapons he chose, the Injuns to leave
the country if they lost, or Colonel Boone to marry into the
tribe, if he lost, and take for his squaws all the bereaved

widows he had made among the tribes in previous depredations. When they sent messengers up the bluff and put it
up to Colonel Boone it seemed fair enough to Daniel.
[*Drinks.*] He . . . chose to fight a gouging match.

LONG JOHN. With three Iroquoy Injuns, Major?

MAJOR. Full-blooded, son, and I do believe to my soul
that two of 'em were rising eight foot tall. [HAIRY *springs
up at this and begins to prowl about the stage.*]

LONG JOHN. He might 'a' whupped three Cherokees, now,
but Iroquoys is different.

MAJOR [*draining his cup*]. Son, at that time there weren't
three Cherokees from the Kaintuck to the Okefenokee who'd
'a' tackled Daniel on his sick-bed. After seven hours o'
gouging, Colonel Boone found himself unable to continue
on account o' two broken arms. . . . He accepted his defeat
with good grace and was instantly adopted into full fellow-
ship by the five nations, showered with weapons, peltries,
an' hosses, and manfully endowed with wives. The Dela-
wares alone sent him a bevy of twenty wives as a wedding
present. Well, sir, Daniel endured the marriage state three
hundred and seven days, keeping the Indian faith and hunt-
ing eighteen hours a day to keep his numerous family in
b'ar-meat. . . . When he escaped, it is said that the lamentations o' his widows started the Elk River out o' its banks
and cleaved its present bed deep enough for flatboat navi-
gation.

LONG JOHN. Did he go back, Major?

MAJOR. Son, he was afeared to—fo' he learned that his
offspring numbered three hundred and fourteen infants, suh,
only seven brace o' them being born twins.

[*Four* BUCKSKINS *come out of barn.*]

FIRST BUCKSKIN. Major, Mister Dozier allows that this

blue-coat monkey disporting himself inside is the identical foreigner who is sent out here to set up North State law in our halls o' justice.

MAJOR.   The identical man!

SECOND BUCKSKIN.   Major, I kain't believe a man is so rash.

FIRST BUCKSKIN.   We sho'ly could not.

SECOND BUCKSKIN.   Air we suckling puff-adders to our bosoms in this Free State of ours?

MAJOR [*rising portentously*].   Gentlemen, you're doubtless aware that Mister Dozier and myself are confronting this young man with weapons in our hands at sunrise.   In my opinion the fate o' the Free State rests on the outcome of our encounter.

FIRST BUCKSKIN.   Major, your honor and your marksmanship air beyond reproach.

MAJOR.   If he fell prematurely, gentlemen, or by any other hand before the set time of our engagement, my name would be irretrievably soiled.   If Mister Dozier has given a contrary impression. . . .

FIRST BUCKSKIN.   Mister Dozier informed us who he was, sir, and no mo'.

THIRD BUCKSKIN.   Major, do you reckon the young man is taking advantage of his coming encounter to flaunt himself in our faces, sir?

MAJOR.   I do not.   In justice to his carriage, I say I do not.   I reckon he holds himself able to take care o' himself anywhere.

FIRST BUCKSKIN.   Then we won't tetch him, sir.

THIRD BUCKSKIN.   No, sir, we won't.

MAJOR.   Gentlemen, I thank you.   [*He sits.*]

THIRD BUCKSKIN.   But we kin question him.

SECOND BUCKSKIN. I reckon we kin question him, Major?

MAJOR. Up to the limits of violence, I jedge it would do no harm to question him.

HAIRY. Then I aim to question him myself, Major, because I kain't set still when he's around. [*He begins to pace up and down with knit brows, near the barn door.* JACKSON *comes out with* CHARITY, *sees the group, turns with her in the opposite direction, she leaning breathlessly on his arm, and runs into* HAIRY.] Good evening, ma'am. [*He bows.*]

CHARITY. Evening, sir.

HAIRY. Would it trouble you none, ma'am, if I mought pester yo' gentleman with a little catechism?

CHARITY. It won't none, Mr. Lake; and I make no doubt it won't trouble him none, either.

HAIRY. May I trouble you, sir? . . .

JACKSON [*bowing*]. Yo' servant, sir.

HAIRY. It remains to be seen.

JACKSON. Truly enough . . . seeing as I am here to press with force and zeal the rights of the old North State in its claims against all transgressors.

HAIRY. Mister . . .

JACKSON [*bowing*]. Cap'n, sir.

HAIRY [*bowing still lower*]. Cap'n it be, sir. Cap'n, I aim to set you right. I 'low a man given to jabbering justice and transgressors just natchelly kain't be my servant, sir.

JACKSON. Are you under criminal indictment, sir?

HAIRY. I am, sir. [*As this dialogue begins,* DOZIER *steps from the door, and one by one the dancers follow until the stage is peopled for the climax.*]

JACKSON. Your charge?

HAIRY. Killin' a rascal, sir.

JACKSON. Then it will be my duty, if there is no palliation, to get you hanged, sir, as high as Haman was hanged in Scripture.

HAIRY. Well, now, Cap'n, it will indeed.

WES. It will, sho it will.

HAIRY. And might I question you now, Cap'n, on a matter a little mo' personal to me?

JACKSON. If this lady accords, sir.

CHARITY. Sho. I'm enjoying myself.

HAIRY. Is North Carolina in the Union, or not?

JACKSON. It is. It is.

HAIRY. Is there a Union law excising a tax on the making of spirits, or not?

JACKSON. There is none yet, but it has been determined upon.

HAIRY. If the Free State was in the Union would I be obliged to pay a tax on my liquor, or not?

JACKSON. Very likely you would, sir. Very likely you will.

HAIRY. Putting that aside, Cap'n, who air the first gentleman o' the land, sir?

JACKSON. His Excellency, General Washington.

HAIRY. To the mark.

WES. Right. To the mark.

HAIRY. Hush, Wes; I'm drivin' him to hit. And does the General ferment the grain and distill it through the worm, sir?

JACKSON. I believe the landed gentry o' the East prefer to make their own spirits, sir.

HAIRY. And does his Excellency?

JACKSON. I believe so.

HAIRY. And does he pay excise tax on those spirits, sir?

JACKSON. He does not.

HAIRY. The President air still in the best o' health?

JACKSON. He is, sir.

HAIRY. He air still addicted to his toddy?

JACKSON. I should conjecture so.

HAIRY. He air still addicted to not paying excise tax on that toddy?

JACKSON. There being no law requiring it, the presumption is in yo' favor.

HAIRY. And he air generally credited with being the wisest among living creeturs?

JACKSON. He is so held in the East, sir.

HAIRY. Then that settles it, sir.

JACKSON. What, sir?

HAIRY. It settles it that if that's all the wisdom they is in the East it's better to be in the Free State than in the North State. It settles it that the Free State will never join up with the excise tax states.

JACKSON. But an excise tax on spirits may be necessary for the maintenance of the armies of Congress, armies for your defense against the British, against the French, against his Majesty o' Spain.

HAIRY. How would our boys fight better if their liquor costs more? What would General Washington say to that?

JACKSON. General Washington has urgently requested the Congress to put a heavy national excise upon distillates of all states, the money to go to the capitol at Philadelphia.

HAIRY. Did the General do that, Cap'n?

JACKSON. I give you my word, he has, sir.

HAIRY. Then the General is a crack-brained, dumb fool, Cap'n.

JACKSON. I agree to that, sir. A scoundrel in his old age, sir, yet my superior officer and yours also, and the Major's likewise.

MAJOR [*rising, swaying*]. You will fight me fo' that, sir! You will fight me first because he is no scoundrel, and second because he has no authority here! [*He sinks down, drunken.*]

JACKSON. You may include that in yo' bill o' particulars, sir. I say he has authority here, and will have. He has authority here under the pledges of the various colonies, the ark o' our liberty, which it is treason and madness to defy.

[*As* HAIRY *has been speaking, the* BUCKSKINS *have grouped about him, evidently dying to join the debate. They take it from* HAIRY *as soon as he is silent, not in the manner of dogs around a bear, but with the utmost gentility and courtesy, which should only serve to give the thing a pall of high, compressed danger.*]

FIRST BUCKSKIN. Whose liberty?

JACKSON. Yours, sir.

FIRST BUCKSKIN. Allowed me, I figger, by your Congress away up yonder, three months away, at Philadelphia.

JACKSON. True, sir, three months away, but a Congress in which you have a voice.

SECOND BUCKSKIN [*a man of forty, ferocious-looking*]. Look here, Cap'n, I allow I have a mighty powerful voice. There ain't another man in the Cumberlands to compare. I have called my dogs three miles to a b'ar-pit on a clear autumn night like this. . . . But I kain't make my holler heard in Congress.

JACKSON. True, sir, but you can send a delegate to make your wishes heard there.

THIRD BUCKSKIN. Supposin' we don't want to. I aim

to be able to do all my own talking, and back it up with
the clostest-shooting rifle, next to Hairy Lake's, in this
here country. I aim to have my share in our own congress
we aim to hold here.

JACKSON. Precisely, sir, and you have thet own congress
in the North Carolina Assembly.

SECOND BUCKSKIN. It ain't ours. I have been down to
the settlements. What's in 'em? Why, a bee-swarm o' galoots, trying to keep alive by selling each other calico cloth
and whisky. All the rules they have air for galoots that
sell calico cloth and whisky.

FIRST BUCKSKIN. Drive him to it, drive him to it.

SECOND BUCKSKIN. And now they are to excise-tax me
fo' making my own whisky. I don't aim to buy their calico
cloth, so befo' long they'll try to excise-tax me for tanning
my own buckskin shirt. . . . I don't believe I'm going to
heed your rules.

THIRD BUCKSKIN. And you air one o' them, Cap'n; it's
you air bringing their laws.

JACKSON. I do, sir. And along with them we shall bring
schools for yo' offspring, protection fo' yo' womenfolks,
guarantees for your liberties.

FIRST BUCKSKIN. Ef you bring protection, how come you
kain't travel the trail to Nashville without long-hunters to
protect you?

JACKSON. Why, gentlemen, as you protect the trails
from the Iroquoy, the North State will protect you from
England and the dastards of Spain. On the trail back a
few days is Judge McNairy, with all the county officers
necessary for law and order, for schools, for militia, for
peace and the pursuit of happiness. The people of North
Carolina contribute these things out of their taxes, sir, and

from the affection they bear her sons on the far frontier.

First Buckskin. Even if I was to put up with North Carolina, Cap'n, because it ain't fur away, and they know me, yet I won't put up with Philadelphia. And if we're in the North State we're under Philadelphia. It's too far away for them to study about me.

Second Buckskin. We won't trust 'em that far fo' our liberty.

Jackson. You have safeguards under the constitution they proffer, sir.

Hairy. Now, Cap'n, you rile me. [*He ascends to anger as his argument progresses.*] Now you tetch me and affect me. When they told me, when they come pleading with me and my eldest boy to rally our boys at King's Mountain and shoot the red-coats there, they told me that we would get shet o' foreigners making rules for free men to follow. I went, and I fit them. I was the hunter that kilt the big fellow in the pink coat and the white wig. . . . But when I come home I hearn that up North they had drawed up another set o' rules, just like the red-coat rules . . . and they tell me [*he is terribly passionate*] they call the thing a constitution, and they'll make me sign it. Well, I'm not going to sign. I'm not going to let anybody in London tell me how I got to make my whisky or tan my shirts, and I'm not going to let anybody in Philadelphia tell me how I got to make my whisky and tan my shirts. And if you've come bringing them rules, I'm not a-going to have ye. I won't put up with ye. I fit ye once and I'll fight ye again. I'll fight ye now.

Jackson. If you want your own congress here, sir, nothing could be nearer Judge McNairy's heart. When you have ten leaders like him you can have your Tennessee country made into a state. Sir, I confide this in you. I can put no heart into my defense of a federal constitution. I am for states' rights. I am for old North Carolina before everything else.

HAIRY. That's what we're trying to teach you, Cap'n. We ain't in the old North State here. We're Free State here—Nolichucky Jack Sevier's Free State, and we reckin it'll take care of us.

JACKSON. Colonel Sevier is a very brave man, but he has lost his dispute with the Governor of North Carolina and is heading an expedition west.

HAIRY. He'll come back.

JACKSON. It would take him a year, sir. And meanwhile, if you have no statehood, who will police your border, ringed with a thousand dangers? Who will punish your Indians?

FIRST BUCKSKIN. We will.

HAIRY. Answer yea or nay, Cap'n. Fur or agin the Free State?

JACKSON. The Free State is disbanded at Jonesborough. How kin I be for it when it isn't there any mo'?

HAIRY. Would ye be for a new state if we got up one?

JACKSON. Yes, if we took in all the Tennessee and Cumberland country and proved ourselves men enough to hold it.

HAIRY. If we told you there was a new Free State at this moment, and told you who was head of it and who was back of it, would you be for it?

JACKSON. It would depend on the men you named, sir.

HAIRY. Then I'll name them, sir. . . .

THREE OR FOUR BUCKSKINS. No, no!

DOZIER. Not to him, sir.

HAIRY. And why not to him? Major! Major!

First Buckskin. He's down, Hairy. [*The* Major *is drunk, asleep.*]

Hairy. Mister Dozier, why not? He's for us, or he never gits to Nashville.

Dozier. Then speak out.

Hairy. There is a new Free State, Cap'n—you hear that?

Jackson. I hear you, sir.

Hairy. A new Free State, sir, officered by Major Singlefoot and Mister George Dozier. Air ye fur it or ag'in it?

Jackson. Against it, sir. One of yo' leaders is a blackleg lawyer, the other—you see him fo' yourself. You are set for failure before you start.

Dozier. When your Judge McNairy reaches Nashville, sir, he will find the government of the Free State in operation and a militia of free men ready to pack him and his followers back to the sutlers who sent them.

Jackson. If you were ever to reach Nashville, sir, which you will not, you would find an officer of the North State at the cote house, and you and your kind excluded from practice. From the moment I set foot in Nashville next week, no Free State license such as yours is valid before the Nashville bar.

Dozier. Leaving you free to run things, your plan, and steal to suit yourself?

Jackson. You have been there some little time, sir. I doubt there's anything left to steal.

Dozier. You hear him, gentlemen.

Hairy. We sho'ly hear him.

Dozier. Stand from between us. We have heard a good many of yo' opinions, sir. When have you a mind to quit opinionating and do some fighting? [*His hands are under his coat, adjusting the priming.*]

JACKSON. Now, sir, now.

DOZIER. What do you propose?

JACKSON. To count three under my breath after I step to this mark and then kill you. [*Bows.*] You may commence firing. [*He steps and stands thin.* DOZIER *draws a flintlock and fires.* JACKSON *flinches slightly. He then, with utter care, extracts a pistol, adjusts the flint, balances the barrel rather awkwardly on his free arm, and fires.* DOZIER *falls face forward, dead.*]

HAIRY [*crossing quickly, turning him over, then putting him back*]. Right in the heart.

MAJOR [*coming to from the sound of the shots, and twisting until he sees the figure; then calling rather stupidly*]. Mister Dozier, Mister Dozier!

HAIRY. He kain't hear no mo', Major.

MAJOR. He fought, Hairy?

HAIRY. He did, Major.

MAJOR. My God . . . I've let a man die in my place. Die for me. . . . I'll never wet my lips to spirits again.

JACKSON. I'm that pained, Major, I kain't say.

MAJOR. I beg pardon for failing you, sir. [*He is rather pathetic.*] I'm ready to meet you now . . . instantly. . . . [*He rises heavily.*]

JACKSON. I regret my being rude to you this evenin', sir. I apologize, sir, and beg to be excused from exchanging shots with you until you appear mo' composed.

MAJOR. Don't crawl like a worm, boy. [*Hard.*] Because I'll kill you, sho. Stand and take my fire.

JACKSON. Any time, sir. It is yo' privilege. Sir, stand and take your fire.

MAJOR. We shall want an umpire with a pocket napkin

. . . a white one, sir, fo' my eyes is dim. [*He is standing as erect as possible.*]

JACKSON. Then make haste, sir. [*Weakly, one shoulder drooping.*]

MAJOR. Quick, gentlemen, a white pocket napkin. [WES *takes his wig, drops it, and the* MAJOR *fires, and stands blind.*]

JACKSON. Hawk [*holding his off shoulder in darkness*], some brandy, and help me git to the tavern. I aim to take the trail this mornin', but I have an errand first, a mile up the road . . . a mile up the road.

HAIRY [*standing over him*]. Why, a wound in the shoulder! Sho, it's too near being out to bother you much.

JACKSON. 'Twas Dozier wounded me.

HAIRY. I marked it. God, Cap'n, that was as polite and mannerly as anything I ever see!

MAJOR [*still blind and swaying*]. Take yo' fire, sir, take yo' fire. Do you want to dishonor me thet-away?

[JACKSON *fires pistol in air.*]

CURTAIN

ACT III

A loft under a triangular cabin roof, on a log floor adzed and puncheoned. A door opening right and swinging wide into the moonlight, with a log ladder running from outside into inside. At rear, heavy outline of chimney, with corner in black shadow. At left a huge fourpost bed, made of logs trimmed and skinned, with stocks of branches still upon the posts, on which are articles of pioneer clothing. A trap door by the bed and against the wall opens from below. Buffalo robe on floor by bed. As curtain rises two children, a boy and a girl, near the ages of twelve and ten, are sleeping in the middle of the bed, which is furnished with a patchwork quilt and a coarse top sheet. No sound, save one call from a whippoorwill, which to the backwoods is the sign of death.

CHARITY *comes breathless up the outside ladder, moves to cubby-hole, listens, moves to bed. The whippoorwill greets her as she moves over to the window. More resigned, she walks over to the bed again. She has moved with swiftness, but not too much excitement.*

CHARITY. Cissy!

CISSY [*turning softly*]. Ummm.

CHARITY. Cissy, wake up!

CISSY. Ummmmmm.

CHARITY. I'll be bound to tell ye, Cissy.

CISSY [*burrowing deeper*]. In the morning.

157

CHARITY. 'Twon't keep. 'Tis turrible.

CISSY [*turning away with finality*]. Ummmmmmmmmm.

CHARITY. A turrible thing . . . oh . . . [*No answer or interest. She moves to the boy.*] Simon Kenton! [*No answer at all.*] Simon . . . I got to tell somebody. [*She lifts him up.*] Simon, a man's been killed account o' me! [SIMON, *released, falls back lethargic.*] A fight, Simon, a turrible fight, and Mister George Dozier's dead! [*No answer. She moves back to* CISSY.] A body's got to tell somebody. [*Desperately.*] Mammy . . . [*She moves to cubby-hole.*] Mammy, Mammy, are ye awake? Answer! [*The whippoorwill answers.*] Hush, you whippoorwill! [*She crosses to the window.*] I know somebody's dead. [*To bedside again, shaking* CISSY.] Cissy.

CISSY. Leave me be, waking a body befo' sunrise. [*Under covers now.*]

CHARITY [*talking to both*]. The little Cap'n was there, dressed like a turkey-cock. He rowed with Mister Dozier over me, and shot him through the breast. Oh, God, but it was turribly quick and hard! . . . They'd 'a' kilt him sho', if he wa'n't such a gentleman to the Major. . . . I'm bound I'll have to run away from here befo' Pappy comes home and finds out. And he was going to bring me a b'arskin . . . promised he would, to cover the hope-chist . . . God, I never see a man so clost-shootin' or so cool . . . said he'd kill him, and did kill him. When he looked at me as he walked away with Hairy, with George Dozier lying there turnin' cold in the moonlight, something sorter came over me like a graveyard rabbit. . . . I was that paralyzed when Rachel Robard and Sairy Bibb came to me. . . . "You'll go home with us [*mimicking*], po' little thing!" they said. . . . "A widder befo' bein' a bride" . . . an' there he was

with the blood running down his uniform coat . . . and
Hairy Lake sayin' he'd put fo' inches o' huntin'-knife into
the man that tetched him, with George Dozier turning cold
under the moon and the little Cap'n walking away to the
tavern to git his horse . . . and not looking at me, Cissy.
[*She touches her.*] He was thinkin' on me, though. I
knowed it, an' my face ran as red as pokeberry juice when I
knowed I was thinkin' on him, too, with George Dozier lyin'
there fish-white from the life-blood that'd left him. . . .
"Po' little thing," they said, "look how she stands it." . . .
I run then, Cissy, run like a turkey right past them all, and
I could feel the Cap'n's eyes on the back o' my head like sun-
shine through a bonnet. He'd kilt George Dozier account
o' me, and I'd kissed him back befo' he done it . . . an' I'll
never lay eyes on the like o' him again. . . . [*She drama-
tizes.*] "I heard you say, Charity, that you ain't never
kissed back to a man" . . . and I was reeling from the cin-
namon bark he'd folded his coat in, like a drunken man,
Cissy. He came up close and said, "Kiss me, Charity," and
when he put his arms on me I couldn't say whether it was his
heart or mine doing the pumping . . . pumping like a rabbit when you take him from a snare, and George Dozier begging me inside just befo' fo' a kiss, when he never knowed it
might be the last one, when we did the hoot-owl in the reel.
. . . Remember how Pappy danced befo' the do' in the
moonlight last spring? . . . The tanbark on the flo' was too
slippery-soft fo' a body to dance on, and if Jackson took my
hand I thought it would stick too fast for a body ever to pull
us apart. . . . "Wouldn't you know, ma'am, even now?"
"Come by . . . ," I told him, Cissy, "come by our place and
climb the ladder and tell me. . . ." But he won't come.
Wake up, Cissy, an' hear me, fo' it's the kind o' thing you

dream about when you ain't too tired. God A'mighty, but
he was cool, Cissy, cool as the churn in the spring-hole. "I
can tell you, ma'am." But he didn't tell me. . . . He kissed
me. You kain't tell by kissin'. You have to come by and
tell, when you're leavin' a place fo'ever. [*She runs to the
cubby-hole.*] Mammy, Mammy, Mammy, Mammy! [*Long
low calls.*]

A Voice. Sh, sh, sh . . .

Charity. You awake, Mammy?

Mrs. Clarkson. Sh! You'll wake the little children down
here, Charity. Git in yo' bed. If you wake 'em I'll never git
'em to sleep again, with their pappy so far away in the
woods and that whippoorwill a-hootin' so chill.

Charity. Mammy, George Dozier's been killed.

Mrs. Clarkson. God A'mighty . . . oh, God A'mighty.
. . . [*Dumb at first.*]

Charity. Killed in a fight.

Mrs. Clarkson [*wringing her hands and sitting on the
side of the bed*]. It kain't be. . . . It kain't be.

Charity. I seed him kilt, Mammy.

Mrs. Clarkson. He kain't be. . . . He was here six
hours ago. . . . [*Cries.*] "I'll soon call you Mother," he
said.

Charity. Don't cry so, Mammy! Don't cry so. . . .
[*She is by her.*]

Mrs. Clarkson [*sobbing*]. Who done it, Charity?

Charity. The little Cap'n from the tavern that I saw.

Mrs. Clarkson. I hope they hang him. . . . Po' George
Dozier! Oh, Charity, God has struck ye a heavy blow!
Po' George Dozier! . . . They'll hang him.

Charity. Hush, Mammy! It were a duel.

Mrs. Clarkson [*crying*]. Why didn't somebody stop it? Why didn't somebody stop it?

Charity. Hit come too quick. He was dead in a second, with a bullet in his breast and his face in the willow leaves, right by the corner of the barn.

Mrs. Clarkson [*with fresh tears*]. Charity, ye're ruined, child, ruined. [*She puts her arms about her.*] All yo' life you'll slave fo' some po' man. Why did God take him from ye. . . . Oh, God, why did Ye take him from her?

Charity. It 'pears that God did, though. And saved t'other man. The little Cap'n gave him first shot.

Mrs. Clarkson [*drying her eyes for details*]. Didn't Mister Dozier take it?

Charity. Hit the Cap'n in the breast bone, but the ball must 'a' turned wide. I seed the blood befo' he fired and killed Mister Dozier . . . I seed . . .

Mrs. Clarkson [*stopping her*]. Don't, Charity, don't! Put that out o' mind. [*Gets up and leads her to bed.*] Don't think on it, no mo'. . . . Who fetched ye home, child? . . . Did Lonny bring ye?

Charity. I was flustered. I run home through the woods by myself.

Mrs. Clarkson. Po' little thing! A widder befo' bein' a bride. [*She is fumbling with the buttons of* Charity's *white dress.*] Undress, sweet thing, and git in the bed.

Charity. I kain't, Mammy, I kain't. I kain't go to bed. I'm flustered.

Mrs. Clarkson. Come down with me, Charity. I'll make a pallet.

Charity. I kain't. I want to stay here.

Mrs. Clarkson [*she has got the dress off*]. Say yo'

prayers, Charity, and ask God to have mercy on George Dozier's soul.

CHARITY. Yes, Mammy, I allow I'll say a long one befo' I sleep. You go now. I ain't lonely any mo'. [*She looks to the window.*]

MRS. CLARKSON. They ought to do something to the man that killed him. He was such a fine figure, too. [*Cries.*] He'd 'a' made ye a lady.

CHARITY [*leads her to the trapdoor*]. I don't aim to be no lady. . . . You go down and git some sleep.

MRS. CLARKSON. I sha'n't close my eyes. [*Pausing at the cubby.*] Have ye cried much?

CHARITY. I ain't, Mammy, they won't come.

MRS. CLARKSON. Lie down, sweet thing, and cry. . . . The funeral's goin' to try ye something awful if ye don't.

CHARITY. I don't aim to break down.

MRS. CLARKSON. You kin live in this house with me an' yo' pappy all yo' days, Charity.

CHARITY. The Cap'n could 'a' killed the Major, if he'd wanted, Mammy.

MRS. CLARKSON. Don't think on it, Charity. The Lord calls us, or He doesn't. We kain't ask why He took George Dozier from ye and let some rascal go on.

CHARITY. I allow he ain't a rascal, Mammy. [*Her voice raised.*]

MRS. CLARKSON. Sh, sh! Don't wake the little ones . . . little Dan'l Boone's gums air a sight from freetin' now. [*She kisses her.*] Git some sleep. [*She goes down; whispers.*] Good night, Charity, say yo' prayers.

CHARITY. Good night, Mammy. [CHARITY *comes to the bed and takes her clothing, looks at the door as if afraid to put them on. Folds them, crosses to the window by the chest,*

*and puts them up. Goes back, resigned, gets into bed, and
tries to sleep. The whippoorwill brings her up again.*]
Cissy! [*Not shaking the child; simply talking.*] I got to
tell somebody. I kain't tell Mammy. I kissed him back. I
kissed him back when I knowed he was lyin' to me. Hadn't
said he loved me. Hadn't said anything at all. Just looked
at me and wanted to kiss me, and I wanted to kiss him. If
he'd 'a' asked me, I'd had to kiss him after he shot Dozier
befo' 'em all. . . . I ran away past the Bibb house fo' fear
he'd come over and say, "Kiss me, Charity," and I'd 'a' done
it. I passed the tavern where I fust saw him when he looked
so pretty an' cool. He was scairt a little by Dozier. 'Twas
why he wouldn't look at me when the boys was pestering him.
I could 'a' cried fo' him then when I saw. I'd 'a' rocked him
to sleep like you rock a rag doll befo' the fire. I'd shut his
eyes, even if they can be sharp as chestnut burrs. . . . He'll
go away and there won't ever be another one in a pretty blue
coat with the moon prying deep into the woods . . . an' he
never said a pretty word. Just looked. Sometimes . . .
they takes us [*she sighs*], and sometimes they leave us. So
cool and springy in his heels, with hair like a painter's ruff
. . . it bristled when he set in at cards and gave George
Dozier his death-look. . . . [*Her head is down and she is
trying to sleep as she croons.*] "Wouldn't ye know, now,
ma'am, wouldn't ye know . . ." [*Pause. The whippoorwill makes her sit up.*] But ye won't know, now. Ye won't
ever know, unless he comes by. Cissy, why couldn't he say,
for me to remember. . . . [*She starts, for she hears sounds
on the ladder. She looks to the window, not sure of her
senses.* JACKSON *comes in, the same as before, except for a
fresh shirt, and stands looking at her from the moonlit doorway.*] I knowed ye'd come . . . I knowed ye'd come . . .

JACKSON [*softly*].   I passed a whippoorwill on the big rock.   Does he set there every night?

CHARITY.   He's come back from mating.   He went away last spring.

JACKSON.   He scared me something terrible when I went by him just now.   [*Smiles.*]

CHARITY.   He scared me, too.

JACKSON.   Are ye scared ofttimes?

CHARITY.   Oft.   Are you?

JACKSON.   Lots o' times.   But try to hide it.

CHARITY.   Ye kain't hide it from me.

JACKSON.   Was I scared at the tavern?

CHARITY.   No.

JACKSON.   When was I scared at the barn?

CHARITY.   'Most all the time.

JACKSON.   All the time.   [*He looks about, sees the chest, goes to it.*]   May I set on this?

CHARITY.   It's the only place there is.

JACKSON.   Looks like a treasure-chest.   [*Sits gingerly.*]

CHARITY.   'Tis a hope-chist fo' me.

JACKSON.   How might a body shet up hope in a chist?

CHARITY.   Backwoods gals do that all o' their life.

JACKSON.   Do they ketch hope with their hands, or shoot it on the wing?

CHARITY.   They sew things fo' it.   When they're dreaming about a fellow they know never will come.

JACKSON.   Have ye sewed long?

CHARITY.   I started an apron when I was rising thirteen, I'm going on to sixteen now. . . .

JACKSON.   When I was going on to sixteen I was hoping fo' nothing in creation but a military uniform.

CHARITY.   At thirteen I was pining fo' a hunter in yaller

buckskin. . . . Law! I was *that* silly. . . . Pappy was pioneering with Colonel Donaldson down the Cumberland and were trailing no'th to French country. I dreamed one night that a hunter came back with him in the fall and brought me a buffalo robe and a white elk's skin . . . and I never even knowed then if they was white elks. . . . Now, wa'n't that something else to dream? . . . But I dreamed it . . . that he brought it to make white shoes fo' the wedding, fo' him and fo' me. He was taller in my dream than Hairy Lake . . . nigh six foot six, and I began sewing on my apron that's in that chist the very next day.

JACKSON. How'd ye know he was so tall?

CHARITY. Because he said, "Charity, my darling thing." Wa'n't that foolish? "Charity, here I've gone and kilt ye a white elk with a six-foot skin. . . . And when he helt it up to spread it around me, it reached from his moccasins to the roots o' his golden beard.

JACKSON [*studiously, enviously*]. I been studyin' fo' six months over raising a golden beard.

CHARITY. Have ye been studyin' about growing to six foot six, Mister Jackson?

JACKSON. I'd 'a' made it, but I reckon I've had mo' than half a foot o' growth a-scairt out o' me, time to time. . . . Back in the Waxhaws where I was born, there come times when I took a thrashing a day.

CHARITY. Who thrashed ye so? Ye must have been an endearin' little redhead.

JACKSON. Red-coats scared me. When Tarleton's horse came dragooning our boys from the settlements, to put red coats on 'em and make 'em fight fo' the Tories and their king. I reckon every boy my age was scairt from time to time. The men would go out in the wood fo' a stand-up fight, and

the leetle boys would trail off after them and try to shoot
bullets a thousand yards. The red-coats ketched me. One
time I was down in a hollow on my belly firing down the
crick to where I'd seen a red-coat in the brush, when I looked
around and two o' them were standing right over me. "What
ye shooting at, little traitor?" they said. I knew 'twa'n't
any use, and I was scairt out o' growth when I knew it.
"You," I said. When they carried me away I was scairt to
death fo' fear they'd hang me for spying, because I was too
po' to buy a Carolina uniform.

CHARITY. If I'd knowed, I'd made ye one and fetched
it to ye.

JACKSON. I expect you were too busy sewing up hope in
a chist. [*A pause.*]

CHARITY. Do ye ever make up things that never happened
to ye at all?

JACKSON. Sometimes, but I didn't make up that one.

CHARITY. When you come into Mister Peevey's at sundown and I saw ye, it was like seeing a soldier in the coulds
at sunset. I said to myself, "Now ye're making up things
again, Charity. Ain't nobody in this tavern like what ye
see, at all."

JACKSON. But I was standing there when you came in,
and I didn't expect you. . . . Likely I looked so taken that
it was a dreamy thing the way we first saw each other. . . .
I had come riding down that glen on the east o' the hill,
through that long bank o' dogwood trees, thinking how white
and shining they'd be, come next April, and when you sailed
through the tavern door in yo' smock, I said to myself,
"Why, cote's over, and April's come again." [*A pause.*]

CHARITY. But I wa'n't wearing my white apron. It was

still in the chist you're setting on, soaking in heart-leaves
I got last April from under the pines.

JACKSON. Was it heart-leaves? I couldn't fetch the
smell to my memory. But now I see 'em plain, just how you
come upon 'em, pushing through last year's needles. Ain't
anything prettier growing.

CHARITY. Pappy allus says, after I've been sowing oats
after him all afternoon and we come in at night, that there
ain't a prettier sight anywhere in the world than a field of
grain, ripe for scything.

JACKSON. Does your pappy farm, too?

CHARITY. Ain't a busier man, or kinder. Mammy says
in eighteen years o' being married to him he ain't never made
her or a child clear an acre o' land or break a sod o' soil.
Do ye like to farm?

JACKSON. I farmed. Worked a place two years near
Salisbury. . . . But I declare, I don't even seem to remember much about it. Nothing ever happening to excite a
body at all. I guess I'd rather be where there's a chance
every coon's age o' being scairt out o' growth.

CHARITY. If ye don't remember how the field smells in
the evening, ye don't like to farm. [*The whippoorwill calls
twice, clearly nearer, and* CHARITY *shudders.* JACKSON *in-
voluntarily starts as she does so, leaping like a cat to the
middle of the floor. There, a worried expression comes on
his face as he works at the clothing under his right armpit
with his left hand.*] Did he scare ye, too?

JACKSON [*still working*]. I suppose he did.

CHARITY [*beginning to see*]. Does it [*she is skirting a
subject they've avoided*] . . . does it pain ye so, po' boy?

JACKSON [*tries to smile faintly*]. None a-tall. None

a-tall. But when ye sighed, it made me jump, and I sorter slipped the poultice.

CHARITY. Why, you po' thing! [*Slides her feet toward the floor.*] And not complaining any!

JACKSON [*moving to her*]. P'raps you kin fix it better. Hitch it fo' me, please. [*Sits on side of bed, his back to her.*]

CHARITY. I've a mind to have you strip yo' shirt and let me wrap it over again.

JACKSON. Thank ye, no, don't take it off; it's drawin'. It's mo' a bruise on the breast-blade than a bleed. Peevey's poulticed it with slippery ellum bark. Smells good enough to chew, don't it?

CHARITY [*her hands are slightly atremble*]. Hit's the best stuff ever [*proximity unsteadies her*] . . . fo' a bruise or a blow. . . . 'Tis so near yo' heart, too.

JACKSON. I reckon it'd clear up quicker, seein' where 'tis near, if Peevey'd used some o' the heart-leaves from a hope-chist.

CHARITY. You better stay here on the hill till it cleans, and get slippery ellum bark and heart-leaves too.

JACKSON [*doggedly, in pain and sweetness*]. As long as I got strength, I got to keep on to Nashville. I got to keep on.

CHARITY [*trembling*]. Because when ye are scairt, ye kin hide it. . . . But ye don't want to tax yo'self. A body ought to rest his strength after what a body's been through.

JACKSON. Not when a body's got strength from a new fountain, tonight.

CHARITY [*dropping her arms*]. How'd ye git new strength?

JACKSON [*turning, husky*]. From yo' lips.

CHARITY [*pause, and then a blushing head*]. Ain't a body making up a thing again that never happen a-tall?

JACKSON. A body disremembers. He never would remember, unless it happen again to prove it.

CHARITY. It does seem like a thing a body's made up. Maybe after all it didn't happen. [*Confessional, head down.*] I been trying to remember, too.

JACKSON. Maybe if I'd put my mind to it I could remember how ye stood against the corn-stalks, and how the moon came down to look at ye! But 'tis all. The rest is cloudy. Maybe you could remember how a body rode through on the trail to Nashville and the wilderness. . . .

CHARITY. Maybe I could recollect how a red-head boy in an ole blue coat, who was born fo' trouble and who could hide it when he was scairt . . .

JACKSON. Went on to Nashville where mo' trouble was awaitin' him, ready fo' it only because an angel-body in a white dress stood under the moon and kissed him, and then . . .

CHARITY [*picking up his thread*]. . . . Then run home and waited fo' him to come by and tell her what he never has told her.

JACKSON. What he never told her because he never told a body befo'. Because he never told anybody befo' and don't know how to say it. . . . Because he ain't flowery enough to tell her [*they kiss*] that she is mo' beautiful than a pink-footed pigeon by a waterfall. [*They kiss again.*]

CHARITY [*in his arms*]. Now ye are makin' up things fo' me to remember.

JACKSON. You eternally believe I'm makin' up things.

CHARITY. I want you to, when a body makes 'em up as

pretty as you do. I'm only afeard you'll begin to tell me what's gospel truth.

JACKSON. What would I say, if I told you what's gospel truth?

CHARITY. If I wouldn't want you to say it, would I admire to say it fo' myself?

JACKSON. I know one thing. . . . [*Close into her ear.*]

CHARITY. What is it?

JACKSON. You put yo' arms around me by yourself.

CHARITY [*playful*]. Was it forward o' me, Cap'n Jackson?

JACKSON. Oh, turrible forward of you, ma'am! [*Kisses her.*]

CHARITY. If it pesters ye, I won't do it no mo'.

JACKSON. It's powerful healing fo' a wound near the heart. . . .

CHARITY. Is it all healed now? [*Moves away two inches.*]

JACKSON. It didn't hurt again till ye moved away.

CHARITY. I wished 'twas so. [*Moving away another two inches.*] But that's one o' the things ye fancy out fo' me to remember.

JACKSON. No; that's scripture.

CHARITY. Ye've made up so many things and called 'em scripture, I 'low ye don't even know.

JACKSON. Do you?

CHARITY. I do.

JACKSON. What is?

CHARITY. Ye don't love me enough to hurt ye none.

JACKSON. Mo' than anything else.

CHARITY. Mo' than law and fighting an' all?

JACKSON. Mo' than anything a-tall.

CHARITY. Po' boy, I knowed ye couldn't know what's in

yo' mind. Don't ye know ye'll ride away again and forget there ever was a Peevey Hill? And the wilderness is so big and wide. . . .

JACKSON. And will ye forget . . .

CHARITY. Not even if I lived to be forty! I'll remember yo' words after ye've forgot ye've said them to me and used 'em again to say to somebody else.

JACKSON. How kin I forget? If the wilderness is big and wide, my heart's the same way. I 'low that I'll hold you in it all my born days. I'd admire fo' you to stop saying that I'll forget ye. [*He kisses her.*]

CHARITY [*husky*]. Are ye kissin' fo' goodbye?

JACKSON. Put yo' arms around me again. 'Tis a heaven-sent ointment to my wound. Don't ye feel ye're curing me? [*Arms around.*]

CHARITY. Po' boy! Po' boy! Only ye don't mean it. Ye're just saying it fo' me.

JACKSON [*kneeling by the bed, taking her into his arms*]. Charity, darling, I mean it so that I kain't leave ye here now. I kain't leave ye this way.

CHARITY [*holding him*]. Ye'd better go, please, sir. It kain't be . . .

JACKSON. Ye don't love me. Ye don't love me a-tall, fo' ye to treat me this way. It's you that don't love me, when ye feel my heart. . . . [*A knocking at the door, at which the two hold closer and kiss profoundly.*]

LONNY'S VOICE. Mrs. Clarkson? Mrs. Clarkson, kin I climb and see if Charity got home?

MRS. CLARKSON'S VOICE. Don't climb the ladder, Lonny. [*Sound of latch and bolt downstairs.*] She's home and to bed.

LONNY'S VOICE. You heard, ma'am?

Mrs. Clarkson's Voice. Oh, Lord, wa'n't it a turrible thing fo' him to be taken that-a-way? It's hard on my child, Lonny.

Lonny's Voice. May I see her for a minute, ma'am? I'm jes' bound to. I kain't let her pass the night without her knowing what I feel.

Mrs. Clarkson's Voice. I reckon it'll have to keep, Lonny, till morning's come.

Lonny's Voice. I kain't come courtin' her, ma'am. I kain't with him not cold. But I kin speak with her tonight and set her mind at rest over something, sho.

Mrs. Clarkson's Voice. Lonny, you kain't come in. I'll see if she's awake. [Jackson *releases* Charity. *She motions to the chimney corner. He walks there as* Mrs. Clarkson *ascends.* Charity *sits quiet.*] There, I knowed ye'd not close yo' eyes! Why didn't you answer Lonny downstairs?

Charity. I don't pertend to feel like seeing him, Mammy.

Mrs. Clarkson. The po' boy's distracted over yo' grief. Lean to the window and bid him home sweetly, Charity. . . . And I'll set here all night by ye. Ye'll sleep by dawn.

Charity. I kain't.

Mrs. Clarkson. Let him climb to the door, sweet thing. He's come as a comforter in yo' trial.

Charity. Let him climb, then.

Mrs. Clarkson [*moving to door but shielding dress.* Charity *gets into bed*]. There, Charity, treat the po' boy kindly. He's sad fo' ye.

Charity. Go down, Mammy! You kain't let him see ye that way.

Mrs. Clarkson [*starts down*]. Lonny . . . [*Exit. Her voice floats from other window.*] Ye mustn't be long.

LONNY'S VOICE. I only want to comfort her, ma'am.
[*He comes up to door and stands pathetic in moonlight.*]
Charity, I had to come by.

CHARITY. I know you did.

LONNY. I had to speak now, and hol' my peace after.

CHARITY. That you did.

LONNY. Charity, after what's happened, I ain't going
away to read for the bar.

CHARITY. It's in yo' blood, Lonny. Ye'll have to.

LONNY. I won't have to. I wanted to tell you . . . that
as soon as it gits daylight, I'm goin' to Cousin Tobe's and
ask him fo' that patch o' land by the bluff. It's good land,
Charity. I'm going to farm, Charity. I'm going to farm.

CHARITY. But yo' folks have been dead set on yo' bein'
a judge like yo' father was, Lonny.

LONNY. But I ain't going to be a judge . . . I came
here to tell you . . . and I won't come again until spring.
. . . I can't visit you fo' a spell now. . . . But I want you
to know I'll be trustin' and hopin' fo' you.

CHARITY. Now, Lonny, I won't have yo' givin' in to me.

LONNY. And when Joe Clarkson gets home I'll ask fo' ye,
and when April comes we'll roll up a log house by that dogwood bank and farm. . . . I got a good mare, and she'll
foal in the spring. I got a young cow, and she'll calve.
We'll make a home together right here, Charity, and I'll love
and protect you, I'll farm for you and hunt for you, all my
life. I'm yours, Charity, and I couldn't sleep without comin'
by and tellin' you. Without yo' promise.

CHARITY. Hit's sweet o' you, Lonny. But you got to
get yo' law papers. I won't study about promisin' until
you git them. Go home, Lonny, and quiet yo'self. We've

had a powerful misfortune. We can't think on anything
else now.

LONNY. You don't have to think, Charity. I just wanted
to tell you.

CHARITY. But I can't promise, Lonny. . . . You got to
be a lawyer.

LONNY. We're in the North State, Charity. It'll take
two years' reading befo' I can practice. I wa'n't fashioned
fo' the law. I was fashioned fo' you, Charity . . . to build
a cabin, break the land, sow the soil, and harvest the crop
fo' you.

CHARITY. Cap'n Jackson'll give you law papers, Lonny.
He will, fo' the askin'. Some day you'd be a judge while
he'd be a general.

LONNY. It ain't his to give. And you can't count on a
man in this country, when he's as hasty as Cap'n Jackson.
You can't count on his surviving a week o' Nashville life.

CHARITY. That you can; if he'll only rest here and quiet
himself fo' a spell. . . . Honey, ye're turrible upset. Please
go home and quit yo' studyin' about me.

LONNY. Nobody'd treat you better, love you sweeter, or
work fo' you harder.

CHARITY. Ye'll have to go, Lonny. I'll tell you in the
morning.

LONNY. Then I set beneath yo' window, Charity. I'll
wait all night fo' an answer.

CHARITY. If ye don't go clean home, Lonny, and go now,
I'll never see ye again.

LONNY. You loved me befo' that little peacock Cap'n
came along. You loved me then. You'd a-been willin' fo'
me to fight George Dozier fo' ye. And it was the Cap'n
turned yo' head and made ye smart. . . . Well, he won't

plow a furrow fo' ye. He won't sow a patch. . . . He'll just go traipsing around, shooting at everybody that gits in his way. . . .

CHARITY. He had to fight. . . .

LONNY. No, he didn't. I been watching him and studying his ways. He fights because he don't know how a decent body does a thing. He's foxy and gambly and full o' loud words just to dissemble that he's worthless. . . .

CHARITY. Ye wouldn't dare to speak yo' mind to him. . . .

LONNY. If he'd stand up to me front to front without shootin' like a rat, I'd dare. He's plain trash, with manners learnt out of a book, and speeches learnt out of a book, and nothin' learnt from his mother. . . . And he's scairt, too. . . . If I walked up to him, just once, he'd be scairt o' me.

CHARITY. Lonny . . .

LONNY. Do you know why he puts on his airs and wears his uniform and talks law and duelin'? Because he's a come-on from a patch o' trash, imitatin' the big-wigs from the settlements and thinkin' he's gentry. If he had blood in him he'd know more than to come into a tavern insulting strangers.

CHARITY. I won't listen to ye. . . .

LONNY. I'm sorry, Charity, I wouldn't say. Only I love ye, and I'm afraid fo' ye until he's shet o' this neighborhood. A traveling sharper, headin' in quick fo' a bad end. And befo' long he'll be known fo' one.

CHARITY [*in anger*]. You git down that ladder and go home where ye belong. . . . Ye git out o' my sight, coming 'round tonight after what's happened. . . .

LONNY [*retreating and starting down*]. I'm a-goin'. But remember that I'll wait fo' you until the end o' time.

CHARITY. Instead o' comfortin' me, you . . .

LONNY [*disappearing*]. Charity, I meant to comfort you. You'll know after while. [*He goes.*]

[JACKSON *comes out.* CHARITY *springs to meet him, flaming with anger.*]

CHARITY. The little white-faced coward, creepin' around here after hit's all over to talk ag'in your back. . . . I thought I'd have to call you out and let you skeer him, befo' I could run him down. I'll never speak to him again so long's I live. To think that he should say such things about a gentleman like you!

JACKSON [*quizzically*]. Wouldn't you allow that he told the gospel, ma'am?

CHARITY [*snatching up the denial*]. Gospel! His saying that you are afraid? . . . Why, you ain't scairt o' the whole kit and bilin' on this low-down Peevey Hill . . . ye ain't afraid o' the whole world. And ye're the finest gentleman God A'mighty ever made. . . . He never saw gentry like you. So mannerly and perlite. Why, no one could have been mo' kinder or sweeter than you have been. To say that you picked a quarrel . . . I guess a body has to defend himself if a whole pot-house o' scoundrels come bearin' down on a body like they did on you. . . .

JACKSON [*with quiet pride*]. I'm afraid I picked that fight.

CHARITY [*with immense pride*]. Of cose you picked it. Why, they won't never be a time when you won't pick yo' fights and carry 'em where you want to, when you see a body o' men bearin' down on ye! . . . That's what made me love you so, standing there carrying it back to 'em when they throwed it up to you. So cool and calm, and not scairt even a little bit. Why, I guess that boy don't know real folks when he sees them! I knowed you, though; I knowed you, and I knowed I wanted you.

JACKSON. Now, Charity, you allowed yourself that I was scared. . . . I reckon there was a world o' truth in what that boy said. I don't know any law. I was sent out here because they couldn't find any other lawyer who'd be risky enough to come. And that hoss and that dog and that pen o' game cocks . . . why, I won 'em at Jonesboro on a cock main, and like as not I'll lose 'em along with that nigger when I git to Nashville. I only won that nigger ten days ago. . . . [*Sadly.*] And I have shot several men.

CHARITY. I don't care. Cose you have. Why, I 'low ye've done ever'thing a man ought to do. . . . I 'low I love ye a heap mo' for it.

JACKSON. I allow I'll get kilt myself before long. And if I didn't, nothing good could come to you from me.

CHARITY. I don't care. I love you.

JACKSON [*wistfully*]. I'd admire fo' you to give me one o' those heart-leaves there in that chist.

CHARITY. What would ye want with it?

JACKSON. So's to shet up hope in a chist.

CHARITY. What chist?

JACKSON [*tapping his breast*]. Here.

CHARITY. Maybe ye'll take all my hope away with ye. . . . But maybe ye'll bring it all back again, when April's come and cote's over.

JACKSON. When I came tonight I 'lowed I'd take it all away, but I kain't.

CHARITY. Ye're mighty pallid. . . . Are ye bleedin'?

JACKSON. My heart's bleeding fo' you, after what I've done.

CHARITY [*putting the leaf in his breast*]. Then hit will be powerful healin', if ye'll only put faith in it.

JACKSON [*touching her arm*]. Then I'll put faith on it. I vow I'll make up something that never happened at all.

CHARITY. I vow something did happen. [*She kisses him fiercely.*] There, kin ye fetch it to your•memory?

JACKSON [*broken*]. Po' little pink foot . . . [*Arms around her.*]

CHARITY [*holding close*]. When spring comes will ye be ridin' through?

JACKSON. I never came back to any place I ever was.

CHARITY. Then ye won't leave . . . for if I let ye leave, there won't never be anything like ye again. And I'll live to be old, and ye'll be the one thing I've wanted, and I won't have never had you. Ye're swayin' tired. [*She leads him to the chest.*] Ye're that weary. . . . [*They sit. He puts his head on her breast.*] Kin ye hear my heart pumpin' fo' ye?

JACKSON [*blind*]. I kain't hear it. What does it say?

CHARITY. Sho, now, it says: Stay here with me; where have ye been so far away; why did ye take so long to come ridin' by; why must ye leave me so soon . . .

JACKSON. I kain't go away from here tonight if ye talk that way.

CHARITY [*on chest, he leaning over*]. No, ye kain't. When a body belongs to another as I belong to you . . . a body doesn't care fo' nothin' else. [*They are poised a moment, then he breaks away and stands.*]

JACKSON. I fooled 'em all pretending I was brave. I was going to cheat you last.

CHARITY. I wouldn't care. I wouldn't care.

JACKSON [*who hasn't the nerve to take the girl, and who*

therefore mouths a moral sentiment as an excuse for running away]. But I'm at the loose end o' cheatin'. And if I leave ye now, ye'll belong to me always . . . above me white and shinin' forever. Goodbye, Charity.

CHARITY. Goodbye. [*She sobs.*] God A'mighty!

CURTAIN

THE BUCCANEER

A Play in Three Acts

The Buccaneer was presented in 1925, at the Plymouth Theatre, under the direction of Arthur Hopkins. The stage settings were designed by Robert Edmond Jones. The cast was as follows:

CARMENCITA	*Jeanne Greene*
MARIA	*Beatrice Maude*
CAPT. MANUEL MONTALVO	*Brandon Peters*
BASILIO FERNANDEZ	*William R. Gregory*
DON JACINTO DE ESMERALDO	*J. Colvil Dunn*
DONNA LISA (Lady Elizabeth Neville)	*Estelle Winwood*
GEORGE CASTLE	*Galway Herbert*
DAVE	*Harry Kendall*
CAPT. HENRY MORGAN	*William Farnum*
AN ENSIGN	*Frank Hearn*
COMMODORE WRIGHT	*Leslie Palmer*
JAMES TOWNSHEND	*Cecil Clovelly*
HENRY MARMION	*Claude Allister*
ELIPHALET SKIPWITH, Esq.	*Edmund Waller*
A HERALD	*Harry Kendall*
LADY PIERSON	*Gene Carvel*
LADY FRANCIS	*Jean Fisher*
MRS. WESTLEY	*Irene Freeman*

THE BUCCANEER

ACT I

*The main hall of a hacienda on the heights of Panama City,
as seen on a late summer evening in the sixteen-hundreds,
is a large, lofty room, with heavy door to left, and a
deep window to the right. A noble stair at the rear
leads to the second floor.*

*Two young women, MARIA and CARMENCITA, are seated at a
refectory table. They are youthful, dark, vivacious
Spanish girls of the Castilian type, both very much
alive. They are flaming in evening dress. MONTALVO,
a cub-like captain, very military, is standing with his
back to the stairway. It is obvious that all are await-
ing dinner. A slave is arranging candles, and the room
becomes lighter.*

MARIA.   What is it like, this pleasure of killing a man?
Does it make you feel cold—or warm?

MONTALVO.   That depends on what you are like, and
what kind of man you like to kill, and what led up to the
killing.   Also, what apprenticeship you've served in the
trade.

CARMENCITA.   How many do you suppose *you* must account for when you face the recording angel?

MONTALVO.   How do I know?   I never take scalps.

MARIA.   But the first time—did you turn cold or warm?

MONTALVO.   Both—and a little seasick.

MARIA.   Was it— [*she points*] that sword?

183

MONTALVO [*drawing sword*]. Yes—do you mark that blade? Mark the sheen of its steel? A Toledo smith forged it for my grandfather. He never used it all his life till the day of his death.

MARIA. He was killed using it, cousin?

MONTALVO. He fell upon it.

CARMENCITA. In a fight?

MONTALVO. No. When he learned that my grandmother had run away to Italy with her confessor—a young priest who had not taken final vows . . . he took my grandmother instead. . . . [*Holding blade toward* MARIA.] Feel that edge. . . . It must have been some satisfaction to know at least the steel was true. . . . [*Sighs.*] My grandmother was not worthy such devotion.

MARIA. Your grandfather was a proud man.

CARMENCITA. But a fool. Were a wife's virtue worth dying for, I fancy all the world would be nothing but Spaniards falling upon swords.

MONTALVO. Sapristi! señorita, but you have a low opinion of your kind!

CARMENCITA. An accurate one.

MARIA. Would you, Cousin Pedro, kill yourself were I to run away with an unfrocked priest?

MONTALVO [*hesitating*]. No. Only the unfrocked priest. You are too pretty to kill . . . unless a man might kill you with his love.

MARIA. Sweet dying, cousin, could I choose the man.

MONTALVO. And who would he be? Some fair-haired Englishman, I'll say, such as Esmeraldo's slave who rode with you to Panama City yesterday?

CARMENCITA. You have her there. She has a letch for that cold, gaunt, ugly groom.

Maria. I have none. But still, an Englishman—a raw Englishman, now . . . a broad man with a heart in his breast . . . none of your slim lieutenants of the Alcalde's guard, Montalvo.

Carmencita. The child would like a pirate, perhaps?

Maria. If he were a great one with broad shoulders and curls.

Montalvo. Doubtless this Morgan would serve you well, Maria. Peradventure you have only to take ship and sail through the Caribbean of a moonlight night, and you will have your Morgan. . . . A heavy price, though, you'd pay . . . it is said he uses women as he does mangoes— once only.

Maria. Can a woman expect more than one night of love? . . . If I thought I should find this Morgan I should take ship at once.

Montalvo. He'd wring your neck and drop you into salt water. Do you fancy that an Englishman has hot blood in him? Has your mistress any hot blood in her?

Carmencita. She is colder than Jacob's pillow. . . . You will see.

Montalvo. Cold? But she has charmed Esmeraldo.

Maria. She is cold like the slopes of a volcano in winter. There is a smoldering hell under that snowcap forehead. . . . Esmeraldo has been nursing the fire for three months, and still his hands are cold. Spaniards take it for granted that a woman knows how to love.

Montalvo. Ah! She thaws a little for him, don't worry.

Carmencita. No, not a degree. I'd know.

Montalvo. You would?

Carmencita. I've watched.

MONTALVO. What fiends you are! . . . Holy Mary, but I'm hungry!

CARMENCITA. What would you have?

MONTALVO. Well, nothing to eat. Drink.

CARMENCITA. Milaga?

MONTALVO. A cask.

CARMENCITA [*goes out of room, up the central stair*]. Trust me.

MARIA. When they are alone together—and it is rarely —what would you say she called him?

MONTALVO. King Phillip?

MARIA. No. Señor Don Esmeraldo.

MONTALVO. Well, that's his name.

MARIA. But one expects a little more than that from one's affianced?

MONTALVO. What she calls him is negligible . . . but, doesn't she—ah——

MARIA. She permits his arms around her, yes; in a very delicate way, that is—but——

MONTALVO. But what?

MARIA. The snow cap is firm.

MONTALVO. But she still will thaw. Imagine Carmencita with her lover—or imagine what you'd do. . . . Show me . . . just once.

MARIA. But I am not affianced . . . and Donna Lisa is . . . and has been married before, too.

MONTALVO. And learned nothing?

MARIA [*as* CARMENCITA *returns with a flask*]. How to keep accounts . . . to lock a wine cellar . . . to give dinners. [*To* MONTALVO.] At any rate, she has not learned to keep her best vintages out of the gullets of returning soldiers.

MONTALVO. I will drink it all. She will never know. . . . I will carry the flask away.

CARMENCITA [*pouring a goblet*]. And the wine, too?

MONTALVO. Does your conscience hurt? One should be willing to do a little thieving for a soldier. . . . I shall be able to tell you in a moment whether you have stolen well. Will you kiss the cup?

CARMENCITA. See, it is too full. I lower it a quarter inch. [*She sips it.*]

MONTALVO. [MARIA *sits.*] There. I shall never know whether or not it had a bouquet of its own . . . you have scented it with your breath.

MARIA. Very pretty! He has come back the courtier, a scoundrel and a gallant. And where did you learn these manners? In the guard?

MONTALVO. From a thousand sweethearts! [*He drinks.*]

CARMENCITA. Faithless!

MONTALVO. But none anywhere near so fair. [*Holding his cup for more.*]

CARMENCITA. Faithless, and a flatterer.

MONTALVO. Better a faithless flatterer than simply faithless.

MARIA. Here's Basilio.

MONTALVO. Not our old Basilio?

MARIA. See for yourself.

[BASILIO, *a dandy, comes in from the right.*]

BASILIO. Ho! Our soldier of fortune, back with his stolen finery! [*He embraces* MONTALVO.] And how did you leave L'Ollanaise?

MONTALVO. We wrecked him.

BASILIO. Prize money? Jewels?

MONTALVO. Moidores. No silver, only gold.

BASILIO. You deserve them. Six ships were in port for fear of him. You could buy half the town with a pocketful of that gold. These pirates ruin trade.

CARMENCITA. Don't talk of pirates again. It has a curious effect on my interior.

[*Servants enter with dishes for table.*]

BASILIO. Talk of food, then. I'm famished.

MONTALVO. There he is. Sit and eat.

BASILIO. I don't dare.

MONTALVO. Frightened of Donna Lisa?

BASILIO. Rather.

MONTALVO. She bites?

BASILIO. I'd hate to put my hand in her mouth when she's angry. So would Don Jacinto.

MARIA. You will see. It's almost time for him. He's always here. She charms him. He cannot move in her presence. Sometimes when he leaves at night, I fear he will sleep outside the door. A loving hound! Head between his paws . . .

BASILIO [*with irony*]. It must be a passionate affair!

MONTALVO. From what I gather, far from it.

BASILIO. But she is marrying him.

MONTALVO. She would marry somebody. It's not an easy situation, being an English widow in a Spanish city.

MARIA. But he is wealthy. What's the adage? Pieces of eight just naturally go to bed with doubloons.

MONTALVO. Shall we bait the Don when he arrives?

CARMENCITA. What about?

MONTALVO. About marrying a frozen saint.

MARIA. You can bait Don Jacinto, but be sure you don't try it with her.

MONTALVO. She'll freeze your entrails.

CARMENCITA. She'll look at you once, and your viscera will turn cold.

MONTALVO. Will some one carry me a challenge to this writing-school mistress and let me choose the weapons? She will blow cold, and I will blow hot.

BASILIO. Tread lightly, warriors all! We don't want to spoil the match.

MONTALVO [*proudly*]. I'll be circumspect. I spent six days with a widow at Porto Bello and learned the most glorious manners.

MARIA. Try them on me.

MONTALVO. They're for widows only.

[DON ESMERALDO, *an elderly gentleman, enters from upstairs, coming down left stairway. MARIA sees him first and rises. They all rise.*]

ESMERALDO. Greeting, Montalvo! You've grown famous. Has it been a year?

MONTALVO. Half a year, anyway.

ESMERALDO. And, Basilio, you haven't climbed the heights for weeks. Something wrong?

BASILIO. Nothing. Just business. Pressing matters of state and commerce. Much seems to have happened since I was here.

ESMERALDO. For instance?

BASILIO. You have won a fair lady.

ESMERALDO. Oh, that! True. . . . Let's sit down. Donna Lisa will be here presently.

[MONTALVO *seats himself in chair at right of table.*]

MARIA. Not there, you forward beast! That's milady's place.

MONTALVO. Mother of Christ, where?

MARIA. Anywhere else. [*They sit.*]

MONTALVO. You're quite in heaven nowadays, of course.

BASILIO. He didn't hear you.

ESMERALDO. Who? I? Oh, yes. That is . . . Why?

MONTALVO. A successful lover, and asking why?

BASILIO. Doesn't that require explanation, Esmeraldo?

ESMERALDO. Explain it any way you like.

MONTALVO. I can't. I simply can't.

BASILIO. They do say the English are cold-blooded.

MONTALVO. But they breed like other races, I suppose? The same, as it were, preliminaries?

BASILIO. Oh, the same. That's established.

CARMENCITA [to MONTALVO]. Surely you know.

MONTALVO. God has spared me the English.

BASILIO. Is it so bad?

MONTALVO. The rumor goes, they make love at a distance of nine paces, like fish, the girl in one corner of the room, her lover in the other. When their affection waxes warm they look at each other and blush, looking away instantly.

MARIA. How daring!

CARMENCITA. What a relief!

BASILIO. After what?

CARMENCITA. I shan't say.

MONTALVO. Don Esmeraldo is, of course, the authority. We should ask him for details. They occasionally kiss, of course?

ESMERALDO. They?

MONTALVO. The English.

ESMERALDO. I suppose so.

BASILIO. I hope we don't embarrass you?

ESMERALDO. Not at all.

MONTALVO. Is it true that the English ladies prefer to receive no intimate attentions from their lords, sending them instead to the restricted quarters of the city for such common pleasures?

BASILIO. Oh, I assure you that must be an exaggeration! The population is maintained.

MONTALVO. But against the best morals and instincts of the race.

BASILIO. Absolutely.

ESMERALDO [*to* MONTALVO]. Have you seen this English buccaneer who has been ravaging the coast of the south?

MONTALVO. Can you ask? Had I seen him only one of us would have lived to tell the tale. Our ship ran away.

ESMERALDO. But you have heard of him.

[MONTALVO *shrugs*.]

BASILIO. One doesn't hear of much else these days.

ESMERALDO. Have you heard that he threatens to take Panama and sack it as the barbarians sacked Rome?

MONTALVO. No. But he'd say it if he thought of it. He might even try it.

ESMERALDO. Do you think he might succeed?

MONTALVO. Take Panama? Never!

ESMERALDO. He took Porto Bello.

MONTALVO. A different matter. He can approach Panama only from the sea. There's no trail overland through the brush. The mountains are impassable except to the Indians.

[*A dull cannon shot is heard from the distance.* MARIA *rises.*]

MARIA. What's that?

BASILIO. That? Do you think it's your Captain Morgan?

MARIA. No. But——

ESMERALDO. Another boat-load of slaves escaped, Maria. They fire a cannon to start the hunt. Two boat-loads. I know it's not from my plantation. I lost a fortune in slaves last year. They drift to the jungle and evaporate. [DONNA LISA *enters by stair. They all rise to greet a beautiful woman of thirty-five, whose light hair and blue eyes, set off by gray silk and pearls, are in quiet contrast to the other women.*] Captain Montalvo, Donna Elizabeth.

[*She bows silently.*]

DONNA LISA. Shall we sit down?

BASILIO. We were talking, Donna Lisa, of English customs.

DONNA LISA. Yes?

MONTALVO. He euphuizes, my lady. We were talking of English love-making.

BASILIO. No—of carp fishing.

ESMERALDO. On the contrary, we were talking of English pirates and escaping slaves. You heard the cannon? [DONNA LISA *seems not to hear.*] I hope it bodes me no more ill luck.

MARIA. But what has this Captain Morgan done that everybody is afraid of him?

MONTALVO. Everybody?

MARIA. Well, I am.

CARMENCITA. They say he's not a man at all. Is it true? I've heard them say he eats broken glass and drinks poison.

MARIA. That isn't the whole story. They say he goes on four legs and roars like a bull, and wears horns on his head.

MONTALVO.   All I can say is I wish he'd come to Panama on his four legs and try roaring like a bull.

CARMENCITA.   Heavens, I don't!

MARIA.   I'm mad to know what he's like, and I suppose I never shall unless he comes to Panama.

BASILIO.   No, and he'll never come to Panama, and you'll never find out.   But take my word for it, he's a very common kind of yellow dog.   They all are, these freebooters.   They took the *Scorzona,* one of our fleet, searched her for valuables, carried off three women, and then scuttled her.

CARMENCITA.   Do they carry off women?

BASILIO.   Does that thrill you?

CARMENCITA.   Beyond words.

MONTALVO.   Well, child, you would be speechless.

ESMERALDO.   Shall we talk of something else, Donna Lisa?

DONNA LISA.   On my account?   Oh, no!

MONTALVO.   We had a perfectly healthy subject going on and were just warming up to it when Don Esmeraldo choked us off with pirates.   Now as to this matter of reciprocal affection among the English, my own opinion is [DONNA LISA *looks at him.   He pauses.*] . . . that is, I know very little about it—but surely, Basilio, you——

BASILIO.   I'm afraid I can't help you.   [*A pause.*]

DONNA LISA [*icily*].   You were about to say something, Señor Montalvo?

MONTALVO.   I?   Oh, no; I think not.

DONNA LISA.   Something about affection among the English.   Do proceed. . . . I am English, you see—and you had a theory to propound?

MONTALVO.   I suddenly remembered your race, Donna Lisa——

Donna Lisa. And paused out of deference? But you must continue. I insist.

Montalvo. Really, I had nothing to say.

Donna Lisa. You a soldier—and so easily frightened?

Basilio. Could he offer flattery more sincere, Donna Lisa? He will tell you himself that he was never frightened before.

Montalvo [*to* Esmeraldo]. You say the governor is really worried?

Esmeraldo. I'm sure he is. And good reason, too. His scouts have lost trace of Morgan's fleet. He may have landed somewhere, and except for the jungle and walls we are almost undefended inland.

Donna Lisa. He keeps strict sentry-watch?

Esmeraldo. Well, he intends to. I sometimes fear our governor is less energetic than the situation demands. In fact, I'm sometimes tempted to call him a pompous ass.

Basilio. Not to his face?

Esmeraldo. It would do no good, either to his face or behind his back. He'd still be the governor. And I have a good deal at stake just at present.

[*An explosion of some magnitude is heard without. All rise except* Donna Lisa.]

Donna Lisa. What was that?

Montalvo [*retrieving his sword, which he had left near a chair*]. Basilio, shall we take a look around?

Basilio. I'm with you.

Esmeraldo. It couldn't have been from the harbor. It was nearer. Dear, do you mind if I go along?

Donna Lisa. It's probably nothing. We may as well finish our meal in peace. Basilio will bring us the news, if there is any. [BASILIO *and* MONTALVO *go out.*] Sit down, please.

> [*Pause. They all seat themselves, but do not eat, waiting rather nervously. There is another detonation. The girls scream.*]

ESMERALDO. I must go.

DONNA LISA. Go if you must.

> [ESMERALDO *starts to kiss her hand; she gives no encouragement, and he goes out.*]

CARMENCITA. Donna Lisa, I'm so frightened. It's something terrible, I'm sure.

MARIA. What can it be?

DONNA LISA. We'll know before long. It's almost certainly of no consequence. I've lived in Panama City three years now, and nothing of any consequence has taken place in that time. [*Rises.*] In England things do happen occasionally. When I came to the Caribbean with my husband I looked forward at first to one long sequence of adventures. The height of extravagant excitement in Panama City is a cock-fight, two ancient and wary birds encountering each other without the slightest animosity. If I fail to die of malaria I shall die of pure lassitude.

MARIA. One can always make violent love.

DONNA LISA. It doesn't amuse me.

CARMENCITA. Have you ever tried it?

DONNA LISA. One doesn't make violent love unless one is violently in love.

CARMENCITA. Oh, I do!

DONNA LISA. And I should imagine even violent love-making would begin to pall after a time.

CARMENCITA. Never.

DONNA LISA. Oh, Lord!

[MARIA *and* CARMENCITA *go to the street door. There is a sound of blows and a sudden confusion outside. The girls retreat hastily.*]

MARIA. Donna Lisa!

CARMENCITA. Oh, oh! The street is full of soldiers.

DONNA LISA [*goes to the door, closes it and stands listening. There is a loud knock*]. Who's there?

[CARMENCITA *retreats to a far corner.*]

ESMERALDO [*outside*]. It's I—Esmeraldo! For God's sake!

DONNA LISA [*opening*]. Quick! [ESMERALDO *slips in. She bolts the door after him.*] What's happened?

ESMERALDO. The pirates have blown up the wall! Basilio's killed!

DONNA LISA. Basilio!

MARIA. Oh, did you hear?

CARMENCITA [*coming forward*]. No.

[*A sudden tumult outside, which dies away.*]

MARIA. It's the pirates. Basilio's dead. They've broken the wall.

CARMENCITA. Basilio! It can't be.

MARIA. Where's Montalvo?

ESMERALDO. The last I saw of him he was chasing two pirates down an alley-way. I think he meant to drive the whole crew out single-handed. It's all useless, though; they have the town. The garrison is surrounded in the castle.

CARMENCITA. What are we to do?

ESMERALDO. They'll search the houses. You must all three be hidden somewhere.

MARIA. Will they come in here?

ESMERALDO. Surely.

CARMENCITA. There's the lower vault. They'd never find it.

ESMERALDO. Are you sure?

MARIA. It has a secret door. I can hardly find it myself.

ESMERALDO. Then carry down what you need at once. There's no time to waste. You'll have to stand a siege, perhaps of some days. And hurry! They may be back at any moment.

MARIA [to CARMENCITA]. Come! Are you coming, Donna Lisa? [They go out.]

DONNA LISA. No, I think not.

ESMERALDO. Dear, you must! You have no conception what brutes they are.

DONNA LISA. I shall not hide in the cellar of my own house—not from anybody. Why should I pretend I'm frightened when I'm not?

ESMERALDO. But I'm frightened for you. These desperadoes will seek every residence and ravish every woman. It's madness not to take what precautions we can.

DONNA LISA. The girls may hide. They may be in some danger, since they are frightened.

ESMERALDO. I must insist—

DONNA LISA. Then insist, since you must.

ESMERALDO. You will come?

DONNA LISA. No.

ESMERALDO. Forgive me, then, if I take matters into my own hands. I shall carry you. [Goes to her.]

DONNA LISA. There will be no carrying. I am quite able to walk wherever I wish to go. I do not wish to conceal myself in the Malaga vault—nor will I, Señor Esmeraldo.

ESMERALDO. Dear, you're mad, quite mad!

DONNA LISA. No.

ESMERALDO.   But what are your plans?

DONNA LISA.   If we are so unfortunate as to receive unwelcome visitors, I shall know how to deal with them.

ESMERALDO.   Deal with them! There's no dealing with these monsters.

DONNA LISA.   Do you, too, credit those servants' fables, about monsters? They are men, like other men, although pirates. And men, in my experience, are credulous creatures, much easier to handle than the gentlest of women.

ESMERALDO.   You haven't answered me. What are your plans?

DONNA LISA.   I shall sit here—and read, perhaps—if you are too unnerved to talk.

ESMERALDO.   I unnerved? My dear, you wrong me! Except that my fear for you would unnerve any one.

DONNA LISA.   If you are not afraid, sit down.

[*He looks at her, speechless for a moment; then seats himself in chair.*]

ESMERALDO [*leaping to his feet*].   Now—will you come? There's still time!

DONNA LISA [*bored*].   Oh, my dear, somebody must answer the door. [*She goes toward the entrance at the right.*] If I don't, they'll break it down, and it would be a pity to spoil the paneling.

[*He leaps to stop her. There is a thundering knock just as she undoes the door.* ESMERALDO *catches her wrist.*]

ESMERALDO.   Are you betraying us to the English?

DONNA LISA.   I shall remember that! [*She wrenches her hand free and flings the door open.* ESMERALDO *draws his sword.*] Good evening, gentlemen!

[*Three English sailors enter; they are in dirty white*

shorts and sandals, with black lanyards about their throats, with rather evil-looking sheath-knives dangling from them. There is a cutlass on the belt of each, and two heavy chased silver pistols above their hips. All have bright red scarves about their heads and wear very fine black pig-tails and incipient beards and moustachios. Two are apparently common seamen, while the foremost is undoubtedly a sailor of consequence. His uniform is better. He wears a brassard with some quaint insignia upon his right arm, bound with a band, for none of the sailors has more on his chest than an armless singlet.]

GEORGE [*the first pirate*]. Stand aside, lady. [*He levels a pistol at* ESMERALDO *over* DONNA LISA'S *shoulder.*] Down, my hearty! Sit down before you lie down. [ESMERALDO *sits.*] That's more like it; that's sensible. There's fifty of us here, and the other forty-nine are rough boys. Out of my way, lady, and stand by for jewel inspection. Go through the house, Davey, attic to cellar.

DAVE [*the second pirate*]. Ay, ay, sir.

GEORGE. Take the upstairs first. I'll stand guard.

[DAVE *and* MITCHELL, *the third pirate, start for the stairs.*]

DONNA LISA. One moment. This is a purely business matter, as I understand it?

GEORGE. No doubt about it, ma'am.

DONNA LISA. It can be accomplished then without firearms, I presume?

GEORGE. Nothing'll suit us better, ma'am. We don't do any more fighting than we have to. We get too much as it is.

DONNA LISA. Very well, then. We shall put nothing in your way. If there is anything here that you particularly value, take it. But kindly leave the room in order, and finish as quickly as possible.

GEORGE. Tell us where the stuff is and we'll get out in five minutes. Sorry about my feet, ma'am. I forgot to wipe them. Your jungle's muddy as hell.

DONNA LISA. As for the stuff, I suppose you can discover it for yourself?

GEORGE. Not without gutting the place, ma'am. You make my work easy for me, and I'll guarantee to leave your quarters shipshape. Make it hard, and we'll wreck it.

DONNA LISA. I see. Well, to be frank, I have a few jewels. No, to be frank, a good many.

GEORGE. That's fine.

DONNA LISA. You'll find them in the first room to the right as you go up the stairs. The jewel-box is on the chest under the window.

GEORGE. And money, now; you keep a stock of Spanish doubloons, no doubt?

DONNA LISA. Money, I must confess, has been rather rare in Panama since the embargo declared in consequence of Captain Morgan's depredations. Our vessels have been swinging at anchor full of merchandise, and the counting houses have had little to do.

GEORGE. But you must have a supply on hand, lady.

DONNA LISA. It has run low, I give you my word.

GEORGE. I'll take your word for it, but where is it?

DONNA LISA. In the chest under the jewel-box.

GEORGE. And if you don't mind my sailor ways, the key is . . . ?

DONNA LISA [picking one out of her girdle]. Here.

GEORGE. Excellent. Lads, you heard that. Get the pretties and the money. I'll keep the señor company. [The

two other pirates start toward the stair.]   No loitering on
the job, Dave.   [*Looks at* ESMERALDO.]

DAVE.   Ay, ay, sir.   [*They go.*]

DONNA LISA.   Will you sit down, George?

[DONNA LISA *sits at the end of the bench before the table.*]

GEORGE.   How did you know my name was George?

DONNA LISA.   Oh, you look like a George, that's all.   I
can tell a George as far as I can see one.   You see, I used
to live in England.

GEORGE.   In England?   What part, ma'am?

DONNA LISA.   Won't you sit down?

GEORGE.   Why, thanks, I will.   [*He sits on stool.*]   Now,
I'm from Yorkshire myself.

DONNA LISA.   Of course.   I might have known.   There
never was a countryman from Yorkshire without some trace
of manners.

GEORGE.   Huh, well, I've known some that had a rather
reckless way with 'em, before women and all that.   Still you
may be right.

DONNA LISA.   Is there any news from England?

GEORGE.   Oh, you'd hear more than I would.   We haven't
touched at a port for months.   You see, I was pressed for
the navy and fought in several actions and then sort of got
lost from my ships, you see—

DONNA LISA.   Yes?

GEORGE.   And then I just ran into Morgan, and there
wasn't much else to do; so I joined up with him.   There's
some money in it, you see, if you're lucky.   But I'm not
really a bad man, ma'am.

DONNA LISA.   No, I'm sure you're not.

GEORGE.   I've been rough; I won't deny that, but I know
a lady when I see one . . .

DONNA LISA. Thank you . . .

GEORGE. I mean you, ma'am. But I'm different from some of the lads with Morgan, I can tell you. Some of them are pretty wild. Morgan himself is pretty wild. But there ain't anything in that, I say. It's discipline and a firm hand that counts. And Morgan gets discipline. He won't stand any foolishness while there's work to do.

DONNA LISA. Really?

GEORGE. Now you'd think from what you've heard that we'd all be drunk tonight, wouldn't you?

DONNA LISA. Yes, I think I should.

GEORGE. I give you my word, not a man in all the crew has had a drink since supper-time last night.

DONNA LISA. How extraordinary!

GEORGE. He insists on it, you see. If he finds a man drinking or if he even thinks a man's been drinking, he lays him out—just like that.

DONNA LISA. But he isn't always so strict?

GEORGE. Oh, no! After it's all over, they'll raid the cellars and get as full as lords. They'll probably get hold of some of the women, too, and I wouldn't answer for what'd happen.

DONNA LISA. Does Captain Morgan allow that?

GEORGE. Why, yes, he kind of does. He goes in pretty strong for women himself, occasionally; and I was just going to advise you, if you don't mind . . .

DONNA LISA. Of course not.

[DAVE *and* MITCHELL *come down with a bag and a chest.
They set down the chest and sit on it.*]

GEORGE. Now, if you'd just stay upstairs out of the way till we're gone—you see, this is the best-looking house in the

village, and Morgan is likely to look into it sometime, and
I'll put a watch over it and it may do some good . . .

DONNA LISA.   You mean . . .

GEORGE.   I mean I'm kind of influential with him, and I
wouldn't like to have anything happen to you; so if you'd
just stay upstairs . . .

DONNA LISA.   I will, thank you.

GEORGE.   You're quite welcome.

[CAPTAIN MORGAN *enters the door quietly, unattended.
He is a fierce man of forty, unkempt, stocky, hairy.*
GEORGE, *who has his back to the door, does not see him.*
DONNA LISA *rises and faces* MORGAN.   *There is a
pause.*]

MORGAN.   You soldiering sailors!   Is madame receiving?
[GEORGE *and sailors spring up.*]   We have one night to sack
a city!   One night, and I find my first mate with a woman!
Castle, you're either drunk or you've run mad.   Who is
this man?   [*Pointing his blade at* ESMERALDO.]

GEORGE.   Don't know, sir.   Found him here.   He seems
peaceable.

MORGAN [*points to the door*].   And what's that?

GEORGE.   Gold and jewels, sir.

MORGAN.   Have you inspected them?

GEORGE.   No, sir.   Haven't had time.

MORGAN.   Do you call that seamanlike?   How can I
keep my accounts straight if I can't depend on my first
officer to look into his seizures?   Do you expect a share out
of this cruise?   Where are the slaves?

GEORGE.   Haven't seen any, sir.

MORGAN.   Have you searched the house?

GEORGE.   Not thoroughly, sir.

MORGAN.   What do you think the English navy's coming

to, with fools like you in command? I thought you were an officer, Castle. [*To* DAVE *and* MITCHELL.] Put down that stuff. Search the house. [*They start toward the stairs.*] No, let the upstairs alone. They'll be in the wine cellar. Look for the concealed doors. Rap the walls. Listen for girls. Fire a pistol and you'll hear 'em squeak. All Hell can't keep a Spanish girl from screaming when she hears a gun. You! [DAVE *and* MITCHELL *go out to the rear.*] As for you, George Castle, you're through. Samson gets your place. Follow me, and bring that grandee with you. [*He goes to the outer door.* GEORGE *hands* ESMERALDO *ahead of him and follows.* MORGAN *turns.*] Fetch that woman along!

DONNA LISA [*rises, trembling with rage*]. Leave my house!

MORGAN [*turning in astonishment*]. What?

DONNA LISA. You cur! You lout! You swaggering two-for-a-shilling bully! Leave my house!

MORGAN. English?

DONNA LISA. Your presence here is an insult.

MORGAN. British, by God! [*Starts toward her.*] Come, milady, I'll have to take you.

DONNA LISA. George, are you no better than your master?

GEORGE. I'm sorry, ma'am. Not much, I'm afraid.

DONNA LISA. Then you disappoint me, and I must show you the door also. Leave Señor Esmeraldo here.

GEORGE. I'm afraid he'll have to come, ma'am, and you, too.

DONNA LISA. You despicable servant! You groom! I am Lady Neville, and I give orders but never take them. Once again—there is the door. [*Pointing.*]

MORGAN [*looking her up and down*]. You hear the lady, you ass? Do as she bids you. [GEORGE, *in utter stupefaction, looks first at one and then at the other, and starts to go*.] A moment, Castle. Tell Samson he's replacing you as second in command. Tell him to comb the city for treasure and keep every man sober till we're three days at sea. Tell him to spread a report that the Spaniards have poisoned all the wine. Tell him to use his judgment. Then put yourself under arrest and sleep in the brig tonight. Your prize money's cut to one-twentieth.

DONNA LISA. Indeed, he should not be put under arrest. He erred only in excessive kindness, and the fault was more mine than his. You are quite wrong.

MORGAN [*ironical, interested*]. And by what right, lady, do you presume to intervene in this matter?

DONNA LISA. Your orders are patently unjust.

MORGAN. And by virtue of what precedent do you claim authority to give me orders?

DONNA LISA. You are a commoner, sirrah—common in blood, in education, and in spirit. You have the look of a hostler's lackey. Can there be any question among us here as to where the authority lies?

MORGAN. I had thought not.

DONNA LISA. Then I refuse to have him punished for treating a lady with courtesy. Restore him his share and his command.

MORGAN [*with a sweep of his hat*]. Lady, to put it bluntly and in plain sailor talk, I'll be blowed. Further than that, I'll be damned. I might be God-damned.

DONNA LISA. You may well be.

MORGAN. As a matter of fact, lady, the very look of you means England to me, and I find myself, steeped in crime though I may be, smelling of blood and only too recently engaged in lewd conversation, unable to refuse your slightest request. Unable, madame, if I may make so bold, because my heart tells me that if I were to step but a pace nearer you I should catch the scent of Devonshire roses from your hair and the fragrance of English hawthorn from your sweet body. England, madame, is a passion with me, and the stench of foreigners is poison to my blood. You are English—we are English together. We are met at the end of the earth; yet there is an indissoluble bond between us. Let us make a compact. Let us be friends. I would to God I were a gentler man.

DONNA LISA. You betray your birth again, Captain Morgan. None but a lout would play the courtier with an effusiveness so indecent. Yet there is a core of truth in what you say. You are a stranger here. If I can befriend you in any way . . .

MORGAN. I thank you. However, I seem to need nothing at present. I have in a way, and I fear somewhat rudely, helped myself to the freedom of your city. But my gratitude is none the less.

DONNA LISA. And as to George, here——

MORGAN. You shall have your way. Castle, you retain your commission. You have my orders. Carry them out.

[*As* GEORGE *goes out, two slave girls run in, screaming, from the rear and throw themselves at* DONNA LISA'S *feet.*]

DONNA LISA [*lifting her skirts and stepping back*]. Don't touch me. Stand up. Do you think you are safer on your hands and knees?

[*They crawl after her, moaning.* CARMENCITA *and* MARIA *are brought in, somewhat disheveled.*]

CARMENCITA. Oh, Donna Lisa! Oh, my lady! We are lost.

MARIA.   English dogs!

DONNA LISA. Captain Morgan, call off your men.

MORGAN. Walk off to the gate and guard this house. Let no one enter or leave. [DAVE *and* MITCHELL *go out.*]

CARMENCITA. Captain Morgan! [*She throws herself at his feet and embraces his knees.*] Mercy! Have mercy on us!

MARIA [*kneeling to him*]. I will pray to the Virgin. I will pray to Maria for you. A thousand white candles. Have mercy.

MORGAN. Damn the Virgin! Don't come to me with your Popish talk. [MARIA *clasps him also. He tries vainly to extricate himself.*] Lady, for the love of God, call off your dogs.

DONNA LISA.   Maria! Are these manners for the daughter of a nobleman of Spain? Carmencita! You are too familiar with the Captain's person. You act like a slave. Rise! [*The girls rise and slip back in terror.*] This is Captain Morgan—a guest. [MORGAN *bows low; they return the greeting.*] You must forgive our country gaucheries, Captain Morgan.

MORGAN. As a commanding officer of some experience, madame, I advise a bit more discipline.

DONNA LISA. I need no advice, sir. Yet in truth you must excuse me on this occasion, which has somewhat disturbed our routine.

MORGAN. My fault, I am sure.

DONNA LISA. Not at all. Maria! Carmencita! It's growing late, and the evening has been exciting. It would be as well if you went to bed.

MARIA. Yes, Donna Lisa. [*The girls go up the stairs.*]

DONNA LISA. Go, girls. [*She waits for them to go and then stands facing* MORGAN.] And now, Captain Morgan, we are glad to have had the pleasure of your company, and we know you are a busy man. We shall not detain you longer.

MORGAN. I was about to ask the favor—

DONNA LISA. Anything . . .

MORGAN. Only this. The town is in considerable confusion. There is, I am afraid, no other household so quiet as your own. I own myself to blame for the conditions; yet I very much need a good night's rest. Could you find it in your heart to lodge a countryman for the night; a countryman notorious for his crimes, yet devoted to your interests and innocent of evil intentions?

DONNA LISA. We shall be glad to shelter you, Captain Morgan.

MORGAN [*kissing her hand*]. I shall not forget your kindness.

ESMERALDO [*starting to his feet*]. For God's sake, Donna Lisa, do you realize the kind of farce you are playing?

DONNA LISA. Perfectly, Señor Don.

ESMERALDO. Do you realize that this barbarian is in possession of the town, that we are at his mercy, that he could cut all our throats at any moment?

DONNA LISA. Perfectly.

MORGAN. But we have tacitly agreed to forget that, señor, and to play the game of chivalrous guest and gracious hostess. I hope it doesn't annoy you, sir.

ESMERALDO. It does annoy me. A game you can forget when it's most convenient for your purposes. What guarantee does your guest give you, milady, that the women are not to be assailed and the rest of our throats cut before morning?

DONNA LISA. And if I were to turn Captain Morgan into the street, what assurance would we have of the safety of our lives and virtue? I prefer to play the game. . . . I have been remiss, Captain Morgan. This is Señor Don Jacinto de Esmeraldo, formerly of Seville, a gentleman whom I hope you will like, for he is my intended husband.

MORGAN [*bowing*]. My felicitations, Señor Esmeraldo.

ESMERALDO. You may rot in chains and stink in hell, you verminous cutthroat, you robber of tills and violator of little children! This game of yours ends here. I know an older game and one more suitable for men. You will step outside with me?

MORGAN. You are in the presence of a lady, sir. Put up your sword.

DONNA LISA. Señor Don! If you have ever valued me, put up your sword. Captain Morgan is a guest in my house —not yours.

[ESMERALDO *leaps at* MORGAN, *who draws. They fence.*
MORGAN, *entirely good-humored, stands on the defensive.*]

MORGAN [*as they play*]. Have you ever done much of this, my friend?

ESMERALDO. Enough.

MORGAN. No, not enough. You must live to take lessons. With a little practice you might do well. [*He drives* ESMER-ALDO *back toward the stairs.*] You should be the better perhaps for a night's sleep. [*He drives him up step by step.*] Let us finish in the morning. [ESMERALDO, *disarmed, turns tail and runs upstairs.* MORGAN *sheathes his sword, comes to table, takes the biggest chair, settles com-*

fortably in it, and looks at Donna Lisa.] How quiet and restful it is here!

Donna Lisa. But you are tired, Captain Morgan.

Morgan. I've often dreamed of a place like this. A perfect city. A perfect woman. A good day's work done. . . . That reminds me. I meant to leave here tonight, until I saw you.

Donna Lisa. Indeed.

Morgan. I put in the first three days of the week escaping from an English fleet sent out here to capture me. Yes; to be safe, I should have left here tonight.

Donna Lisa. We shall be pleased if you can stay, of course. Yet, if you must go . . .

Morgan. Oh, I shan't go now! I don't think they'll catch up with me. I don't think they know where I am. And as I say, I've often dreamed of a place like this— and a woman like you. Isn't it strange—out of all this Indies—here we are together alone.

Donna Lisa. Do you fear capture?

Morgan. I dare say it's fate.

Donna Lisa. That you will be captured?

Morgan. Oh, no: that we should be together.

Donna Lisa. I fear you waste time here, Captain Morgan. You have taken Panama City. Surely you have orders to give and much to do. I will excuse you.

Morgan. It is my business to take towns, my dear, and George's business to sack them. I leave all that to your friend George. A good officer, George, except when you are around. . . . Sit down, please. [*She sits. He hitches his chair closer to her.*] What a grand place this would be to settle down in!

DONNA LISA. Have you thought of giving up—er—the sea?

MORGAN. Oh, often. I've often dreamed of a place like this. Here we are, as I said—

DONNA LISA. Yes, I know.

MORGAN. —alone together.

DONNA LISA. Yes; you have said that, Captain Morgan. But did you not say you were tired, and in need of a good night's rest?

MORGAN. I was tired of the others; not of you. [*Pause; he helps himself to the Malaga.*]

DONNA LISA. When you wish to retire, you will find your room at the head of the stairs to the left. You do look weary.

MORGAN. I've had a very trying week. Will you have some of the Malaga?

DONNA LISA. No, thank you.

MORGAN. It's excellent.

DONNA LISA. Thank you, no.

MORGAN [*drinks*]. I don't know when I've had such a pleasant evening.

DONNA LISA. We have a surplus of pleasant evenings here. They grow monotonous.

MORGAN. You find this one like the others?

DONNA LISA. Oh, precisely.

MORGAN [*hitching his chair still closer*]. With you and me together alone?

DONNA LISA. You are easily entertained.

MORGAN [*rising*]. Not so easily.

DONNA LISA. Oh, finish your wine, sir, finish your wine! It's my best, and you taste it. There is nothing in the world like Malaga to induce a refreshing sleep.

MORGAN. Sleep, lady, with you under the same roof?
You do me a great injustice.

DONNA LISA. Captain Morgan!

MORGAN. You have said you look upon me as a rogue,
a person of low origin, not of your world . . . but I am no
common man, lady. I am, though it is I who speak it, one
of the great of the earth. An admiral of genius, a leader
of men, even—at heart—something of a poet,—and most
of all a devotee of beauty. Lady, it was at your shrine that
I worshiped. It was for *you* I hoped as I cut my way
through Spanish lines to Spanish gold. It was *you* I longed
for. I long for *you* now!

DONNA LISA. Do you expect me to believe this?

MORGAN. No; I expect you to be moved by it.

DONNA LISA. But it happens I'm not. [*Takes up a
book.*] Have you read any Chaucer? Here is a most interesting volume, containing *Troilus and Cressida* and the
Legend of Good Women. Shall I read to you?

MORGAN. From a legend of good women? No, I thank
you.

DONNA LISA. Do you wish to retire immediately? I hope
I'm not keeping you.

MORGAN. It seems that I bore you?

DONNA LISA. I am a trifle bored, yes, Captain Morgan.
I had no idea pirates were so sentimental. You will pardon
me?

MORGAN [*his face going black*]. By God!

DONNA LISA. No, no—don't swear, I beg—there's nothing more childish than swearing. You will find your room,
sir, at the head of the stair, at the left. . . . I imagine your
conquests must have been mainly among kitchen maids?
Your technique is bad. [*A pause.*] Truly, sirrah, you had

best go to bed before I laugh at you outright. [*She goes
back to her book; he stands irresolute.*] Oh, you must listen,
Captain Morgan! You would love Hector. [*She reads.*]

> Now was this Hector piteous of nature,
> And saw that she was sorrowfully bigoon,
> And that she was so fair a creature;
> Of his goodness he gladed her anoon,
> And sayed, Lat your fadres treson goon
> Forth with mischance, and yes yourself, in joye,
> Dwelleth with us, whyl you good list, in Troye.

[MORGAN *goes to the stair.*] Oh, but this next stanza!

> And all the honour that men may doon you have,
> As forforth as your fader dwelled here——

[MORGAN *starts upstairs.*] You aren't going, Captain
Morgan? [*He makes no reply.*] But if you must . . .
good night.

MORGAN [*low; without turning*]. Good night, hell! [*He
disappears.*]

DONNA LISA [*dropping her book and laughing*]. Good
night, hell!

CURTAIN

ACT II

The same scene, early the next morning. The room is as it was left, DONNA LISA's copy of Chaucer lying face downward, open, on the table. The chest brought down by the pirates stands where they dropped it, and a particularly villainous-looking low-grade pirate is kneeling at it, patiently trying one skeleton-key after another on the lock. He is ill at ease, and once, at a slight noise, looks around stealthily. As he works with renewed interest, having found a key that promises to do the trick, MONTALVO appears in the doorway at the rear, unseen by the lonely marauder. MONTALVO draws his dagger and advances silently. At his thrust the pirate slips to the floor without sound or sigh. MONTALVO wipes his blade on the bandanna which the dead man was wearing, tiptoes to the window, looks out, then starts to ascend the stairs. MARIA enters from the rear, carrying a small water-jar. She sees the fallen pirate, stifles a scream, sets down the jar, and retreats to the wall, her hand to her throat.

MONTALVO. He won't bite you, Maria.

MARIA. Oh! Montalvo!

MONTALVO. Be quiet. Are there more of them?

MARIA. How did he get in here?

MONTALVO. The way I got in. By the lower passage. I caught him at Donna Lisa's chest.

MARIA. You killed him?

214

MONTALVO. He's my third. Why are there sentries about this house?

MARIA. Morgan's here.

MONTALVO. Here? Where?

MARIA. Upstairs. Asleep.

MONTALVO. He was here all night?

MARIA. Yes.

MONTALVO. But, my God! where's Donna Lisa?

MARIA. In her room. Sound asleep.

MONTALVO. Remember—I've been hunted like a rabbit all night, Maria. I've killed three men in one way and another. My eyes ache from looking steadily at one doorway these last four hours. I can't endure much more. Don't try to be amusing.

MARIA. Do I look amused? Go up and look for yourself.

MONTALVO. Where's Carmencita?

MARIA. Sleeping, I think.

MONTALVO. Well, *Cien nul diablos,* I am crazy! Did you give him lodging for the night?

MARIA. Just that.

MONTALVO. And then go quietly to bed?

MARIA. Just so.

MONTALVO. And nobody hurt?

MARIA. Only Don Jacinto.

MONTALVO. Well, at least, the Don made trouble! How did it happen?

MARIA. You see, they sent him to bed——

MONTALVO. They?

MARIA. Morgan and Donna Lisa.

MONTALVO. Wait a minute—wait a minute! Morgan and Donna Lisa sent Don Jacinto to bed?

MARIA. Yes.

MONTALVO. And he went?

MARIA. Under protest, yes.

MONTALVO. And then?

MARIA. Then Donna Lisa sent Morgan to bed.

MONTALVO. What? And *he* went?

MARIA. Yes.

MONTALVO. How do you know?

MARIA. I was waiting in the hall upstairs to see how she came out with him.

MONTALVO. And then?

MARIA. Then Donna Lisa went to bed herself.

MONTALVO. And to sleep?

MARIA. She always sleeps well.

MONTALVO. But Don Jacinto was hurt——

MARIA. Yes.

MONTALVO. How?

MARIA. About the middle of the night he went to Morgan's room and assailed him by surprise. They fought it out, and Don Jacinto was wounded in the groin; but not seriously. Morgan has a slight touch in the shoulder.

MONTALVO. Um! You seem to be getting along pretty comfortably here. The whole house seems to have a slight touch of insanity. . . . On the whole perhaps I'd better go.

MARIA. But you're much safer here.

MONTALVO. With Morgan in the house?

MARIA. Oh, he's as much a gentleman as yourself!

MONTALVO [*pointing to the sailor's body*]. And what will he say to that?

MARIA. He'd say you were quite justified. The fellow had no right here. He was robbing his own company.

MONTALVO. You think so?

[Carmencita *appears on the stairs.*]

Maria.   He says himself there's always a rough element that gets out of hand when they're sacking a city.

Montalvo.   Oh, he does!   You appear to be familiar with the great man's conversation.   You find him agreeable?

Maria.   Not half bad.

Montalvo.   You had a chat with him?

Carmencita [*sweeping down*].   A chat with him!   I don't know what you call a chat, but if she didn't spend the night with him, I'm no judge of manners.   [*She sees the body.*] Holy heaven, what's that?

Montalvo.   Just a dead pirate, Carmencita.

Carmencita.   Who left it here?   It must be taken out at once.   Where are the porters?

Maria.   There isn't a slave in the house.   I've looked even through the vaults for them.   They're simply gone.

Montalvo.   So we are to congratulate you on a conquest, Maria.   When a buccaneer captures your town you proceed to capture the buccaneer.   Neatly done, neatly done!

Maria.   She knows nothing about it.   She was asleep.   I merely went in to bandage his wounds.

Carmencita.   It's well you've learned to lie with a straight face, my dear, for you'll need all your talents in that direction.   Don Jacinto tells another story.   He told me while I was bandaging *his* wounds that he found you there.   Yes, and it was you who roused Morgan and saved his life.

Maria.   I have nothing to say except that Don Jacinto lies.   [*She sets her jar down on the table with finality and goes out.*]

Montalvo. Has Donna Lisa heard of this? [*Crossing toward her.*]

Carmencita. She didn't wake, and I didn't like to wake her. I knew she'd be angry.

Montalvo. At whom?

Carmencita. Don Jacinto. She had instructed him that Morgan was her guest and was to be given every courtesy.

Montalvo. Ah, yes! She's English, of course. And so is he. Doubtless a buccaneer is as good as anybody else, in England.

Carmencita. Or better.

Montalvo. Why, yes. In a nation of pirates such a one should be a sort of nobleman. [*He turns.*] You needn't tell Donna Lisa I was here. I'm going.

Carmencita. But where?

Montalvo [*pausing*]. I don't know. [*He sits down disconsolately.*] My place is a wreck. The whole city's a wreck. I saw them carrying out my gold plate last night. By the way, there are three English ships in the harbor; came in at dawn and sent a boat ashore.

Carmencita. Morgan's?

[Donna Lisa *is descending the stairs from the right.*]

Montalvo. I suppose so. Came to carry my gold plate to England. That's where all the gold plate goes.

Donna Lisa. Montalvo!

Montalvo. Donna Lisa! Am I welcome? [*Rises.*]

Donna Lisa. Need you ask? We were fearful for you.

Montalvo. I had my misgivings about this house, Donna Lisa, but you seem to have been fortunate. You are at the center of the storm and therefore undisturbed.

Donna Lisa. We are involuntary headquarters, Señor Montalvo. . . . Be quick with breakfast, Carmencita. Captain Morgan will no doubt leave early. . . . Oh, and there is something on the floor here. Will you call the slaves to take it away?

CARMENCITA. The slaves have vanished, Donna Lisa.

DONNA LISA. This is hardly an object for the breakfast room. [MARIA *enters with a tray of food as* MORGAN *descends the stairs.*] Maria, what unexpected industry! Good morning, Captain Morgan. [MORGAN *bows.*] May I make you acquainted with a friend, Señor Don Manuel Montalvo?

MORGAN. Most happy, sir. What's this?

MONTALVO. My doing, Captain. I caught him at the chest.

MORGAN. Ah, yes. Quite right. I know the rascal. [*He stirs the body with a foot.* [*To* MONTALVO:] Will you take his heels, sir? [*They carry the sailor out at the back.* MARIA *and* CARMENCITA *busy themselves with the arrangement of the table.*]

DONNA LISA. You slept well, Carmencita?

CARMENCITA. Perfectly.

DONNA LISA. And you, Maria?

CARMENCITA. Yes, Maria, did you sleep well?

MARIA. Beautifully, little one, beautifully. [CARMENCITA *gives* MARIA *the lie with a look.* MORGAN *and* MONTALVO *reënter.*]

MORGAN. I regret this little annoyance, my lady. And yet I'm very glad you've disposed of him, sir. [MORGAN *seats himself behind the table.*]

MONTALVO. It is only fair to tell you that I'd have done the same to you if I'd had the chance.

MORGAN. And what Spanish gentleman would not, Señor? You need not explain.

Donna Lisa. Your place is here, Montalvo.

Montalvo [*standing*]. Thank you. I never breakfast with pirates.

Morgan. But I am no pirate.

Montalvo. I must contradict you, Captain Morgan. You are.

Morgan. We are guests here, my friend, and I take no offense. Nevertheless, I am no pirate, but a commissioned officer in the navy of his gracious majesty, Charles II, save his Grace. I would have you remember that.

Montalvo [*standing*]. And if you think you are no pirate, I would have you look about you at this city when you have breakfasted, Captain Morgan. I think it will convince you to the contrary.

Morgan. You are young. The difference between war and piracy is legal, not actual. One captured city looks like any other, no matter by what authority the assault is ordered.

Montalvo. Does the king get all my gold plate—or do you?

Morgan. Did all the gold plate go to the king when you Spaniards sacked Algiers?

[Don Jacinto Esmeraldo *appears at the head of the stairs, white as a sheet and walking with difficulty.* Montalvo *and* Carmencita *run to assist him. He comes with them to the foot of the stairs.* Morgan *rises.*]

Esmeraldo. So you break bread with him and serve him with your own hands. You are for the winning side, I see. [Montalvo *goes upstairs.*] It is like a woman, to throw herself in the way of the conqueror. You and I shall never break bread together again. I am not conquered. I have still some blood in me. False of heart, faint of courage, *go* with your race. Go back to your English. Betray them as you have betrayed our city. You were not frightened? No—you knew you had no reason to be frightened. As for me, I can still draw a sword— [*He attempts to unsheathe his weapon and falls back into the arms of* MONTALVO *and* CARMENCITA.]

MONTALVO. Let me take him.

DONNA LISA. Here, Maria, my smelling salts! He is ill.

MORGAN [*rises*]. No, not ill, madame. Wounded.

DONNA LISA. How wounded?

MORGAN. Not badly, though he lost blood. He will recover.

DONNA LISA. No, but by whom?

MORGAN. I must take the blame for that. He came to my room in the night.

DONNA LISA [*starting upstairs*]. Why had I not heard of this?

MORGAN. It's nothing, Donna Lisa.

ESMERALDO. Nothing, no, not this time. But it shall be something before I end.

DONNA LISA. Montalvo, will you help him to his bed? [*To* MORGAN.] You must pardon us.

[MORGAN *bows.* MONTALVO, *assisted by* CARMENCITA, *carries* ESMERALDO *up.* DONNA LISA *follows.* MARIA *lingers at the foot of the stairs;* MORGAN *kisses her across the rail.*]

MARIA. Take care they don't see.

MORGAN. They've gone. Do you love me?

MARIA. Too much.

MORGAN. Impossible.

MARIA. Too much, for you will go away and what will become of me?

MORGAN [*lightly*]. What will become of you? Why, darling, what will become of me? Think of me, my dear Maria, sailing lonely over the Spanish Main, longing always for my little Maria and walking up to death gladly at last because I don't know where to find her.

MARIA. I think you're very cheerful about it. And we'll never see each other again——

MORGAN. That's the loveliest thing about it. That's what makes it perfect.

MARIA. Not seeing me again?

MORGAN. Not growing tired of you. Wouldn't you rather wait for me eternally than see me so often you grew tired of me?

MARIA. When you say that you are tired of me already.

MORGAN. I don't know how much of Panama there is left to sack, Maria. I don't know whether I shall be here or ten leagues from here this evening . . . but if I am here—wait for me.

MARIA. And . . . if you are not here?

MORGAN. If I am not—why—just wait for me. Will you?

MARIA. Yes.

MORGAN. And now be a good girl and kiss me once more and run upstairs. There's some one coming.

MARIA [*kissing him*]. This evening——

MORGAN. Good-bye.

[*She runs upstairs, passing* CARMENCITA.]

CARMENCITA. What were you saying to Maria?

MORGAN. What is the first maxim of a gentleman?

CARMENCITA. You mean to tell me you were saying to Maria, "What is the first maxim of a gentleman"?

MORGAN. The first maxim of a gentleman is, never discuss one woman with another.

CARMENCITA. It seems that you and Maria get along very well together.

MORGAN. I'd much rather talk about you than Maria.

CARMENCITA. What could you say about me?

MORGAN. About your flashing eyes, your rose-sweet mouth . . .

CARMENCITA. I don't believe you.

MORGAN. But make an effort to believe it, darling! Make an effort! You aren't trying! Is this affair to be entirely on my side?

CARMENCITA. You flatter yourself, sir. So far there is no affair.

MORGAN. And do you think we two could part without so much as an affair, my dear? You underestimate us both. Come, kiss me! [*They kiss.*] This evening, in the patio, little Carmen. At moonrise. Kiss me again. Quick! There's some one coming. [*They kiss again. They hear footsteps above and separate.* DONNA LISA *appears at the stair-head.*]

DONNA LISA. Carmencita!

CARMENCITA. Yes, Donna Lisa. [*To* MORGAN:] This evening! [CARMENCITA *runs upstairs, passing* DONNA LISA, *who descends to* MORGAN. *She bends toward him in an instant, then withdraws.*]

DONNA LISA. I offer my apologies for the wound you have sustained under our roof, Captain Morgan. I realize that your code authorizes summary vengeance in such cases. We owe our lives to your forbearance.

MORGAN [*approaching her*]. My dear Donna Lisa——

DONNA LISA. You forget yourself, sir.

MORGAN. True, true! But as you know, I have fallen in love with you, violently and disastrously, and if it becomes noticeable you must forgive me.

DONNA LISA. Must I listen to that sort of thing at breakfast also?

MORGAN. I am not one of your cuckoo-clock gallants that spend the morning at his toilet, the middle of the day in siesta, the afternoon gaming, and the evening with his mistress. I make love when I can't help it—and if it happens to be at breakfast, why not?

DONNA LISA. Because it bores me . . . if that matters.

MORGAN. You are posing, my lady; posing elegantly and with skill, but posing. No woman was ever bored with it, morning, noon, or night.

DONNA LISA. Oh, you little know—

MORGAN. You may have been bored with that walking stick they have carried upstairs. . . .

DONNA LISA [*she rises and walks about*]. Oh, a woman is the most unfortunate thing!

MORGAN. What woman?

DONNA LISA. Any woman! A man can do as he pleases, but a woman can do nothing but accept compliments until she is so sick of them, she marries to escape.

MORGAN. I gather you have led a melancholy existence? Nothing but one man after another.

DONNA LISA. Nothing but one man after another. [*Sitting again.*] First in England, when I grew tired of dancing at country parties, my relatives must needs push me into a match; and in Panama City, when I became a widow, my friends will have it that my situation requires an alliance.

And no sooner is that alliance broken off, than the very free-booter I put up for the night thrusts his attentions on me. You think there is nothing in the world for a woman save a man—some man . . . any man. Is not the world as wide for one sex as the other? I came to Panama City for adventure . . .

MORGAN. And you call this no adventure? [*Sitting near her.*]

DONNA LISA. Single, married, or widowed, in England or the Caribbean, among enemies or among friends, still a woman may take part in nothing but courtship and domesticity.

MORGAN. Your own fault, I assure you.

DONNA LISA. Mine?

MORGAN. I tried marriage a while, though you wouldn't think it. Very pleasant it is back in Wales with the mountains turning gold in autumn and green in spring. A man comes home peacefully every night but Saturday, kisses his decent little wife a frugal little kiss, and before he knows it, he's dead and done for. That's domesticity for you. I decided that I didn't want to die that way. I took ship.

DONNA LISA. It sounds so easy! You took ship. . . . But suppose I wanted to take ship and sail away and keep on going?

MORGAN. Nothing to prevent you.

DONNA LISA. Everything.

MORGAN. Nothing except that you're frightened to death of your precious virtue. Forget that and you can do as you please.

DONNA LISA. You do as you please and keep your reputation. You even win reputation by it. Suppose I forget my virtue, where would my reputation be?

MORGAN. You must lose your reputation for virtue before you can gain a reputation for anything else, dear lady. All men have lost their reputations for virtue. That's the first thing they do. Then they can start. Not before.

DONNA LISA. Not all men.

MORGAN. No! Not all. But all that count. All that get more out of life than a housewife gets.

DONNA LISA. But to take an instance. Could any woman make a place for herself in your company? You know better.

MORGAN. It depends on the woman. You could—if you wanted to.

DONNA LISA. You know better.

MORGAN. You have presence, a good head in emergencies; you'd command respect.

DONNA LISA. Among pirates?

MORGAN. I'd not advise piracy. I've never gone in for it myself.

DONNA LISA. No, I forgot.

MORGAN. Call it privateering. Of course you'd have to go into it head over heels, forget everything else, use your influence as a woman as I use mine as a man, play your officers against each other, distribute favors, build up a name for courage, charm your mates, put your men in their places . . . you'd know how when you got there——

DONNA LISA. Oh——

MORGAN [rising]. If you want life you can have it. There's plenty of it lying around. [Rises and goes to her.] Of course you might get too much of it before you were through, with men killing each other for you every week or two. Still . . .

DONNA LISA. And I might be killed. Had you thought of that?

MORGAN. Any time. . . . And as for losing your virtue, you simply wouldn't have any.

DONNA LISA. In a way, that might be a relief.

MORGAN. Oh, it is.

DONNA LISA [*still seated*]. It's almost . . . attractive. And—although I wouldn't enlist with you, remember—what, if I were going to enlist, would you have me do first?

MORGAN. Love me.

DONNA LISA [*rising, turns away from him*]. So it was only courtship again!

MORGAN. Courtship if you will, madonna, but not domesticity. To love most men is domesticity; to love me is an adventure. I offer you no hacienda among the foothills, no cottage by the sea. I offer only arms that are more familiar with tiller and sword than with soft encounters.

DONNA LISA. Why do you choose to tell this tale to me?

MORGAN [*going to her*]. I'll tell you that when you tell me what it was that passed between us like a flame when I came in that door last night, madonna. We knew then, quite as well as we know now, what this would come to. I knew I must have you. Something it is of the mind, something of the body—swift as tropic lightning, not to be explained.

DONNA LISA. No, no! You are wrong.

MORGAN. You are wrong to trifle.

[GEORGE *enters from the right.*]

GEORGE. Whenever you're at leisure, Captain Morgan. Your pardon, lady. Those ships, sir.

MORGAN. What ships?

GEORGE [*standing at the door*]. There are three English ships in the harbor that weren't there last night.

MORGAN. Our own?

GEORGE. No.

MORGAN. Then what ships?

GEORGE. Commodore Wright's fleet.

MORGAN. Now may he rot in his own scuppers, the dirty hound! I thought you said he was three hundred miles south?

GEORGE. So it was reported, sir. The scouts must have been in error.

MORGAN. Damn them, damn their eyes; damn them blind, and you too, you bungling, headless total loss! Have you no other excuse?

GEORGE. None, sir.

MORGAN. Have they sent boats ashore?

GEORGE. One, sir. The commodore's on shore looking for you.

MORGAN. It's damned early for a commodore.

GEORGE. I gave him considerable misinformation as to where you were. We aim to lose him and keep him lost till we've had time to get the stuff together.

MORGAN. He won't find this place?

GEORGE. He's looking under the wharves for you along the water-front.

MORGAN. I suppose several of them followed you here?

GEORGE. No, I judge you're safe on this side of town.

DONNA LISA. But who is this? [*Comes down between them.*]

MORGAN. Commodore Wright of his Majesty's navy, who's been chasing me around the Caribbean for the last half year with a warrant for my arrest.

DONNA LISA.   But what have you done?

MORGAN.   Nothing but serve the king. Nothing but take Porto Bello for him from the Spanish. But there is a pan-handling clique about the king, a mangy pack of dogs-in-the-manger that will neither do anything themselves nor suffer others. They've proved to him by some chancery legerdemain or other that my captain's commission gives me no sanction for land actions. Hence the warrant; hence my own ship dragging anchor somewhere off the coast, un-able to enter and transport spoils. And to please these cos-metic browsers and lip-stick suckers I and my men must now find our way back overland with what little we carry.

GEORGE.   We go back overland?

MORGAN.   Yes. Cache all valuables at the church. Get together enough food and water for a three-day march. [GEORGE *starts to go out by a small, concealed door at the right.*] You'd better not go out the same way you came in. Isn't there a rear exit?

DONNA LISA.   There's an underground passage. Let him take that, and no one will see him leave the house.

MORGAN.   And if there are any back alleys in this town, use them. [GEORGE *goes.*] So . . . I've lost Panama.

DONNA LISA.   I'm sorry. I don't know why—and it's silly of me—but one always takes sides.

MORGAN.   You could make up for it. No one else.

DONNA LISA.   Tell me how?

MORGAN.   Come with me,

DONNA LISA.   But you must know that's out of the ques-tion. Where are you going? What would become of me? Three days through the jungle—

MORGAN.   Wear dancing slippers if you like. Your feet

won't touch the ground till we've reached the anchorage. But come.

Donna Lisa.   And never see England again?

Morgan.   Never step another minuet—never bow to another dowager—never listen to the addresses of another perfumed fop—set your teeth into life—be the first woman that ever was a man.

Donna Lisa.   One wants so many things.

Morgan.   You want nothing that you can't take for yourself.

Donna Lisa.   What I can have—is England.   What I want . . . I have no idea.

Morgan.   But I know what I want and know what you want.   You want escape, and I offer it.

Donna Lisa.   It's easy to talk of these things.   But to do them . . .   [*Walking toward the window.*]

Morgan.   . . . needs only courage.   [*Following her.*]

Donna Lisa.   Oh, if I had the courage!   If I had longer to think about it——

Morgan.   You'd play safe, of course.   Now you know why in England or in the Caribbean there's nothing for a woman but domesticity.   They're afraid.   All afraid.   Even you, who met and turned me so easily last night, even you who know how to play a new game and invent the rules as you go—you are afraid.   You'd rather a minute at a time, one secondhand day after another, than take one step for yourself.   Is it true?

Donna Lisa.   It may be.

Morgan.   Can't you for once be different from the others?   [*Looking into her eyes.*]

Donna Lisa.   You're right, I'm afraid!

MARIA [*appearing at the head of the stairs*]. A romantic scene of a bright spring morning! The birds mating in the trees! The pirate making love to the lady of the house! Most delicate and touching!

MORGAN. It's only farewell, Maria. I've had bad news. Ten to one I shan't be here again.

MARIA. Oh!

[CARMENCITA *follows her down the stairway.*]

MORGAN. Would you give me your hand in such a case?

MARIA. No! No . . . [*Running to his arms.*] Good-bye.

MORGAN. Be happy and live long.

CARMENCITA. Will you tell my fortune too? [*Approaching him.*]

MORGAN [*kissing her*]. May you never have a lover with arms weaker than your own.

CARMENCITA. Odious!

MORGAN. Then it's good-bye, Donna Lisa?

DONNA LISA [*not answering him*]. Carmencita, will you show him the way?

[MORGAN *and* CARMENCITA *go out by the door at the right.* MARIA *goes to the window.*]

DONNA LISA. You appear to have been deeply affected by Captain Morgan's threat of departure. Console yourself, my dear. Unless I gauge him incorrectly, he is returning.

MARIA. I know.

DONNA LISA. Yes? [*Turning toward her.*] You also have an instinct for these matters. No doubt you will find opportunity for further parley with the gentleman. I shall be at pains to leave the field clear for you.

MARIA. You are very kind. It will not be necessary.

DONNA LISA. But to further your happiness, my dear, I would do anything within reason, or even beyond.

MARIA. You think yourself very clever, Donna Lisa. Well, you're not as clever as you think.

A VOICE [*outside the street door*]. Captain Morgan's headquarters?

DONNA LISA. No. Your business, sir?

THE VOICE. May I come in a moment, ma'am?

[DONNA LISA *steps back, and an ensign of the king's navy appears.*]

ENSIGN. I'm looking for Captain Morgan, ma'am.

DONNA LISA. Captain Morgan is not here.

[MONTALVO *and* ESMERALDO *appear at the head of the stairs.*]

ENSIGN. He's been here?

DONNA LISA. Before I answer your questions, may I ask who you are?

ENSIGN. Why, you see, I'm his Britannic Majesty's ensign. I'm glad you speak English. It makes it easier, and it's very embarrassing, breaking in this way. You see, I have a word for Captain Morgan's ear, and if he's been annoying you, why you may be glad to learn that Commodore Wright has a warrant for his arrest. Now, if you could tell me where he is . . .

DONNA LISA. I'm afraid I can't.

ENSIGN. I don't doubt your word, you see—but the officer who just came in . . . that wasn't Captain Morgan?

DONNA LISA. No.

ENSIGN. And you have no idea where he might be found?

DONNA LISA. I can tell you nothing.

ENSIGN. Thank you very much.

ESMERALDO. And why not? You had breakfast with him, if I'm not mistaken. [*Starting down the stairs.*]

ENSIGN. Then Captain Morgan has been here, ma'am?

DONNA LISA. He has made this house his headquarters.

ENSIGN. Against your wishes, I'm sure, ma'am. Now, if you could tell me when he's likely to be back, we could relieve you of him, and I dare say we'd be happier. He'll be here again?

DONNA LISA. I think not.

ENSIGN. Could you tell me where we might find him?

DONNA LISA. I have no idea.

ESMERALDO [*descending with* MONTALVO]. Why, yes, betray your king as well as your household! Run up the pirate's colors on the tower! I wronged you, my lady, when I accused you of siding with the English! It's your buccaneer! Sir, this house not only has been Morgan's headquarters, it is his headquarters now. He not only has been here, he has been made welcome here, trebly welcome, and he will be here again! He may be here now!

MONTALVO. I was about to suggest that if this young man wishes to find Captain Morgan it would be a good plan to search the house. [*Coming downstairs.*]

DONNA LISA. Yes, by all means.

ENSIGN. Well, now, I doubt that I ought to try it alone. However, I'm greatly obliged by the information, and we'll throw a guard about the place at once, begging your pardon, ma'am.

DONNA LISA. Oh, I'm sure a guard would be an excellent device.

ENSIGN. Yes, ma'am. You see, that way we'll get him either going or coming.

DONNA LISA. You think of everything.

ENSIGN. You see, I've studied tactics, ma'am.

DONNA LISA. I might have known.

ESMERALDO [*at the door*]. Come, Montalvo. There are too many English here. [ESMERALDO *and* MONTALVO *go out.*]

ENSIGN [*bowing*]. I thank you for your courtesy, ma'am.

DONNA LISA. Your own courtesy, sir, is like your tactics: irreproachable.

ENSIGN. Thank you, ma'am. [*He starts for the door.*]

DONNA LISA. I wonder if I might ask a favor of you?

ENSIGN. Why, surely.

DONNA LISA. I have been more or less stranded in Panama City since the death of my husband, and being English, I find my position growing more intolerable from day to day. If Commodore Wright could arrange passage for me back to England, I should be more than grateful. Do you think it could be managed?

ENSIGN. Well, now, I doubt it, ma'am. The commodore will be here in a few moments, ma'am. And he will answer for himself. [*He comes back to her.*] Of course, if you could help us to lay hands on Captain Morgan, I doubt if there would be any difficulty about that passage to England.

DONNA LISA. Again, I must compliment you on your knowledge of tactics.

ENSIGN. Think it over, ma'am. [*He goes.*]

DONNA LISA. Carmencita! [CARMENCITA *enters.*] Carmencita, run at once to the church and find Captain Morgan. Tell him this house is watched and he must not return.

CARMENCITA. This house——

DONNA LISA. No questions! Quick!

[*As* CARMENCITA *turns to go she meets* MORGAN *in the*

doorway. She glances at DONNA LISA *and runs out quickly.*]

DONNA LISA. Oh, you here! I have just sent Carmencita to warn you. The commodore's ensign has been here. They are throwing a guard about the house. [MORGAN *walks toward the window.*] Don't go to the window. They're there now.

MORGAN. You sent to warn me?

DONNA LISA. Yes.

MORGAN. Thank you.

DONNA LISA. How did you enter?

MORGAN. I did not leave, my dear. I have been walking in the patio, trying to make up my mind to leave you.

DONNA LISA. If you stay longer the commodore will find you here. Then let us say, shall we not—that we shall remember each other kindly, and . . . perhaps . . . with some regret?

MORGAN. Would it not be better to remember each other kindly without regret? We are met by chance at a far corner of the earth and in a far corner of an obscure century. It is unlikely that we meet again. We are still young, or young enough; but we shall not be young forever. And when my bones lie white in the sunlight somewhere between Mexico and Peru, and when your hands and lips are dust in an English churchyard, would it not be better that we had taken what we wanted of each other and gone away singing?

DONNA LISA. You speak well and poetically on the most incredible subjects, Captain Morgan. What more can a man desire when he knows himself master of such magnificent rhetoric?

MORGAN. Ay, you can mock, Donna Lisa, but that's no answer.

Donna Lisa.   What answer could I make you in the morning sunlight?

Morgan.   When the moon rises I shall be gone.   The town is no longer mine, but tonight the Caribbean is yours and mine.

Donna Lisa.   I fear you need the moon for such an overture; for by day, I hope you realize, it is a most immoral proposal.

Morgan.   Quite immoral and reckless, dear Donna Lisa.

Donna Lisa.   Surely there are others in the city who could find it in their hearts to love for a night the conqueror of Panama?

Morgan.   And after seeing you—with you in my mind—do you think I should want them?   And are you proud, after all, of the comparison?   It is you that I love.   [*He lays a hand on her shoulder.*]   I can stay but a moment longer. You will come?

Donna Lisa [*pausing*].   Yes.   [*They embrace and kiss.*] Let's steal one night out of eternity.   But on one condition . . .

Morgan.   It's too late for conditions, sweet.   [*He kisses her again.*]

Donna Lisa.   . . . That we swear no oaths and take no vows to love forever.   That we love while we can, and part when we must, without pretending.

Morgan.   I shall never need to pretend.   [*He kisses her again.*]

Donna Lisa [*in utter surrender*].   If I take you, it is because you are real, too real to perjure yourself to save my pride.   You will love me a little while, and I shall love you a little while . . . and when it's gone that's the end.

Morgan.   When you start to argue I must stop you thus,

with a kiss, for you are better at it thán I am. There has never been another girl like you. There never will be. No conditions.

Donna Lisa. No squabbling, no complaints, no recriminations when it's over. Only this day . . .

Morgan. Very well. This day, and forever—and then another day.

Donna Lisa. Yes. Yes to you. [*They melt into each other's arms.*] Have your way always.

Morgan. For it was you I always wanted.

Donna Lisa. Oh, it *was* true, what you said!

Morgan. What was true?

Donna Lisa. When you came in that door, I knew. But I had to try you. Did you mind?

Morgan. You marvelous woman! Mind! [*In embracing him she touches the wound in his shoulder, and he flinches slightly.*]

Donna Lisa. I've hurt you?

Morgan. Only this scratch.

Donna Lisa. Does it trouble you much?

Morgan. Not at all.

Donna Lisa. And is it well bandaged? Who did it?

Morgan. Maria.

Donna Lisa. Maria's a precious child. I thank her for it.

Morgan. You can thank her for saving me from worse.

Donna Lisa. From worse?

Morgan. Yes. [*Realizing the slip.*]

Donna Lisa. She warned you?

[Carmencita *enters at the rear.*]

Morgan. Yes.

Donna Lisa [*breaking away*]. But where was she?

Morgan. I think, by accident, she just happened—

Donna Lisa. She was in your room!

Morgan. No . . .

Donna Lisa. I might have guessed when she flashed out at me and ran upstairs. It's well I learned in time. And it was I who believed you cared nothing for these others after you had seen me. [*Catching sight of* Carmencita.] And no doubt Carmencita is one of your light-o'-loves.

Morgan. What has all this got to do with us?

Donna Lisa. Carmencita!

Carmencita. Yes.

Donna Lisa. Was Maria with Captain Morgan last night?

Carmencita. You haven't been without considerable competition, Donna Lisa, if I do say it. . . .

Donna Lisa. Then you, too, I dare say . . .

Carmencita. When you are quite through with him, señora mia, you might remind him of a rather particular appointment for this evening . . . by moonlight.

Donna Lisa. With you? . . . Oh, you are welcome.

Carmencita [*going out*]. No hurry, I'm sure.

Donna Lisa. You dared, you dared, to make me a laughingstock to my whole household! Oh! Oh! And I believed you. Oh! [*With a cry of hatred*, Donna Lisa *rushes at him and begins to beat him savagely in the face with both fists, not so much a woman's blows as a man's*.] You scoundrel, you liar, you cheap knave! Liar! Liar!

Morgan [*laughing under the blows*]. Now I know you love me.

Donna Lisa [*renewing the attack*]. You, coming to me with your sighs of eternal love! Your free life! Liar and knave! Debaucher, thief, with the morals of a dog-pound.

. . . I'll kill you! I'll fix your lying face so no other woman will ever believe you . . . so all other women will find my scars there, and know that they were made by a woman who did not believe your lying.

MORGAN. Ho! Ho! [*Only half warding off her blows and laughing uproariously.*] Who would have thought the woman had so much fire in her? What a pair we'll make together, you and I! Hit me again, my little one. 'Tis sweet, your fury. Hit me again!

DONNA LISA [*still beating*]. What a pair we shall make! You tap-room seducer. You raping cutpurse catchpenny of a tin-soldier! Do you think I'd go with you farther than I could find pretense to kill you? Do you think we shall ever pair together? That I shall mate with such a vulture as you? You twisted, lying old goat-face of a brothel master!

MORGAN [*catching her hands*]. With none other. Only your pride is hurt now.

DONNA LISA [*struggling*]. Let me go. Let me go, and I'll kill you.

MORGAN. Enough, my pretty one. Enough. Don't struggle so. I let you go, after all this sweet fury? Why, I shall carry you off to the ends of the world now!

DONNA LISA [*furiously, almost breaking away*]. You coward and bully! You clown who thinks himself a lover!

MORGAN [*picking her up and starting for a door at the right*]. I shall carry you off now, precious dove. No more ruffling your feathers.

DONNA LISA [*breaking away*]. And you'll be carried into the flames of hell. [*Running to the window and giving a signal.*] Morgan's here! Morgan's here! [*Turning on him.*] I've given you over to the commodore and he'll hang you up by your ugly neck until your lecherous eyes start from your lying face, you coward and bully and upstart of a tavern romance!

MORGAN [*rushing after her and picking her up again*]. If the commodore fools with me I'll feed his guts to the sharks, my little white porpoise! Let them try to take me— let them try to take you from me. [*The door flies open and* COMMODORE WRIGHT, *a pompous sailor, bursts in with the* ENSIGN *and boat's crew.*] Hell, guts and molasses! [*He drops her and runs to the base of the stairway, setting his back against it and whipping forth two blunderbusses.*] Stand fast, my silks and laces, or you'll be maggoty before another tropic day is past.

THE ENSIGN.   Captain Morgan?

MORGAN.   At your service, Jack man.

THE ENSIGN.   Stand attention.

MORGAN [*whirling and then louting with his hat*].   An English commodore at Panama City. Now, that is odd, by God it is! How come you here, who could not take it in seven years of planning? Did you take the Spanish by surprise? No. You didn't take it. Come to think of it, I took it. And now, I suppose, you have come to offer me your commission, to tear off those epaulets of yours and give them to a better man.

WRIGHT.   I arrest you in the king's name, Captain Morgan, for exceeding your commission on the high seas.

MORGAN.   Why, yes—arrest me. Arrest me when you can, and I wish you joy of me before you're done.

WRIGHT.   Before you're done, let us say. With eighteen feet of hempen rope, and thirteen knots of it under your ear, while you dance on the thin air of the Execution Dock.

MORGAN.   Swing me? What ingratitude! Here, by my kind permission, you walk the streets of the richest city in

the Indies. But perhaps you'd like to hang me to close my
mouth, lest I tell that you did not take for yourself the city
where you now draw warrants signed by your silly king.

WRIGHT. Shall I put you in irons, Captain Morgan, or
will you come peaceably?

MORGAN. Come where, milord?

WRIGHT. To ship with me, and then to England.

MORGAN. I don't like the climate of England. Some
other time, milord, some other time.

WRIGHT. No other time. This warrant charges you with
acts exceeding your commission. If you will not subscribe
to it, we shall be charged to change your offense to robbery
and piracy. For by resisting the king's arrest, you subscribe yourself guilty and lose all status in his Majesty's
navy. You must choose between piracy and surrender.
[MORGAN *frets.*] Come, I am not a patient man.

MORGAN. Nor I. [*He turns to* DONNA LISA.] Lady,
did I not tell you that a man must take what he will, and be
damned to all the world? Unless this royal governess ordered me, it was unpatriotic for me to be the scourge of
Spain. I have exceeded my commission. [*He turns upon*
WRIGHT.] Take care, sir, that I do not exceed it so far
that you will never have use for yours again.

WRIGHT. And supposing you were successful? You
know that ten others would begin where I left off, and in
the end, older perhaps and somewhat more grizzled and worn,
you would still have that dance on thin air from eighteen feet
of cord. Morgan, there are those in this service who admire
your seamanship, though none envy your reputation. Are
you not man enough to face a court and begin again? Would
you waste your talents brawling in every brothel in the rim
o' the world, scorned by such women as this lovely creature

here? Look at her; look at you. Can you stand there and know her contempt for you and not wish to be a more honorable man?

MORGAN. I may live to be honored. I may even live to be a hundred years old. But God save me from talking like a commodore! [*He turns toward the door, brushing aside two sailors. At a signal from the commodore, a third sailor leaps on his back from the stairs. There is instantly a heap of struggling men on the floor.* MARIA *and* CARMENCITA *enter from above.*]

DONNA LISA. Don't let him get away!

WRIGHT. Quickly, men!

[MORGAN *rises, but the men cling to him like burs. They spreadeagle* MORGAN *on the floor.*]

DONNA LISA [*leaping to her feet*]. Dog—dog! [*She kicks him.*]

MORGAN. Madam, madam! May not a fallen but faithful lover kiss your hand?

WRIGHT. You've brought this upon yourself, Morgan. There is no other way. You will face charges greater than those I brought.

MORGAN. How do I know you're all you pretend to be? Have I seen your damned warrant with your pimping king's seal? Am I answerable for every popinjay who boasts a cocked hat? Serve your warrant, and if I then judge it genuine, I may submit. But take these verminous dogs off my neck.

WRIGHT. Carry him to the brig. And you, lady?

DONNA LISA [*to* MORGAN]. I hate you! I hate you!

MORGAN [*throwing off the sailors*]. Oh, darling, I love you, I love you!

DONNA LISA. I hate you, I hate you!

MORGAN [*as they catch his arms*].   Ho, ho, she hates me!
How she hates me!   I tell you, you love me—you love
me——

DONNA LISA.   You beast!   Oh, you beast!   [*Half hysterical.*]

MORGAN.   She loves me!   [*He surrenders.*]

DONNA LISA.   Oh, must I listen to him?   Stop his mouth!
Beast!

MORGAN.   Ay, ay!   We will be together, darling.

DONNA LISA.   Never, never!

MORGAN.   Never . . . No, no.   Forever!

CURTAIN

ACT III

Scene One

*An audience chamber at Whitehall. CHARLES II sits on a
bench in the center of the room. A councilor is standing before him, reading a long-winded document to
which the roomful of courtiers, naval officers, and
ladies—for MORGAN is under fire, and DONNA LISA is
materially concerned—pay various degrees of inatten-
tion.*

THE COUNCILOR. . . . It being further attested that the
said Henry Morgan, being at that time commissioned a private captain in the navy of his Majesty, Charles II of England, did attack, seize, and loot the city of Porto Bello, the
said city being at that time in the possession of the king of
Spain, and did lay waste, loot, and burn churches, treasure-
houses, and individual domiciles, parceling the loot among
his men, without royal warrant permitting an extension of
his sea-commission to actions against the organized enemy
ashore——

CHARLES. My God, stop it! That's enough. . . . You
swear to that, Commodore?

WRIGHT. I do, sire.

CHARLES. What had you seen of Captain Morgan previous to his arrest?

WRIGHT. Why, I'd never laid eyes on him personally,
sire, but in obedience to your Majesty's commission I tracked

him from Porto Bello to Panama City—a trail of robbery, arson and bloodshed. We found Porto Bello looted of treasure. We found Panama City sacked and ruined. On the high seas between the two we encountered four Spanish ships gutted by this marauder. We took him in the very act of carrying off a woman!

CHARLES. You have the good name of the navy at heart, Commodore. What would you say was necessary to clear it of blame in this matter?

COMMODORE. To clear the navy, sire, and the kingdom, it will be necessary to hang him, and to publish his crimes.

CHARLES. Come, come! Have you no milder method? Name the minimum which would satisfy honor.

COMMODORE. He defied and resisted the king's officer, your Majesty. He is a notorious criminal. His record blots the whole history of your Majesty's victories by sea. Hanging, sire, is the minimum.

CHARLES. But would you not be inclined to admit, Commodore, that he has been useful, and in some instances practically indispensable, to the sea power of the kingdom?

COMMODORE. Your Majesty, it were better to swallow a hundred years' defeat than to recognize a pirate's victory.

CHARLES. You would rather be virtuous than victorious?

WRIGHT. If that is the alternative, your Majesty.

CHARLES. Very well, sir; you have spoken. And now, Captain Morgan . . . you exceeded your commission in the taking of Porto Bello?

MORGAN. I took Porto Bello by a very plausible extension of my commission which any judge on your bench could legalize in five minutes.

CHARLES. Oh, as to that, any judge on any bench could legalize any crime in five minutes.

MORGAN. Then let them legalize it.

CHARLES. We are met here to determine that.

MORGAN. Has it occurred to your Majesty that if England has no use for Porto Bello you might give it back to Spain?

CHARLES. My seafaring friend, in the international game of snatch, cities are taken but never returned.

MORGAN. Then, your Majesty, since you are to hang me for taking Porto Bello, why shouldn't you hang yourself for keeping it?

WRIGHT. Your Majesty, will you listen to this?

CHARLES. I am conducting a hearing, Commodore. It is my business to listen. You suggest hanging Captain Morgan. Captain Morgan suggests hanging me. No offense, of course. All in good part, I'm sure.

MORGAN. Quite, your Majesty, quite.

WRIGHT. Sire, when we found Captain Morgan at Panama City he flung himself upon my officer, delivered himself of abusive language, mocked at the authority of the Crown and made light of your Majesty's warrant. His conduct on that one occasion proves him a pirate in act and belief!

CHARLES. Answer, my buccaneer. Talk yourself out of that.

MORGAN. Your Majesty, the officers of the navy are gentlemen and seamen; but unfortunately the gentlemen are not seamen, and the seamen are not gentlemen. The British navy used to be feared without being much respected. If our commodore here has his way, it will end by being respected but not much feared. I am accused of taking Porto Bello and Panama City without legal sanction. So much the better for you, for if you were to take them legally you'd have to declare a costly war on Spain. I am accused of

pocketing the loot and distributing it among my men. I
did pocket it. The laborer is worthy of his hire. . . . I
offer you two Caribbean ports in exchange.

WRIGHT. He offers a robber's title to stolen goods, sire.

MORGAN. A robber's title! As if we weren't all robbers
and thieves! As if there was an acre of land owned in Eu-
rope, to say nothing of the New World, that wasn't founded
on a robber's title! As if there was a port in England that
didn't make what margin of profit it gets by preying on
Spanish trade! I've lived up to your law a thousand times
closer than these foxy gentlemen who live near enough the
courts to buy them when they need them! They sit at home
and distract and gouge and burrow under those who are
bold enough to strike out for the king!

CHARLES. True, Captain, quite true; but one of these
inadmissible truths. If we were to admit all this publicly,
you know very well the kingdom would go to the devil.

MORGAN. Why, then, at least act on it, sire. Let me go
back to the Caribbean and finish my job in the king's name,
or in God's name hang me. [He turns.]

CHARLES. Another moment of your time, if you can
spare it, Captain. There's one more charge against you.
[To the COUNCILOR.] Can you find that passage concern-
ing Lady Elizabeth Neville?

COUNCILOR [reading]. Upon which, deponent sayeth
that Captain Morgan did wilfully and violently attempt to
carry off this woman, using contemptuous and insulting language to those present and chiefly to the king's officer.
And further, deponent sayeth that—

CHARLES. Enough. Where is this king's officer?

THE ENSIGN. Here, sire.

CHARLES. You attest this?

The Ensign. Yes, sire.

Charles. You recognize the incident, Lady Elizabeth?

Donna Lisa. In the main, sire.

Charles. Do you wish to bring an indictment?

Donna Lisa. No, your Majesty. Captain Morgan is already under indictment for piracy and in a fair way to be hanged. That should serve.

Charles. But you accuse the Captain of this crime?

Donna Lisa. It is true that he attempted to carry me away. It is also true I had planned to go with him—and would have gone had not a certain matter come to light.

Charles. That would seem to palliate the offence.

Donna Lisa. Yes, sire.

Charles. And this certain matter—if I may ask—what was that?

Donna Lisa [embarrassed]. It is of no moment, sire.

Charles. But I have asked!

Donna Lisa. It concerned his intimacy with my maids-in-waiting.

Charles. And what was your attitude toward this, my dear?

Donna Lisa. I resented it. [Morgan smiles. Charles smiles at him.]

Charles. I understand. . . . Monsieur of the Council, you may blot that paragraph of the record dealing with Lady Elizabeth. And I believe this concludes our session. Captain Morgan, it appears that I shall be obliged to remand you for execution. The audience is at an end. The witnesses may retire. The prisoners remain. [All but Morgan go out.] Morgan, I've put off this hearing six months in hopes these sea pirates at the Admiralty would forget you, but, damme! they still insist on hanging you.

What am I to do? I can't hang you to satisfy the honor of these petticoat admirals and placket commodores. You've done more to rid the sea of our enemies than all of them put together.

MORGAN. May I venture a suggestion, your Majesty?

KING. That's why I got them out—to ask your advice, Captain, as to how I am to hang you without killing you.

MORGAN. Why, my advice is this, Majesty. If you don't want to hang me, did you ever think of hanging them instead?

KING. You wouldn't want me to hang that pretty widow. Tell me, Morgan, what have you done to this lady that she blushes when she looks at you?

MORGAN. I captured Panama, sire.

CHARLES. I'll warrant. And what else did you capture?

MORGAN. Porto Bello, Majesty.

CHARLES. So you won't boast of your light-o'-loves! Damme, you're a rum sort of seadog. Not an admiral in my fleet that doesn't come homing from the isthmus with a chart of lies about the Spanish women and the Indians he's charmed.

MORGAN. I never tell tales, Majesty.

CHARLES. Not even at royal command?

MORGAN. Sire, I could tell a hundred better than you ever heard from your nincompoop admirals in their popinjay coats. But, sire, if I were to talk of such matters I'd begin to feel downright sorry that I'm to be hanged.

CHARLES. But this pretty widow, what did you do that makes her so skittish when you're around? You must have a method worth knowing.

MORGAN. Before God, Majesty, I did nothing.

CHARLES. You didn't try?

MORGAN. I did, sire, but I made one great mistake. I fell in love with her.

CHARLES. I see. And it made you seem insincere. Damn the creatures!

MORGAN. And so I remained a moment too long in Panama City, and your Majesty's commodore caught and sacked me, and your Majesty's hangmen will stretch my neck. I was always a devotee of beauty, and now I'm a martyr to it.

CHARLES. Damme, Captain, I hate to see a good seaman hanged over a wench! They aren't worth it. I hate 'em all, this morning.

MORGAN. Majesty, this one comes damned near being worth it.

CHARLES. You should have stuck to buccaneering, Captain, and let the women alone.

MORGAN. Majesty, as a lover I've lost my good opinion of myself.

CHARLES. And as an admiral, now?

MORGAN. As an admiral, Majesty, I'm still a man of genius.

CHARLES. Tell me, Morgan, do you ever find much trouble beating these Spaniards?

MORGAN. There's no trouble giving them the actual beating. It's my commission hampers me. I chase 'em ashore, and they get away.

CHARLES. Morgan, why couldn't you serve me if I sent you out to catch the tide with the commodore's fleet tonight?

MORGAN. Under that silver-hooped barrel of ship's grease? No man could serve you well under that, sire.

CHARLES. Damme, Morgan, you're a problem to me. I

can't stand you, because you're needed. If I reward you,
I'll have half the town around my ears. . . .

MORGAN. I won't sail under him, sire. He's no seaman.

CHARLES. Well, then, if I sent you in command, could you
teach him seamanship?

MORGAN. In command over the commodore?

CHARLES. Ay, over the commodore.

MORGAN. By God, I'd either teach him or wear out a
rope's end on him!

CHARLES. Then take him, Morgan. Take his fleet, and
take him with you. He's been underfoot around here for six
months, ever since he brought you back, and we're all sick
of him. Take him along and make him jump overboard in
that iron shirt he wears.

[A HERALD *enters with a robe.*]

HERALD. Sire——

CHARLES. I've got to give the accolade to three duns this
afternoon. What a life, Morgan! There are three note-
shavers to be knighted at four o' the clock, in a room that's
colder than the hinges of hell, and the most I know of any
of them is that I owe them money. [*He puts on his robe.*]
And then I've got to sit like a mummy for three quarters of
an hour afterward, talking to the ugliest lot of royal females
that ever wore a farthingale. Come in with me, Morgan.
I always feel better when I can see one more man in the
room.

MORGAN. In this uniform, Majesty? . . . And if I'm
commanding the fleet. I'll need two or three hours before
sailing.

CHARLES. To bother the widow, eh? [*He stops, reflecting.*] By the rod of Aaron, I'll knight ye first! 'Twill

work wonders with the jade. They can't withstand the titles.

MORGAN. Sire, I beg leave to decline the honor. I'd lose my grip on my men if I went back to the Caribbean a gentleman.

CHARLES. The devil take your declination! I'll knight you if I like. I'll knight you, first because I like you, and second because it will anger these money-lenders to be knighted along with a pirate. Gad, it will bother them! I can hear them chatter. With a skull and cross-bones, gad! [*He rises and goes to the door.*] Get ready for the ceremony, Morgan. And oh, yes, write me a confidential dispatch and tell me how the widow was affected. [*To the* COUNCILOR.] Tell them inside there's been a slight change in plans, sir. We knight four instead of three. [*The* COUNCILOR *goes out.*] We'll have a drink after the ceremony, Morgan; and don't forget that confidential dispatch. It's important.

MORGAN. I haven't authority to send a confidential dispatch, Majesty.

CHARLES. Oh, I forgot to tell you! If you take Commodore Wright's place you'll be my deputy out in Jamaica— governor of Jamaica. I'll send your papers to the ship. How's that for authority over the widow?

MORGAN. Governor of Jamaica!

CHARLES. Surely! Jamaica! Where the ginger comes from. [*He goes off.*]

CURTAIN

Scene Two

An antechamber. Through the door at the left it gives on the audience chamber. Donna Lisa *and her ladies enter from the right, in something of a flutter.*

Donna Lisa. Remember, you two must stand in front of me, especially if he comes through, so I won't be known. Thank heaven the court enters from the other wing! I'll sit here. Maria, spread your skirts for a screen. [*Moving back to the wall.*] Oh, my heaven, here come two of them now, dressed and trussed up, and God help us to escape!

Maria [*moving with her*]. Is Morgan with them?

Donna Lisa. Call him Henry, child. Having been intimate with the gentleman, you are entitled to dispense with formality.

[Townshend *and* Skipwith *enter.*]

Townshend. Marmion not here at this late hour?

Skipwith. He is always late. It runs in the family.

Townshend. Ay, and has done ever since his mother was one year later than her husband's death with the birth of a posthumous heir. [Marmion *enters.*] Cousin, we two were going in alone.

Marmion. Alone? Now by St. Dunstan's clock, I doubt that I shall go in at all in the face of this insult! Do you know what the king has done? There is a fourth to be gartered with us—his name is Morgan, and he has just been taken from a dungeon underneath the Tower.

Townshend. A jailbird?

Marmion. A jailbird! Why, damme, a jailbird would be good company compared with this customer! A brigand, a pirate, a murderer on the high seas, a villainous cutthroat who has been six months in the lower keep for mayhem and rape among the Caribbean isles.

TOWNSHEND. By any rule of common courtesy is it not an insult to be knighted in a buccaneer's company?

MARMION [*with an eye on* DONNA LISA's *group.*] Softly, softly; we are overheard. Is there a lady to be gartered with us, I wonder?

TOWNSHEND [*turning so the women may hear him*]. Oh, the ladies have garters to give! They need no decorations from monarchs.

MARMION [*to* CARMENCITA]. Your mistress hides her face. Am I correct in assuming that your mistress would not be spoken with?

DONNA LISA [*rising*]. Her mistress will speak for herself, sir, since you insist. We appear to be in the way?

MARMION. Oh, on the contrary!

DONNA LISA. And what is your excuse for this parley?

MARMION. Can you deny audience to a slave?

DONNA LISA. Oh, I give you back your liberty without ransom, gentle warrior! But on condition that you make use of it by running away.

TOWNSHEND. Dismissed, cousin, dismissed!

MARMION [*bowing*]. Still at your service—and adieu.

DONNA LISA [*courtesying*]. Adieu, O flower of chivalry!

[MARMION *retreats in discomfiture.* MORGAN *enters from the right, and* DONNA LISA *is screened again.*]

MORGAN. Well, gentlemen, I understand we four are all in the same boat. Thank God I'm not to make a monkey of myself all alone.

TOWNSHEND [*half turning*]. You are addressing——?

MORGAN. You, sir, among others.

Townshend. Oh, I beg pardon. [*He turns back to* Marmion.] Had we concluded our arrangements, Cousin Marmion?

Marmion. You have elected yourself to take precedence, cousin.

Morgan [*hail-fellow-well-met*]. Do I gather there's an election with this affair?

Townshend [*to* Marmion]. Have you met the gentleman, cousin?

Marmion [*smoothly*]. This is Captain Morgan, I believe?

Morgan. Right the first time, sir.

Marmion. Allow me to introduce myself, sir. One Marmion, a poor relation of the Marmions of Essex.

Morgan. Most happy, I'm sure.

Marmion. This gentleman here claims descent from the Townshends of Essex, Captain Morgan, and though there is no proving these matters, let us hope his mother was honest, for he bears the Townshend name.

Morgan. Most happy, sir.

Marmion. As for the melancholy knight-to-be on his left, sir, you may identify him by the name of Skipwith, a name made glorious by some remote ancestor who skipped with something, perhaps with the contents of the king's exchequer, perhaps with another man's wife. At any rate, it is no matter, for this last scion has nothing to show for it but some acres of Kentish earth.

Morgan. Your most humble. He speaks truth, Sir Dolorous?

Marmion. Oh, more, sir; and then again, less.

Townshend [*distantly, withdrawing a step*]. You will

pardon us, Captain Morgan, if we continue our conference?

SKIPWITH [*following*]. By your leave, sir. [MARMION *hesitates.*]

MORGAN. Why, before you go into silence, might a plain seaman ask a plain question?

MARMION. Doubtless.

MORGAN. It seems we are fated to be knighted together, worse luck, for I see you don't like it any too well. But since it must be so—I've never put a deal of study on these furbelows—is there much that I should know to avoid stumbling?

TOWNSHEND. There is nothing, Captain, which should not come natural to a gentleman born. [*A pause.*]

MORGAN. My birth, sir——

TOWNSHEND. Is not in question. You will excuse me?

MORGAN. Why, no, I won't. By God, there are men in Wales, my masters, with hats as high as your own—and parentage not so doubtful! I tell you——

MARMION. My cousin means no reflection on you, Captain Morgan, none in the world.

MORGAN. As for you, young olives and vinegar, there's too much oil on your tongue. You talk like so much French dressing.

MARMION. I have been known to talk to some purpose, Captain Morgan.

MORGAN. Not since I've known you. When you choose your arms, take an eel rampant, with a yellow belly and a white flag in his mouth.

TOWNSHEND. You are well paid, Marmion. You waste kindness on an understrapper.

MORGAN. I want none of your kindness.

TOWNSHEND. Oh, so we understand, sirrah. A remarkable specimen, would you say, Skipwith?

SKIPWITH [*bored*]. Genus homo, peasant class, tavern manners.

TOWNSHEND. Voice loud, carriage braggart, language tending, one might say, toward the piratical.

[MORGAN *lays a hand to his sword. Then, reconsidering, turns his back and walks away.*]

SKIPWITH. By inference, an untidy feeder, one who tucks his napkin, and, God save us, shovels.

TOWNSHEND. In short, a most singular animal.

DONNA LISA [*still seated, speaking to her maids in a low voice, yet loud enough that all may hear*]. There is about the court, you may have noted, Carmencita, a species of tinseled worm, more familiar with under plackets than with the weapons of the duello, a nest of impotent, varnished wasps, who sting with the tongue only, live by the laws of bawds, boast no schooling save in the college of heraldry, set the fashions in public about the central table of a favorite tavern, self-instructed in the latest stages of super-finical perversion. [MORGAN, *whose back is to* DONNA LISA, *pauses to listen, but does not turn.*] A rotten, dying population of compost, reeking in the nostrils of a whole city, specialists only in quips and disgraceful diseases.

MARMION. My lady has found her tongue!

SKIPWITH. This room is reserved, I believe. We should call a sergeant-at-arms to clear it of fishwives.

MORGAN. Donna Lisa!

DONNA LISA. Lady Elizabeth Neville, sir.

SKIPWITH. Oho, a camp-follower of the privateer! So I suspected.

MARMION. A word with you two. [MARMION, TOWNshend, *and* Skipwith *go toward the left.*] The herald will call us. We tender our excuses, sir and madame, wishing you no worse luck than each other. [*The three go out.*]

Morgan. Lady Neville, you have been kinder to me than I deserve.

Donna Lisa. I did not come willingly, Captain Morgan.

Morgan. Yet when you came you were kind, and for that I thank you. I leave England tonight. . . .

Donna Lisa. Yes?

Morgan. I had hoped to see you again. . . .

Donna Lisa. It will be unnecessary. [*They bow.*]

[*A bugle sounds from within, and a* Herald *comes through, droning almost unintelligibly. They hear only the end of his proclamation.*]

Herald. . . . The king summons Captain Morgan, Henry Marmion of Essex, James Townshend of Essex. [*The* Herald *pauses and looks in a puzzled way at* Morgan, *who is still kneeling; then asks aside, in a speaking voice:*] Captain Morgan, sir?

Morgan. Righto.

Herald. The king's commands, sir! [*He continues in his singsong.*] Eliphalet Skipwith, Esq., of Kent, Captain Henry Morgan, Henry Marmion. [*His voice is lost as he goes out.* Morgan *goes out.*]

Donna Lisa [*in sudden terror*]. George, George! Why didn't you follow your master?

George. You said nothing about that, ma'am.

Donna Lisa. Oh, my God! He's gone in to the king without his squire. Didn't you see the others following?

George. Yes, ma'am, I saw them, but how was I to know?

Donna Lisa. You might have guessed, you zany.

GEORGE. I know it, ma'am. I might have, but I didn't. You see, I thought maybe the others was all wrong. I could go now, ma'am.

DONNA LISA. No, no, it's too late now. Oh, why am I such a fool?

GEORGE. I don't know, ma'am.

DONNA LISA [*too broken to rejoin*]. Call the carriage, George. I can't bear to be here when they come out.

GEORGE. Carriage for Lady Neville, ma'am?

DONNA LISA. Yes, yes—Lady Elizabeth Neville.

CARMENCITA [*who has been watching through the door at the left*]. Donna Lisa!

DONNA LISA [*on her way to the door at the right*]. Come, Carmencita!

CARMENCITA. You must see. He's doing beautifully! He carried it off with such an air.

DONNA LISA. Carmencita!

CARMENCITA. Oh, oh, the terrible Townshend has tripped over his sword! Oh, heavens, what a mess! . . . Quick, quick, come here! [MARIA *and* GEORGE, *then* DONNA LISA, *go to the door at left.*]

MARIA. Why, he must be injured. The pages are picking him up!

DONNA LISA. Has the captain fallen down? I might have known he'd fall down or something!

CARMENCITA. Not Morgan! It isn't Morgan, Donna Lisa, it's that great beast Townshend. He fell into his own scarlet cloak, and they haven't got him out yet. Saints deliver us! Did he break a leg?

MARIA. No, he's going on again.

CARMENCITA. He had to go first, and he fell over his own shins. Oh, Lord! Oh, Lord! I shall die of joy.

GEORGE. You see that little fellow with the black mustache? That's the king.

MARIA. How do you know?

GEORGE. Oh, I know him. I met him.

DONNA LISA. George, did you call that carriage?

GEORGE. No, ma'am.

DONNA LISA. And why not, sir?

GEORGE. I sort of got interested, you see.

DONNA LISA. Call it now.

[GEORGE *takes one more look at the proceedings on the left; then, with no good grace, goes out.*]

MARIA. They're all coming this way. . . .

CARMENCITA. No, not all. Not the king's retinue.

MARIA. Sir Terrible Townshend is limping.

CARMENCITA. Something must have happened to him. Surely a courtier doesn't fall flat on a carpet without provocation.

DONNA LISA. Come, girls; we shall be trapped here again.

CARMENCITA. It doesn't matter, Donna Lisa. Everybody will be here.

[*The room begins to fill with soldiers, courtiers, ladies. MORGAN enters. TOWNSHEND emerges, followed by his squire; then by MARMION and SKIPWITH with their squires.*]

TOWNSHEND [*fuming*]. Before you leave, sir, I have the honor to challenge you for that insult.

MORGAN. On what ground, chevalier?

TOWNSHEND. You are aware of the ground, sir.

MORGAN. Oh, better aware of it than yourself, chevalier, since you have so much trouble keeping your feet; but still far from certain of your cause.

TOWNSHEND. Do you deny that you tripped me from behind as we entered the king's presence?

MORGAN.   Surely, chevalier, you must be mistaken. *I* trip
a knight like a charity scholar—*I* trip up a portly gentleman by the heels as he walks in line? George! Where's
George? [GEORGE *enters at a word*.] George, where have
you been? Come, give me a reputation—do I trip?

GEORGE.   Trip, Captain?

MORGAN.   Yes, trip.

GEORGE.   Why, I should say not much, Captain, if any.

MORGAN.   There, you see, chevalier! George has been
with me these many years. If I tripped, George would know
it. And what is the worst George can say of me? He says
not much, if any.

MARMION.   This is no laughing matter, Captain Morgan——

MORGAN.   Sir Henry Morgan, my Lord Marmion; Sir
Henry Morgan, Deputy Governor of Jamaica.

MARMION.   As you please, Sir Henry, with all the further
additions your imagination conjures. Still is this no laughing matter.

MORGAN.   It has caused considerable merriment, to my
certain knowledge.

MARMION.   My cousin has turned his ankle, sir, as a result
of your rudeness, and is therefore in no condition to meet
you. I offer myself in his place.

TOWNSHEND.   Quite unnecessary, cousin.

MARMION.   I insist. There lies my gauge. [*He tosses a
glove at* MORGAN'S *feet*.]

MORGAN.   There's a kind of spunk in you, Marmion, boy,
and I take it up on two conditions.

MARMION.   And when has a knight taken up a gauge on
conditions?

MORGAN.   It happens that I am leaving England within
six hours, chevalier. We catch the tide at midnight. Before

that hour I am at your service, providing—and this is the
second condition—that if you are disarmed and unhurt you
come with me as a volunteer. I do you the honor, you will
perceive, of coveting you for my officer.

MARMION. There lies my challenge, Sir Henry. As for
your conditions, I have not heard them.

MORGAN. Then I won't fight you, sir. I will not fight
you because I am in a hurry, because I have nothing to gain
by it, and because you have no chance against me. Do you
think I would hold my ships at the whim of a younger son
who has at last saved enough out of his allowance to buy
him a garter?

MARMION. Then formally, sir, and in the presence of this
assembly, I dub you a coward, and you cannot deny it.

MORGAN. A fig for your dubbing and your assembly!
Henry Morgan a coward! Walk up to a few fortresses as
I have done, take a few towns and a few Spanish treasure
fleets; then come back and call me a coward, and I promise
to listen to you. You prattle, child. You should see some
service.

MARMION. This will please the king.

MORGAN. Ay—tell the king and the court and London
town and the kingdom! Tell them you challenged Morgan,
and he ran away. I'm through with the king and the court
and London town and this side of the world. I'm through
with your flowers and ribbons and fancy talk and fancy
morals. It means nothing to me what you think of me in
this woman's town, this lackey's paradise. Judge me by
your standards and be damned to them—I've better standards of my own. Must I fight every boy who owns a sword
and doesn't like my conversation? I'll fight when I have a
cause worth fighting for and an antagonist who's won his

spurs. Am I a game cock, to put on exhibition? I'll tell you what I think of this town and of you all. You're a scrambling of all the petty thieves and faint hearts that don't dare go out and loot for yourselves, a heap of leaners and hangers-on, afraid to go your own way, dragging on each other for support and licking the king's boots for him, so he'll let you live. And look at your courtiers—how long would they last on the deck of a man-o'-war? The deck of a man-o'-war's the place for a man. There's beauty and courage and fighting blood on the deck of a ship of the line. You, Sir Marmion, you're the one gallant here with the makings of a man in you. You ought to go out and take a look at my ships. I'll duel you on that issue. [*A pause. Marmion disdains to answer.*] No? Then I'm off for Jamaica, gentlemen and ladies, and God forgive you for a parcel of nincompoops. Unless, by chance, I'm mistaken, and there's a man among you—just one. On that chance, gentlemen, a call for volunteers, a last call for volunteers! Who'll follow Sir Henry Morgan to the Caribbean and the Spanish Main? Who's sick of living at the rotten center of an empire? Who'll see Jamaica with me, and a thousand ports of call? [*A pause.*] Not one! I thought so. George, we go as we came. [Morgan *and* George *start toward the door at the left.* Morgan *tosses his glove to the center of the stage.*] There lies my challenge! [Morgan *and* George *pause at left. There is a silence, then a slight stir and whispering.* Donna Lisa *rises slowly, walks deliberately to the glove, pulls it on, and goes up to* Morgan.] Lady Elizabeth!

Donna Lisa. Lady Elizabeth Morgan!

CURTAIN